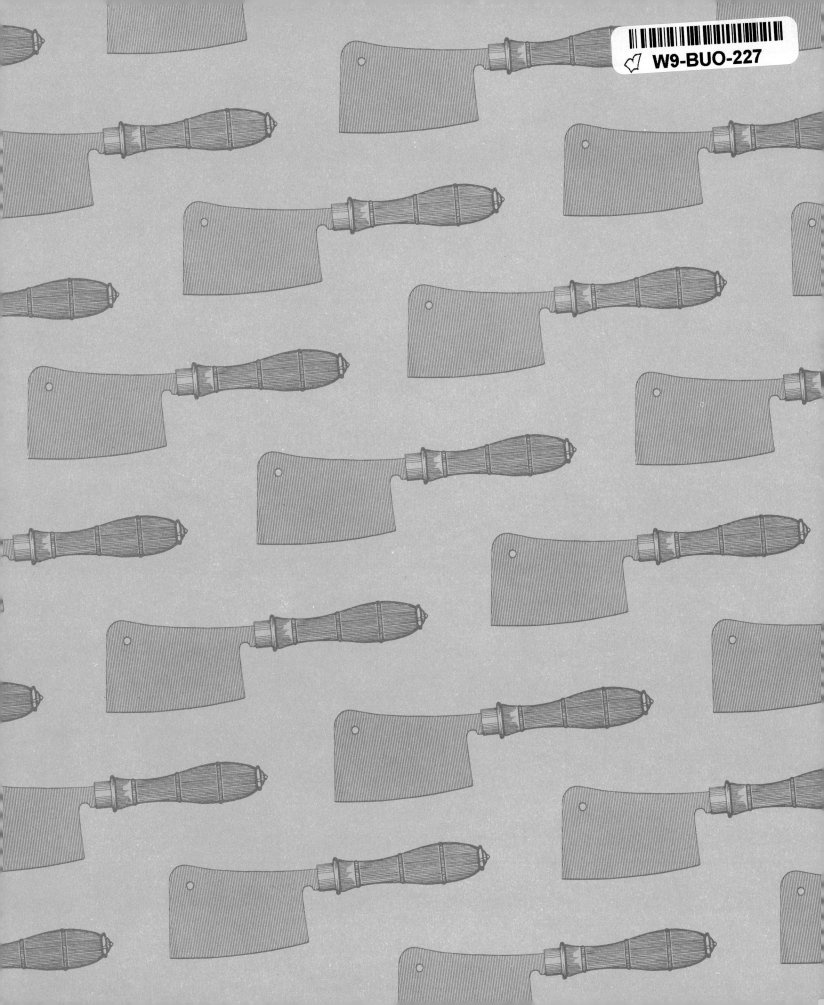

TIME LIFE® BOOKS

Other Publications:

THE CIVIL WAR
PLANET EARTH
COLLECTOR'S LIBRARY OF THE CIVIL WAR
LIBRARY OF HEALTH
CLASSICS OF THE OLD WEST
THE EPIC OF FLIGHT
THE SEAFARERS
WORLD WAR II
HOME REPAIR AND IMPROVEMENT
THE OLD WEST
LIFE LIBRARY OF PHOTOGRAPHY (revised)
LIFE SCIENCE LIBRARY (revised)

For information on and a full description of any
of the Time-Life Books series listed above, please write:

Reader Information
Time-Life Books
541 North Fairbanks Court
Chicago, Illinois 60611

*This volume is one of a series that explains and demonstrates how
to prepare various types of food, and that offers in each book an
international anthology of great recipes.*

Pork

BY
THE EDITORS OF TIME-LIFE BOOKS

Cover: A roasted pork loin, first boned and then rolled around a stuffing flavored with sage and onion, is carved into neat slices. During roasting, the loin was basted repeatedly with its pan juices, creating a lustrous, mahogany-tinged glaze.

Time-Life Books Inc.
is a wholly owned subsidiary of
TIME INCORPORATED

Founder: Henry R. Luce 1898-1967

Editor-in-Chief: Henry Anatole Grunwald
President: J. Richard Munro
Chairman of the Board: Ralph P. Davidson
Executive Vice President: Clifford J. Grum
Editorial Director: Ralph Graves
Group Vice President, Books: Joan D. Manley

TIME-LIFE BOOKS INC.

Editor: George Constable. *Executive Editor:* George Daniels. *Director of Design:* Louis Klein. *Board of Editors:* Dale M. Brown, Thomas A. Lewis, Robert G. Mason, Ellen Phillips, Gerry Schremp, Gerald Simons, Rosalind Stubenberg, Kit van Tulleken. *Director of Administration:* David L. Harrison. *Director of Research:* Carolyn L. Sackett. *Director of Photography:* John Conrad Weiser. *Design:* Anne B. Landry (art coordinator), James J. Cox (quality control). *Research:* Phyllis K. Wise (assistant director), Louise D. Forstall. *Copy Room:* Diane Ullius (director), Celia Beattie. *Production:* Gordon E. Buck, Peter Inchauteguiz

President: Reginald K. Brack Jr. *Senior Vice President:* William Henry. *Vice Presidents:* George Artandi, Stephen L. Bair, Peter G. Barnes, Robert A. Ellis, Juanita T. James, Christopher T. Linen, James L. Mercer, Joanne A. Pello, Paul R. Stewart

THE GOOD COOK

The original version of this book was created in London for Time-Life Books International (Nederland) B.V. *European Editor:* Kit van Tulleken. *Photography Director:* Pamela Marke. *Chief of Research:* Vanessa Kramer. *Special Projects Editor:* Windsor Chorlton. *Chief Sub-Editor:* Ilse Gray. *Production Editor:* Ellen Brush

Staff for Pork: *Series Editor:* Alan Lothian. *Series Coordinator:* Liz Timothy. *Head Designer:* Rick Bowring. *Text Editor:* Tony Allan. *Anthology Editor:* Markie Benet. *Staff Writers:* Gillian Boucher, Jay Ferguson, Mary Harron, Thom Henvey. *Researcher:* Eleanor Lines. *Sub-Editor:* Katie Lloyd. *Permissions Researcher:* Mary-Claire Hailey. *Assistant Designer:* Mary Staples. *Design Assistant:* Cherry Doyle. *Quality Control:* Douglas Whitworth. *Editorial Department:* Anetha Besidonne, Pat Boag, Debra Dick, Philip Garner, Margaret Hall, Joanne Holland, Molly Sutherland, Julia West

U.S. Editorial Staff for Pork: *Series Editor:* Gerry Schremp. *Designer:* Ellen Robling. *Picture Editor:* Adrian Allen. *Text Editor:* Ellen Phillips. *Staff Writers:* Carol Dana, Malachy Duffy, Bonnie Jo Kreitler. *Researchers:* Cecile Ablack, Eleanor Kask. *Assistant Designer:* Peg Schreiber. *Copy Coordinators:* Allan Fallow, Tonna Gibert, Ricki Tarlow. *Art Assistants:* Robert K. Herndon, Cynthia Richardson. *Picture Coordinator:* Alvin Ferrell. *Editorial Assistants:* Audrey P. Keir, Patricia Kim. *Special Contributor:* Karen M. Bates-Logan (research)

CHIEF SERIES CONSULTANT

Richard Olney, an American, has lived and worked for some three decades in France, where he is highly regarded as an authority on food and wine. A regular contributor to such influential journals as *La Revue du Vin de France* and *Cuisine et Vins de France,* he also has written numerous articles for other gastronomic magazines in the United States and France. He is, too, the author of *The French Menu Cookbook* and the award-winning *Simple French Food,* has directed cooking courses in France and in the United States, and is a member of several distinguished gastronomic societies, including La Confrérie des Chevaliers du Tastevin, Les Amitiés Gastronomiques Internationales, and La Commanderie du Bontemps de Médoc et des Graves. Working in London with the series editorial staff, he has been basically responsible for the planning of this volume, and has supervised the final selection of recipes submitted by other consultants. The United States edition of The Good Cook has been revised by the Editors of Time-Life Books to bring it into complete accord with American customs and usage.

CHIEF AMERICAN CONSULTANT
Carol Cutler, who lives in Washington, D.C., is the author of three cookbooks, including the award-winning *The Six-Minute Soufflé and Other Culinary Delights.* During the 12 years she lived in France, she studied at the Cordon Bleu and the École des Trois Gourmandes, and with private chefs. She is a member of the Cercle des Gourmettes, a long-established French food society limited to just 50 members. She is also a contributing editor to *The International Review of Food & Wine* and frequently lectures about food.

PHOTOGRAPHERS
Alan Duns was born in 1943 in the north of England and studied at the Ealing School of Photography. He specializes in food, and has contributed to major British publications.
Aldo Tutino, a native of Italy, has worked in Milan, New York City and Washington, D.C. He has won a number of awards for his photographs from the New York Advertising Club.

INTERNATIONAL CONSULTANTS
GREAT BRITAIN: *Jane Grigson* has written a number of books about food and has been a cookery correspondent for the London *Observer* since 1968. *Alan Davidson* is the author of several cookbooks and the founder of Prospect Books, which specializes in scholarly publications about food and cookery.

FRANCE: *Michel Lemonnier,* the cofounder and vice president of Les Amitiés Gastronomiques Internationales, is a frequent lecturer on wine and vineyards. GERMANY: *Jochen Kuchenbecker* trained as a chef, but he has worked for 10 years as a food photographer in several European countries. *Anne Brakemeier* is the co-author of three cookbooks. ITALY: *Massimo Alberini* is a well-known food writer and journalist, with a particular interest in culinary history. His many books include *Storia del Pranzo all'Italiana,* *4000 Anni a Tavola* and *100 Ricette Storiche.* THE NETHERLANDS: *Hugh Jans* has published two cookbooks and his recipes appear in a number of Dutch magazines. THE UNITED STATES: *Julie Dannenbaum,* the director of a cooking school in Philadelphia, Pennsylvania, also conducts cooking classes at the Gritti Palace in Venice, Italy, and at The Greenbrier in White Sulphur Springs, West Virginia. She is the author of two cookbooks and numerous magazine articles. *François Dionot,* a graduate of L'École des Hôteliers de Lausanne in Switzerland, has worked as a chef, hotel general manager and restaurant manager in the U.S. and France. He now conducts his own cooking school. *Judith Olney* received her culinary training in England and France. She conducts cooking classes from her home in Durham, North Carolina, and has written two cookbooks. *José Wilson,* a former food editor of *House & Garden* magazine, wrote many books on food and interior decoration.

Correspondents: Elisabeth Kraemer (Bonn); Margot Hapgood, Dorothy Bacon (London); Miriam Hsia, Lucy T. Voulgaris (New York); Maria Vincenza Aloisi, Josephine du Brusle (Paris); Ann Natanson (Rome).
Valuable assistance was also provided by: Jeanne Buys (Amsterdam); Hans-Heinrich Wellmann, Gertraud Bellon (Hamburg); Karin B. Pearce (London); Diane Asselin (Los Angeles); Bona Schmid, Maria Teresa Marenco (Milan); Carolyn T. Chubet, Christina Lieberman (New York); Michèle le Baube (Paris); Mimi Murphy (Rome).

CONTENTS

The Prodigal Pig

Few animals have been as useful to man as the pig. Easily fed, cared for and housed, this creature has always been one of the main dietary props of civilization, both in the Western world and in the Orient. For centuries, the pig provided Europe's peasantry with practically the only meat they ever ate. In China, pork was so universally prized that a symbol representing a pig beneath a roof became the ideogram for "home." Despite the wide range of meats available to most consumers today, pork remains popular worldwide. Estimates of the global pig population range between 400 and 500 million—roughly one pig for every 10 people on earth.

The pig's ancestor, the wild boar, was first used for food by man some time in the Stone Age. From killing boars as they came to scavenge around human settlements, man gradually learned to supervise herds of half-wild pigs that could be caught and slaughtered when meat was needed. The truly domesticated pig may have made its first appearance in China. Certainly the earliest surviving pork recipe is Chinese. Dating from before 500 B.C., it describes the roasting of a suckling pig—stuffed with dates and enclosed in a jacket of straw or reeds mixed with clay—in a heated pit. Similar methods are still used to roast pigs in the Polynesian islands.

The domesticated pig can live on almost any feed, and, compared to other livestock, is amazingly prolific: A sow can produce two litters of seven or more piglets—the average is 11—a year. It is not surprising, then, that in Classical Greece, whose countryside lacked sufficient fodder for cattle raising, pork was so important to the diet that Demeter, the goddess who protected agriculture, was usually depicted with a pig for a companion. The Romans, too, esteemed pork. The Roman harvest goddess, Ceres, was said to have inaugurated the eating of pigs in reprisal for their trampling a field of corn.

The Romans drew up detailed laws that regulated the butchering of the meat, and they excelled at curing—preserving the meat by salting and smoking. A recipe of the Second Century B.C. specified that the meat be covered with salt and left for 17 days, dried in a draft for two days, then rubbed with oil and vinegar and, lastly, smoked for two days. Preserved by such methods, pork kept sufficiently well to be transported throughout the Roman Empire.

Since pork could be preserved almost as easily as pigs could be fed, the household pig remained a crucial food source well into modern times. Because it was difficult to find fodder, even for pigs, through the winter months, Europeans evolved a tradition of killing the family pig toward the end of the year. The

killing and butchering developed into a village ceremony of feasting and work, and the pork, once salted down, became a staple of the winter diet—usually poached with dried beans, as described on pages 52-55.

These festive pig killings produced much more than salted meat; virtually every part of the pig was put to use. Cuts that were not salted or cooked fresh became patés and sausages. The blood also went into sausages, and the tongue, heart and intestine were transformed into brawn, chitterlings and other products of the pork butcher's art. The soft fat was rendered into lard—the principal cooking fat for people who had few or no cows to produce cream for making butter, and no oil-bearing vegetables such as olives or corn. Indeed, pigs were valued as much for their lard as for their meat.

As early as the 18th Century, landowners sought to improve their pigs' yield of lard by supervised feeding and breeding; their ideal pig was an almost spherical creature tipped by tiny extremities. With the increasing availability of vegetable oils and other sources of fat in the 20th Century, however, the demand for obese pigs declined, and there has been a countertrend toward a leaner pig, bred principally for its meat. Today's pig has a long loin—the portion of the animal that produces the least fatty, most expensive cuts—and well-developed hind legs.

Pig breeding has become a major industry in the United States. The 13 hogs that Hernando de Soto brought to Florida in 1525—the first pigs on this continent—were the predecessors of huge droves that today collectively comprise nearly 60 million animals, a pig population second only to that of the People's Republic of China. The great majority of these animals are raised in the Corn Belt states: Indiana, Illinois, Iowa, Missouri and Minnesota. On a typical modern pig farm, four to five hundred animals live together in clean, heated buildings, known somewhat coyly as pig parlors, and feed on dried corn plus a variety of supplements designed to enhance growth and control disease. At the age of six months or so, the animals—now weighing about 200 pounds and known as hogs—are shipped off to packing houses. There they are slaughtered and divided into the so-called primal sections—and sometimes the retail cuts—described on pages 8-9.

Ham and bacon

Only about a third of each animal's meat will be sold fresh; the rest is turned into processed products such as sausage, or is cured by salting and smoking. Although it is possible to cure any cut of pork, the process is most frequently applied to the fatty belly, which produces bacon and salt pork, and to the hind legs, which produce hams.

Most modern curing techniques *(pages 10-11)* serve only to impart a desirable flavor and texture to the meat; they do not preserve it, and the meat must be refrigerated. There are, however, exceptions to this rule, among them some of the world's best-known hams: France's *jambon de Bayonne,* Westphalian *Schinken* from Germany, and Italian prosciutto. In America, the equivalents are Smithfield and country hams. Smithfield hams—the term Smithfield is applicable only to hams cured in the Virginia town of that name—are the stuff of culinary legend. Actually, the same curing process is widely employed elsewhere to produce similarly delicious country hams.

In the past, hogs that produced Smithfield hams were fed for at least part of their lives on peanuts, a local crop. This diet gave the hams a rich sheen and a delicately nutty taste. Today, the meat for Smithfield and country hams usually comes from corn-fed hogs raised on farms all across the South. The meat is salted in two stages: a process that takes about four weeks. Next the meat is washed and coated with crushed peppercorns; peppercorns do not affect the curing process, but are a legacy from a time when pepper was used to repel insects. Then the meat is refrigerated for two weeks and smoked for 10 days. The smoke once was produced by fires of aromatic hickory wood; but since this wood is now scarce, the fires are today fueled almost exclusively with white oak, occasionally augmented with apple wood or with hickory dust. After smoking, the meat is aged for six to 12 months at a temperature of 75° to 80° F. [24° to 27° C.]. Meat cured by this process will keep for up to two years unrefrigerated. However, it must be hung in a cool, dry place to prevent it from absorbing water and thus rotting.

Smithfield and similar hams are most readily available at specialty butchers. They are expensive, but their salty, smoky flesh and sweet, translucent fat make them hams beyond compare—so flavorful, in fact, that they must be carved paper-thin.

Smithfield and country hams are not, of course, the only cured hams available. Other versions are simply salted or brine-cured, but not finished by smoking or aging. Most common of all are brine-injected hams that have been steamed or poached by the manufacturer and are consequently designated "precooked" or "ready-to-eat." Unlike Smithfield and country hams, these hams must be refrigerated as if they were fresh meat.

All cured hams except brine-injected smoked hams should be soaked in cold water before cooking to rid them of excess salt. The soaking period will vary according to the size of the ham and the nature of its cure; specific instructions are given on the chart on pages 10-11. After this preliminary treatment, hams are best cooked by slow and gentle poaching, which ensures that the meat remains moist *(pages 54-55);* they may be finished by brief braising *(pages 64-65)* or by baking to create a glaze on the meat *(box, page 40).*

Pork and health

The notion of the pig as an unclean animal is an ancient one, still sufficiently deep-rooted to permit the total interdiction of pork eating in Jewish and Muslim societies. It is true that the pig has a greater capacity than other domestic animals to survive—and even thrive—in unsanitary conditions, and any food produced in an unhealthy environment may spread diseases. In modern times, however, the increasing awareness of food hygiene among pig breeders has greatly reduced the scope of the problem. The only hazard to health still associated with the eating of fresh and salted pork is trichinosis, a parasitical disease that is impossible to detect in living animals but that can be transmitted to humans.

The incidence of trichinosis has been substantially reduced over the past years; prepared pork products are now spot-checked for evidence of contamination before they are put on sale. But the parasite responsible for trichinosis has not yet

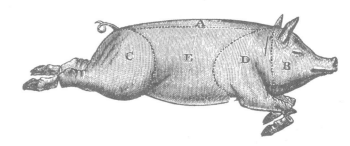

been eliminated from all fresh pork, and the meat must still be cooked thoroughly to protect against infection. Unfortunately, fear of the disease has often led to overcooking. The parasite is killed and the meat made safe to eat when the internal temperature of a cut reaches 137° F. [59° C.]—about the temperature of rare beef. To allow an adequate margin for uneven cooking within a cut, however, food authorities recommend cooking pork to an internal temperature of 165° to 170° F. [75° C.]. Cooks without meat thermometers should test pork for doneness by piercing the thickest part with a skewer or other sharp instrument; the juices will run clear, with no tinge of pink, when the meat is fully cooked.

Other health considerations—both pro and con—surround the use of sodium nitrate and sodium nitrite in sausages and cured meats. These compounds serve to develop color and flavor in the meat and to protect against the growth of toxins responsible for botulism. Some evidence, however, suggests that these chemicals may be carcinogenic. Food authorities have consequently recommended reductions in the amounts used in the preparation of cured meats. Pork, bacon and sausages cured without the aid of sodium nitrate or sodium nitrite are available in some health-food stores and specialty markets.

Buying and storing pork

Color and consistency are the two best guides when you are purchasing pork. The prime loin cuts should be pale but tinged with pink, and the fat should be pure white. Cuts from the shoulder and legs generally are darker and more coarsely grained. Both the flesh and the fat of all fresh cuts should be firm to the touch. Similarly, when buying ham and bacon, look for clean, white fat and firm, pink meat. Smithfield and country hams are usually covered partly or wholly with harmless black mold; this can be easily scrubbed off after the meat is soaked.

Like all meat, pork should be stored in the coldest part of the refrigerator. Before refrigerating the meat, remove any loose paper in which it may be wrapped. Set the meat on a wire rack above a plate or platter and cover it loosely with foil or a large bowl; the plate will catch draining meat juices, while the covering will help to prevent the meat from drying out. Ground pork will keep in these conditions for one to two days, cuts of fresh pork for three to four days, and bacon and cured ham (excluding Smithfield and country hams, of course) for five to seven days.

To freeze fresh pork, wrap it snugly in freezer paper and seal the package tight with freezer tape. It can be kept for three to six months. Cured ham and bacon should not be stored in a freezer for more than a month because of the danger that their salt content may turn their fat rancid.

Cooking and serving pork

There have long been two complementary but distinct traditions of pork cookery. On one hand, the meat has been treated as fare for banquets and celebrations; on the other, it has served as a mainstay of family cooking.

The Roman satirist Juvenal described the pig as "the animal born for feasting." The time of boar's-head centerpieces for banquets is long past, but Juvenal's description is still borne out by such glorious dishes as a roast suckling pig *(pages 46-47)* or a massive roast fresh ham, its succulent flesh covered by a golden layer of crackling—rind crisped by the oven's heat *(pages 40-41)*—or by a rich glaze of pan juices *(pages 38-39)*.

Despite its festive uses, fresh pork has occupied a relatively small place in France's haute cuisine. The great French chef Auguste Escoffier noted in his *Guide Culinaire* that "however deservedly pork may be praised, it could never have been included among the preparations of first-class cookery (except subsidiarily) had it not been for the culinary value of ham." Part of the reason for such neglect may have been the overfat pigs that were the only kind available until modern times; part of it may also be attributed to the slightly sweet savor of the meat, which is not to every taste.

Pork meat today is lean, however, and any sweetness can be easily counterbalanced by salting the meat down for a relatively short time before cooking it *(pages 14-15)*. The tender flesh, in consequence, becomes amazingly delicate in flavor, suitable for such classic dishes as the poached loin roast chilled in jelly demonstrated on pages 56-57, or the deep-fried loin slices—tender as scallops of veal—demonstrated on pages 30-31.

Pork lends itself equally well to humble but hearty dishes—the many combinations of pork and sauerkraut found in Germany, for example, or the assemblage of poached cuts known as *potée (pages 58-59)* that has graced French farmers' tables for centuries. The range of pork dishes is enormous, and one of the pleasures of exploring pork cookery lies in experimenting with garnishes and flavorings. You can, for example, scent roast pork with rosemary, in the Italian manner, or garnish paprika-spiced pork with sour cream and chopped gherkins, a favored Central European combination, or cook it in an Oriental sweet-and-sour mixture of soy sauce, ginger, and sugar or honey. More than 200 recipes appear in the anthology that makes up the second half of the book, yet this international selection should be regarded as no more than an outline of pork's possibilities.

Beverages with pork

The choice of drinks to serve with pork also is wide, but it should be approached with some care, since a suitable beverage depends not only on the type of pork served, but also on the other ingredients that help flavor the meat.

Substantial *potées (pages 58-59)* and poached salt pork, for example, call for beer, as do spicy sausages. A heavy German lager, dark and mellow tasting, admirably sets off this hearty food. Or, to lighten the meal, choose a Northern European—Dutch, Danish, Swedish or Norwegian—lager. These slightly acidic, faintly sharp-tasting beers provide a fine contrast to the taste of the meat.

Hams—particularly country and Smithfield hams, whose saltiness might overcome a wine—are also effectively accompanied by beer or by hard cider. If you wish to serve wine with these rich-tasting meats, choose a dry, full-bodied rosé: a Tavel from the Rhône Valley, or a Côtes-du-Rhône rosé. California produces a rosé wine from the Pinot noir grape; this, too, could be served with ham.

If the ham has a sweet glaze, however, or if you are serving a cut of pork that is cooked with sweet ingredients, a fairly sweet white wine is in order: A dry wine would taste acidic if served with a sweet-tasting dish. Elegant, fruity Rheinhessen wines from Germany or Rieslings from Alsace would enhance a loin of pork stuffed with apricots *(pages 42-43)*. With a richer glazed ham *(pages 64-65),* a fuller, fruitier Rheingau would be complementary, as would a soft, fairly full Verdicchio from Italy.

Many pork dishes are quite delicate in flavor, often displaying the mild sweetness characteristic of the meat itself: A suckling pig *(pages 46-49)* and roast leg of pork or a cold loin encased in aspic *(pages 56-57)* are cases in point. Such dishes are most

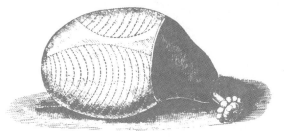

pleasingly partnered by dry white wines with an undercurrent of sweetness. Gewürztraminers possess these qualities. A more complexly flavored wine would be a Pouilly-Fumé. And a less expensive possibility is the white wine made in California from the Sauvignon grape.

It is not, of course, imperative to serve white wines with pork and ham. Reds that are fruity but not too robust—Beaujolais or, from California, Zinfandel—make excellent accompaniments. The rule to remember is that there are no set rules; in this, as in all aspects of pork cookery, experience and your own palate will prove the surest guides.

A Guide to Fresh Cuts

If you know which part of the carcass fresh pork comes from, you will know how tender it is and, therefore, how to cook it. The front of the animal contains small muscles with many connective tissues. This tough, fibrous meat is best tenderized by poaching or braising. The rear section contains large muscles and little connective tissue; its meat is tender enough to roast or fry. The back muscles are little used; this very tender meat may be cooked by any method. Belly cuts are poached or broiled to render their fat.

Pork carcasses are split, then divided into the primal cuts shown in the central diagram (the loin is shown cut in three). Primal cuts are further divided into retail cuts, identified here by their standard meat-industry names.

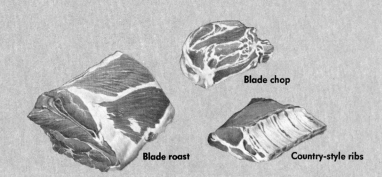

Blade roast

Blade chop

Country-style ribs

Blade end. The fattiest part of the loin, this cut is meaty and tender. Blade roasts, cut from the front of the blade end, contain three to nine ribs and may be sliced into single-rib blade chops. Country-style ribs are made by sawing across the ribs into the muscle, then splitting the meat lengthwise into halves.

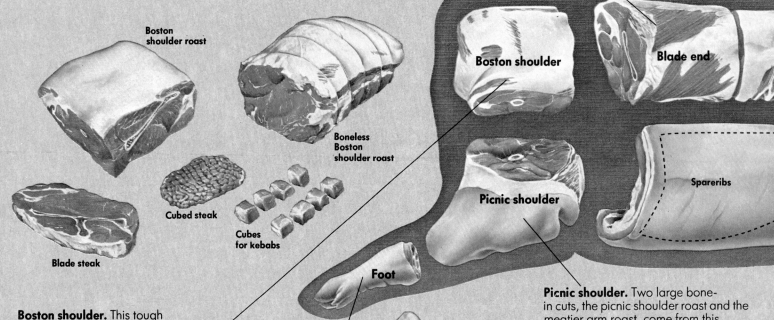

Boston shoulder roast

Boneless Boston shoulder roast

Cubed steak

Cubes for kebabs

Blade steak

Boston shoulder

Blade end

Picnic shoulder

Spareribs

Foot

Boston shoulder. This tough primal cut yields bone-in or boneless roasts or bone-in blade steaks. Some meat is scored to tenderize it, then sold as cube steaks; any of the larger cuts may be cubed to make kebabs.

Picnic shoulder. Two large bone-in cuts, the picnic shoulder roast and the meatier arm roast, come from this tough, fatty section. The arm roast may be divided into steaks, and the lower part of the shoulder — the animal's leg — is divided into cross sections to make hocks. The remainder of the picnic shoulder is used for ground pork.

Pig's feet

Pig's feet. Cut from the forelegs or hindlegs, feet contain little meat. Although they may be served alone (page 78), they are mostly used in stock.

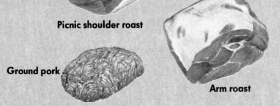

Picnic shoulder roast

Ground pork

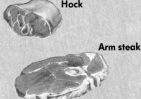

Arm roast

Hock

Arm steak

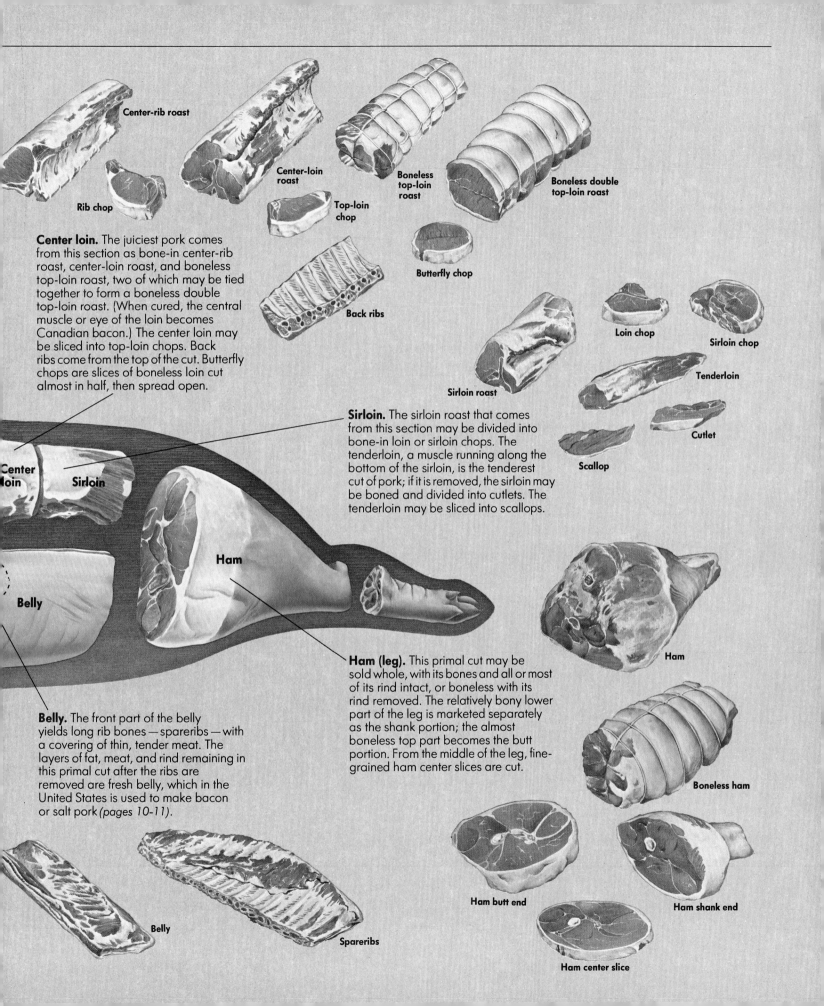

Center-rib roast

Rib chop

Center-loin roast

Top-loin chop

Boneless top-loin roast

Boneless double top-loin roast

Butterfly chop

Back ribs

Center loin. The juiciest pork comes from this section as bone-in center-rib roast, center-loin roast, and boneless top-loin roast, two of which may be tied together to form a boneless double top-loin roast. (When cured, the central muscle or eye of the loin becomes Canadian bacon.) The center loin may be sliced into top-loin chops. Back ribs come from the top of the cut. Butterfly chops are slices of boneless loin cut almost in half, then spread open.

Center Loin

Sirloin

Sirloin roast

Loin chop

Sirloin chop

Tenderloin

Cutlet

Scallop

Sirloin. The sirloin roast that comes from this section may be divided into bone-in loin or sirloin chops. The tenderloin, a muscle running along the bottom of the sirloin, is the tenderest cut of pork; if it is removed, the sirloin may be boned and divided into cutlets. The tenderloin may be sliced into scallops.

Ham

Belly

Ham

Boneless ham

Belly. The front part of the belly yields long rib bones — spareribs — with a covering of thin, tender meat. The layers of fat, meat, and rind remaining in this primal cut after the ribs are removed are fresh belly, which in the United States is used to make bacon or salt pork *(pages 10-11)*.

Ham (leg). This primal cut may be sold whole, with its bones and all or most of its rind intact, or boneless with its rind removed. The relatively bony lower part of the leg is marketed separately as the shank portion; the almost boneless top part becomes the butt portion. From the middle of the leg, fine-grained ham center slices are cut.

Belly

Spareribs

Ham butt end

Ham shank end

Ham center slice

Understanding Cured Cuts

The curing processes used to turn fresh pork into ham, bacon or salt pork all begin with salt, applied to the uncooked meat either as crystals or as brine. The salt draws out moisture, thus concentrating the meat's taste and firming its texture. Other ingredients—sugar and various chemical compounds, among them sodium nitrite and nitrate *(page 6)*—may be added to give the meat flavor and color. The longer the salting, the drier the meat. After about 40 days, the salted meat contains so little moisture that decay-causing organisms cannot grow.

Preservation of the meat was the purpose of salting for centuries. Today, however, most hams and bacon—described in the first three columns of the chart at right—are not, in fact, preserved. They are salted, and sometimes smoked, only long enough to give them the robust flavor that the old preserving methods imparted. The modern processes draw out little fluid, and the meat stays moist and mild-flavored. Cuts cured this way must be refrigerated as if they were fresh.

Country or Smithfield hams are quite a different matter. They, too, are salted or brined, but the salting period is followed by aging, smoking, or both. The procedure may take as long as a year, by which time the meat will have lost as much as 30 per cent of its weight in fluids. Its flesh will be firm, dark and rich in flavor. And this meat can last as long as two years without refrigeration.

	Dry Salt Cure	Wet Salt Cure
Method of Curing	The meat is rubbed with a mixture of salt and sodium nitrate, then refrigerated for up to seven days per inch [2½ cm.] of thickness.	The meat is covered with a brine of salt, sodium nitrite and water, then refrigerated up to nine days per inch [2½ cm.] of thickness. Or the meat is injected with brine, then refrigerated 24 hours.
Retail Label	Salted or corned ham; salt pork.	Corned ham; salt pork.
Advance Preparation	Soak hams in cold water for six to 12 hours; parboil them in fresh water for 25 to 30 minutes. Parboil salt pork for five minutes.	Soak hams in cold water for six to 12 hours; parboil them in fresh water for 25 to 30 minutes. Parboil salt pork for five minutes.

The chart above describes the standard methods of curing pork and gives the retail label name

Smoked country-style ham

Smoked brine-injected ham

Identifying cured cuts. The varying colors in this array of cured meats reveal the techniques used in their curing. Country and Smithfield hams have dark rinds—sometimes flecked with a harmless mold—and wine-red meat. Smoked, brine-injected hams have brown rinds and pale pink flesh, whereas salt-cured or corned hams have almost white rinds. Salt pork and smoked slab—or unsliced—bacon are streaked with firm, white fat.

Brine-injection Cure	Smoked Country Cure	Air-dried Country Cure	Smithfield or Virginia Cure
The meat is injected with a brine of salt, sodium compounds and sugar, aged at room temperature for one week and smoked for six to 48 hours. If then heated to an internal temperature of 155° F. [68° C.], the meat is sold as "ready-to-eat" or "fully cooked."	Large cuts are coated with salt, sodium nitrate and sugar, refrigerated 30 days, washed, and refrigerated 14 to 28 days. Or they are brined three days per pound [½ kg.] and refrigerated 15 to 20 days. All are then smoked 18 to 24 hours and aged 20 to 30 days. Bacon is dry-salted for 10 days or brined for 15 to 21, then smoked.	Large cuts are dry-salt cured for about 30 days, then washed, and refrigerated for 14 to 28 days. Or they are brined for three days per pound [½ kg.], then refrigerated for 15 to 20 days. Finally, large cuts are aged for 40 days. Bacon is dry-salted for 10 days or brined for 15 to 21 days, then sold.	The meat is coated with a mixture of salt, sodium nitrate and sugar, refrigerated for five days, resalted, refrigerated for one day per pound [½ kg.], then washed, and refrigerated for 14 days. Finally, the meat is smoked for 10 days, and aged for six to 12 months.
Smoked or sugar-cured ham, Boston and picnic shoulder, loin, hock, Canadian bacon, bacon.	Smoked country-style ham or picnic shoulder; country-style bacon.	Air-dried country-style ham; country-style bacon.	Smithfield or Virginia ham or picnic shoulder; Smithfield bacon.
No advance preparation needed.	Soak for 12 to 24 hours in several changes of cold water. Scrub off any mold with a stiff brush. Sliced bacon needs no soaking.	Soak for 12 to 24 hours in several changes of cold water. Scrub off any mold with a stiff brush. Sliced bacon needs no soaking.	Soak for 12 to 36 hours in several changes of cold water. Scrub off any mold with a stiff brush. Sliced bacon needs no soaking.

associated with each method. It also shows the preparations needed to rid each type of meat of excess salt before baking, braising or poaching.

Corned ham

Smithfield ham

Smoked brine-injected bacon

Salt pork

The Basics of Boning

Pork cuts can be bought already boned, but if you do this rather simple job yourself, you save money and can prepare the meat exactly as you want it. Moreover, you can then use the bones for a stock base *(page 16)* or to enrich a braising or poaching liquid *(pages 56-57 and 62-63)*. To do the boning, all you need is a cutting board, a sharp-tipped knife with a slender, flexible blade, and a general knowledge of the animal's skeleton.

Whole hams or butt portions often contain an irregularly shaped portion of the pelvic bone—the aitch bone—that will impede a carving knife. To simplify slicing hams, this bone can be removed before cooking *(top row, right)*. Do not try to remove embedded leg bones, however: The deep incisions needed would allow valuable juices to escape.

If you wish to produce a completely boneless piece of meat to roll into a roast or fill with stuffing *(pages 42-43 and 62-63)*, choose a center-rib loin, center loin, blade end or Boston shoulder roast. The center-rib loin, center loin and blade end all contain a section of backbone and ribs; it is removed by the steps shown here with a center-rib loin *(middle row)*. Additionally, the center loin contains a section of tenderloin, and the blade end often has a flat section of blade bone at one end. Before these cuts are boned, the tenderloin must be detached from the backbone, but not cut off, or the blade bone must be cut out. Boston shoulder contains only a single portion of shoulder blade and is perhaps the simplest cut to bone *(bottom row)*.

Though the details of the boning vary with each cut, there are certain basics that apply to all. Refrigerate loin cuts or Boston shoulder for six hours and ham for at least 12 hours to firm the flesh and fat so that the meat will be easy to cut. Work slowly, cutting as close to the bone as possible to avoid wasting meat. After you have loosened the flesh from the bone, use your free hand to pull it aside, so that you can see where to place the knife as you cut deeper into the meat. Since the knife can get slippery, make sure you keep the fingers of your free hand away from the edge of the blade, and keep the tip of the blade pointed away from your body.

Preparing a Ham

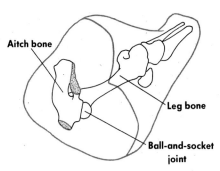

Ham bones. Visible as protrusions on the meat surface — the shaded areas here — the aitch bone is linked by a ball-and-socket joint to the leg bone, which runs through the ham.

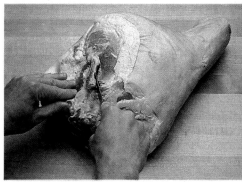

Beginning the cut. On the butt end of the ham, insert the knife into the flesh on the right side of the visible aitch bone. Cut in about ¾ inch [2 cm.] to free the flesh from that side of the bone.

Dealing with a Center-Rib Loin

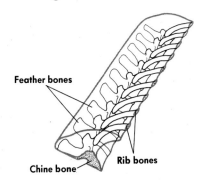

Loin bones. The chine, a part of the backbone, runs the length of this cut; the ribs arch out from it. Thin feather bones may extend from the chine at a right angle to the ribs.

Separating the ribs. Lay the loin, chine side down, on a work surface. Working close to the bone, slice between the ribs and the flesh, pulling back the freed meat as you cut.

Boning a Boston Shoulder

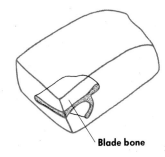

Boston shoulder bones. The shoulder blade in this cut appears on the surface as a straight line on one side, and as a hook surmounted by a straight line on the adjacent side.

Beginning the cut. Place the Boston shoulder fat side down so that you can see a straight line of bone on the surface. Slice into the meat along the top edge of the bone.

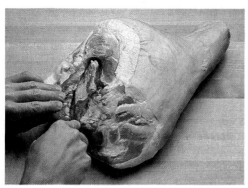

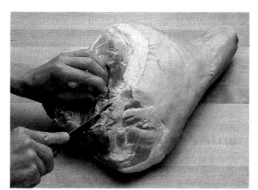

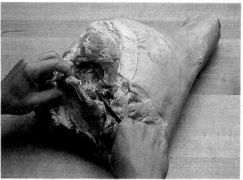

2 **Continuing the cut.** Cut around the top of the bone and down the left side, keeping the blade parallel to the bone surface. As you work, pull the flesh gently back from the bone.

3 **Freeing the bone.** When you have cut completely around the bone, deepen the cut and pull back the flesh to expose the joint that connects the aitch bone to the leg bone.

4 **Removing the bone.** Grasp the aitch bone and twist it to loosen it in its socket and expose the cartilage at the base of the joint. Cut through the cartilage and pull out the aitch bone.

2 **Freeing the ribs.** Complete the cut along the inner surface of the ribs. Make sure to slice all the way down to the base of the ribs so that the knife comes in contact with the chine.

3 **Freeing the chine.** Working from the end closest to you, angle the knife to follow the shape of the knobby top of the chine, freeing the meat from each knob.

4 **Completing the boning.** Cut along the chine until all the meat is free. If the loin has feather bones (this one does not), angle the knife to cut over them.

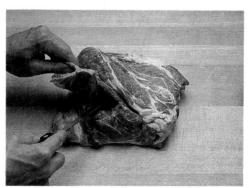

2 **Freeing the top meat.** Lifting the flesh, work inward until the entire top of the shoulder blade is exposed. Then cut under the bone, sliding the knife around the curves of the hook.

3 **Freeing the underside.** Continue to cut around the curves of the hook on both of its surfaces, lifting the bone away from the flesh as you go.

4 **Removing the blade bone.** Adjust the position of the bone with your hand to facilitate the work, and cut behind the bone to free it completely from the meat; then pull out the bone.

Advance Infusions of Flavor

Two techniques are used to endow fresh pork with flavor before it is cooked: salting and marinating. Salting, a simplified home version of the professional curing process described on pages 10-11, can be done in two ways: either by packing the pork in salt crystals or by immersing it in brine. When done at home, neither method is intended to preserve the meat, but both will alter its flavor and texture. Those who consider pork unduly sweet will find that it loses that quality after a minimum salting period of 12 hours. Treated longer—up to seven days with dry salt, nine days with brine for each inch [2½ cm.] of thickness—the pork becomes progressively drier, firmer and, of course, saltier.

Dry salt crystals liquefy as they absorb moisture from the pork; this liquid must be discarded and the salt replenished every three days or so. Brine, on the other hand, needs only to be stirred occasionally. When the salting time is minimal, these two methods produce much the same results with equal ease. If the salting is to be lengthy, however, most cooks find that brine is the more convenient medium for thick cuts such as Boston shoulder *(opposite)*. They reserve dry-salting for thin cuts such as spareribs or the belly shown below.

In either case, the salt of choice is coarse-ground: sea salt, pickling salt or kosher salt, all of which are free of the additives that diminish the flavor of fine-ground table salt. Some cooks include saltpeter (sodium nitrate) in their salting mixtures to heighten flavor; it has been omitted in these demonstrations because it toughens meat and may be a health hazard.

The salting vessel must be porcelain, stoneware, glazed earthenware or glass; a metal vessel may react with the brine and flavor it. To ensure that the meat does not spoil during salting, refrigerate it. If there are jointed bones in a large cut such as ham, insert a needle into the center of the joint so that the salt or brine penetrates to the bone before microbial action can start.

After being salted for 12 hours or so, pork can be wiped dry and cooked as if it were fresh meat. After three days of salting, soak it in fresh water for four hours before cooking it; after five days, soak it for six hours; and after a week or more, soak it overnight and parboil it in fresh water for 15 to 30 minutes *(pages 10-11)*.

By contrast, marinating is a brief process: The recommended times are one to three hours at room temperature and up to 30 hours in the refrigerator. If the marinating period were longer, the acids in the mixture would impart a gamy taste to the pork.

Marinades not only flavor uncooked meat, they also tenderize it. Marinades may consist of almost any combination of flavoring ingredients, but they usually include an acid element—such as vinegar or wine—that breaks down tough fibers in the meat. The acidity also adds a touch of piquancy that contrasts with the other more aromatic flavorings such as onions and herbs.

Dry-Salting with an Herbal Fillip

1 **Salting the pork.** In a bowl, mix coarse salt with various flavorings: Ground allspice and cloves, crushed juniper berries and bay leaf, pepper and dried herbs are used here. Spread a layer of the mixture in a glass or glazed-earthenware dish. Put the pork—in this case, belly—in the dish. Rub the mixture over the meat, then pack more salt around the pork.

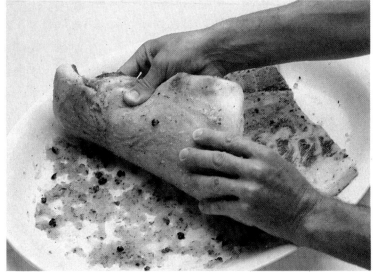

2 **Turning the pork.** Cover the dish and refrigerate it, turning the pork now and then and rubbing it with the salt in the dish. Leave the meat in the salt for at least 12 hours; for recipes calling for salt pork, it should be left for three to seven days. After about 10 hours, brine will form. At three-day intervals, discard the brine and rub the pork with additional salt.

Bathing Meat in Brine

1 **Preparing the brine.** Fill a large pan with cold water. Use muslin or cheesecloth to wrap spices and herbs — in this case, juniper berries, cloves, thyme, bay leaves and mace. Drop the bag into the water. Pour in salt and sugar. Bring to a boil over medium heat. Skim off any scum. Take the pan off the heat when the salt dissolves.

2 **Submerging the pork.** Cool the brine. With a butcher's needle, pierce the meat — Boston shoulder, here — ¼ inch [6 mm.] deep in several places to help the brine penetrate it. Put the meat in a deep crock or pot. Remove the wrapped seasonings from the brine and discard them. Pour the cold brine over the pork (above).

3 **Weighting the pork.** To prevent the pork from floating to the surface, place a plate on top of it. Weight the plate with a stone or a ceramic or glass weight, such as the water-filled preserving jar shown here; a metal weight would react with the brine. Check that the meat is completely submerged, then cover the pot.

4 **Brining the pork.** Put the pot in the refrigerator and let the pork steep in the brine for at least three days. For stronger flavor, brine the pork for up to nine days per inch [2½ cm.] of thickness, stirring with a wooden spoon every three days. When the pork is salted to your taste, lift it from the pot and rinse it in a bowl of cold water.

An Aromatic Wine Marinade

Immersing pork in liquid. Set the pork to be marinated — cubed picnic shoulder is shown — in a bowl. Sprinkle with herbs and aromatics — in this case, parsley, thyme, bay leaf, garlic and onions. Add enough red wine to cover (above). Cover and leave at room temperature for one to three hours, or refrigerate overnight.

A Green-Pepper Coating

Enveloping the pork. Seed and chop green peppers and put them in a mortar with salt and garlic or fresh ginger root and onion. Pound the mixture to a pulp, then moisten it with dry white wine. Spoon the mixture over the pork — cutlets are shown. Turn the meat to coat it. Cover the dish, and refrigerate it for up to 24 hours.

Capturing Meaty Essences in the Stockpot

A good stock, made by simmering meat and bones in water with aromatic vegetables and herbs, is one of the foundations of pork—as of most meat—cookery. It can be used equally well as a rich cooking liquid for braising and poaching or as a base for sauces *(opposite, below)*.

The stock can be made with any uncooked pork bones and meat trimmings provided that the meat is fresh rather than salted or smoked. Chicken or veal scraps may be included for extra flavor. If you add fresh pork rind, hocks, pig's ears or feet—all of which contain a good deal of natural gelatin—the stock will set to a jelly when chilled and can then be used to coat cold dishes *(pages 58-59)*.

In the preparation of the stock *(below)*, the meat and bones should first be covered with cold water and slowly heated. As the water approaches a boil, proteins drawn from the meat coagulate and rise to the surface in a gray scum. Skim repeatedly; if scum is present when the water reaches a rolling boil, it will cloud the stock. To produce the clearest cooking liquid, add a little cold water to the pan, then bring the liquid back to a boil, skimming off the scum again as it forms.

After herbs and aromatic vegetables are added, the stock should simmer for at least three hours. Finally, it should be strained and cleansed of all fat.

You can make the stock in advance and store it in the refrigerator; it will keep for three to four days if it is boiled for a few minutes every day to prevent the growth

Making the Basic Stock

1 Preparing the stock. Set a rack in the bottom of the pot. Put meaty pork trimmings and bones—in this case accompanied by the gizzard and wing tips of a chicken—in a stockpot; cover with cold water.

2 Skimming the stock. Place the pot over low heat. With a ladle, skim off the scum that forms as the water comes to a boil. Add cold water, return to a boil and repeat until no more scum rises.

3 Assembling flavorings. Tie fresh herbs and vegetables—leek tops, celery, thyme, parsley and bay leaves are used—into a bundle to make a bouquet garni. Peel garlic, carrots and onions; stick one onion with cloves.

4 Simmering the stock. Add the bouquet garni and vegetables to the stock along with a dash of salt. Set a lid ajar over the pan. Adjust the heat and simmer for about four hours.

5 Straining the stock. Discard the large pieces of meat and vegetables. Strain the stock into a bowl through a colander lined with a double layer of dampened muslin or cheesecloth. Discard the solid ingredients.

6 Cleansing the stock. Cool the stock, then refrigerate it overnight. The next morning, lift off the solidified fat with a spoon. Remove the last traces by blotting the stock gently with a paper towel wrung out in hot water.

of bacteria. Stock can be stored in a freezer for months if it is tightly covered.

Pork stock is a natural starting point for a variety of sauces to accompany pork. The most straightforward is a velouté ("velvety") sauce *(recipe, page 166)*. It is made by blending stock with roux, the cooked mixture of flour and butter often used to thicken sauces. To achieve the smooth texture that its name implies, the velouté should be whisked to remove any lumps, then simmered for at least 40 minutes. Long cooking reduces the sauce and gives it extra body, as well as eliminating the taste of raw flour.

A velouté sauce can, in turn, be used as a base for other sauces associated with pork cookery. In the demonstration below, it is combined with onion, white wine and mustard *(Steps 4 and 5)* to make a piquant *sauce Robert (recipe, page 166),* one of the oldest of French sauces. The addition of sour gherkins *(Step 6)* transforms the *sauce Robert* into a *sauce charcutière:* literally, "the sauce of the pork butcher's wife." These sharp-flavored sauces make excellent accompaniments to broiled or poached pork.

Though the *Robert* and the *charcutière* are the velouté-based sauces most often associated with pork, other variations are worth exploring. Puréed tomatoes stirred into a velouté make a rich sauce suitable with broiled or poached cuts, while a velouté sauce flavored with a Madeira braising base is a classic accompaniment to braised ham *(recipe, page 149).*

Velouté and Its Variations

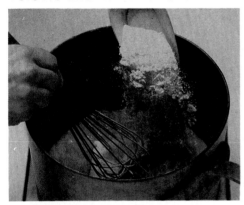

1 **Making a roux.** In a heavy saucepan, melt butter over low heat. Whisk flour into the butter. Stirring continuously, cook this roux for three or four minutes, until it turns golden.

2 **Adding stock.** Pour the stock — it may be either hot or cold — into the roux, whisking as you pour. Whisk until the sauce begins to boil. Move the pan half off the burner, and reduce the heat so that the sauce simmers.

3 **Cleansing the sauce.** Skim off the fat that repeatedly forms on the cooler side of the liquid. After no more fat appears, continue to simmer the sauce for at least 40 minutes. At this stage you can serve it as a velouté.

4 **Preparing a sauce Robert.** Sauté a finely chopped onion in butter over low heat until it starts to color. Stir in a little dry white wine. Ladle in the velouté sauce *(above)* and stir with a wooden spoon to blend all of the ingredients.

5 **Finishing the sauce Robert.** Skim the sauce *(Step 3, above),* if necessary, to remove impurities. Stir a spoonful of prepared mustard into the sauce. To complete the sauce, adjust the seasoning to your taste.

6 **Making sauce charcutière.** Slice sour gherkins lengthwise into thin strips. Add the gherkin strips to the hot *sauce Robert,* and stir them in. Serve the *sauce charcutière* immediately.

A Quartet of Savory Stuffings

Stuffings give extra substance to pork dishes, and help cuts such as boneless Boston shoulder retain their shape during cooking; but their principal function is to contribute flavor. They are particularly useful for enlivening the mild, slightly sweet taste of fresh pork. Although pork can be stuffed with simply a handful of herbs or with dried fruit *(pages 42-43)*, most stuffings—including the four demonstrated here—are based on bread and eggs. The bread adds body and the eggs bind the mixture together.

Almost all mixed stuffings include a sprinkling of herbs, but in the aromatic sage-and-onion preparation demonstrated at right *(recipe, page 100)*, the herb is given a more prominent role. Fresh sage leaves have a strong, slightly acrid flavor; they may be blanched—plunged into boiling water for a few seconds—to mellow their taste. The natural sweetness of onions balances the acerbity of the sage; before being chopped and added to the stuffing, the onions can be baked in their skins to concentrate their flavor.

The flavor of onions is subordinate in stuffings made with *duxelles*—a combination of finely chopped mushrooms and onions sautéed in butter *(opposite, top; recipe, page 130)*. To bring out the mixture's essence, it should be cooked until the moisture that the mushrooms contain has evaporated and the vegetables start to stick to the bottom of the pan.

Many stuffings include meat and thus tend to emphasize the pork's own taste. They may simply consist of raw or leftover, cooked meat trimmings and flavorings added to an egg-and-bread-crumb base *(opposite, center; recipe, page 128)*, or they may contain some vegetable ingredient such as spinach *(opposite, bottom; recipe, page 103)*. In either case, the meat will not require precooking, provided that the final timing of the pork takes account of the extra bulk.

To prevent such a stuffing from drying out as it cooks, include some fatty meat along with the lean. The meat will be more succulent if it is chopped by hand rather than ground; grinding crushes the fibers of the meat, forcing out the juices.

A Blend of Sage and Onion

1 **Preparing the ingredients.** Bake unpeeled onions in a 325° F. [160° C.] oven for one hour until soft; let them cool. Trim the crusts from firm, dry bread and soak it briefly in warm water, then squeeze it dry and put it in a bowl. Add eggs and chopped beef suet; season with salt, pepper and spices. Blanch and drain sage leaves. Peel the onions.

2 **Mixing ingredients.** Chop the peeled onions into small pieces. Bunch the sage leaves and chop them fine. Add the onions and sage to the mixture in the bowl. Use both hands to mix all the ingredients *(above)*.

3 **Adjusting consistency.** Knead the mixture together until you form a moist paste. If the mixture seems runny, add a few dry bread crumbs to soak up excess liquid; if it seems too crumbly, add another egg. Sprinkle a handful of flour over the stuffing; it will absorb fat and juices during cooking.

4 **Working in the flour.** Using both hands, mix the flour with the rest of the ingredients, making sure that it is distributed throughout the stuffing. The mixture should be even textured and firm enough to hold its shape.

Duxelles: A Mushroom Concentrate

1 **Cooking the duxelles.** Sauté chopped onions in butter until soft. Add chopped mushrooms and stir until the liquid evaporates — about five minutes.

2 **Combining ingredients.** Mix the *duxelles* with bread crumbs, eggs and herbs. Season with salt, pepper, nutmeg and lemon juice.

3 **Mixing the stuffing.** Work the ingredients together lightly: Too much force will produce a pasty stuffing.

A Pork-based Mixture

1 **Chopping.** Pound garlic with seasonings. Chop fresh pork trimmings into fine bits. Assemble parsley, an egg, herbs and bread crumbs.

2 **Stirring the mixture.** Chop the parsley, then add all of the ingredients to the mortar. Using a fork, stir until the egg has been absorbed.

3 **Kneading the stuffing.** Gently knead the mixture to distribute the ingredients. The stuffing should have a supple, pastelike consistency.

A Meat-and-Vegetable Alliance

1 **Preparing the spinach.** Parboil stemmed spinach leaves and drain them. Cool them under running water, then squeeze the leaves dry.

2 **Assembling ingredients.** Chop the spinach. Chop fresh pork and mix it with eggs, bread crumbs, herbs, parsley, onion and seasonings.

3 **Mixing the stuffing.** Add the spinach. With your hands, mix the ingredients, adding more bread crumbs for a firm texture if necessary.

The Simple Art of Sausage Making

Fresh pork sausage consists of chopped or ground meat that may be shaped into patties for frying or encased in some natural material—cleaned pork, lamb or beef intestines, usually—for cooking by any method. The meat texture may be varied at will, as may the flavorings *(recipes, pages 86-90)*.

Little special equipment is required for making sausages. A sharp knife can be used to chop the meat, but a food grinder is faster. If you have a grinder, a sausage-stuffing attachment is convenient but not essential: Sausage casings can easily be stuffed by hand with the aid of a wide-tubed sausage funnel.

As a general rule, lamb and pork casings yield sausages of the right size for frying and broiling: about 1 inch [2½ cm.] in diameter. Larger beef casings are best used for coarse-textured poaching sausages 1½ to 2 inches [4 to 5 cm.] thick *(box, opposite, bottom left)*.

These casings are available in bulk from wholesalers and in smaller quantities from butchers. They generally have been either brined or dry-salted, in which case they must be soaked beforehand to remove salt *(Step 1, right)*. Buy twice the amount of casing you need; the material tears easily. Leftover casings may be repacked in coarse salt and refrigerated almost indefinitely for later use.

A less familiar but delicious natural covering is pork caul, a fatty stomach membrane obtainable at butcher shops. Wrapped around sausage meat by hand, it will adhere of its own accord *(box, opposite, bottom right)*. The French word for caul—*crépine*—has given these sausages the name *crépinettes*.

Sausage fillings must include not only meat but fat, which will keep the meat moist. The proportions of meat to fat can vary widely, but one part fat to two parts meat is a sensible starting point. Boston and picnic shoulders are good, inexpensive sources of lean meat. The fat may come from the belly or the back, but it must be fresh and cut about ¼ inch [6 mm.] thick. Both meat and fat should be chilled thoroughly to firm them for easy chopping and grinding.

If wrapped snugly in foil or plastic, homemade sausages will keep in the refrigerator for three days.

1 Soaking the casings. Place brined or dry-salted casing—in this demonstration, pork casing—in a bowl of tepid water. To remove any strong odor, add 1 teaspoon [5 ml.] of vinegar or lemon juice for each quart [1 liter] of water. Soak until the casings absorb some of the water and become soft and elastic—about 30 minutes.

2 Rinsing the casings. Run cold water from a faucet—or pour it from a pitcher through a funnel as shown here—into each casing to rinse and open it. Drain the casings in a colander, but do not dry them; moisture will keep them supple.

6 Filling the casing. Ease a few more inches of casing off the tube, grinding in more meat. Continue until the casing has been stuffed tight to within 3 inches [8 cm.] of its end. Detach the casing from the tube and knot the open end. If the casing tears as you fill it, cut it off, knot the end and begin again with the remaining casing.

7 Forming links. With your hands, roll the sausage on a table to distribute the filling evenly. Leave the sausage in one long cylinder and coil it for cooking as demonstrated on pages 28-29. Alternatively, form links by twisting the sausage through *(above)* at regular intervals. To prevent unwinding, twist successive links in opposite directions.

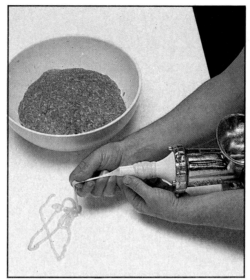

3 **Preparing the stuffing.** Trim connective tissue from lean meat, then chop the meat and about half as much fat into coarse pieces. Pass the meat and fat through a food grinder's medium disk. Mix the ground mixture with salt, pepper and flavorings — in this case, mixed herbs, grated nutmeg and ground cloves and allspice.

4 **Fitting on the casing.** Fit a sausage-stuffing attachment onto the grinder. Gently push one end of a casing 2 yards [180 cm.] long onto the tube of the stuffing attachment. Gather the casing over the tube until a section only 6 inches [15 cm.] long hangs free. Make a knot in the casing 3 inches [8 cm.] from the free end.

5 **Starting the grinding.** Fill the bowl of the grinder with the sausage mixture, and turn the handle to push a small amount of meat into the free-hanging length of casing. Push the meat toward the knot with your fingers to be sure no air pockets form in the casing between the tube and the knot.

Stuffing Casings by Hand

1 **Varying texture.** Trim any fat from lean pork. Cut the meat into ½-inch [1-cm.] cubes. Grind two thirds of the meat, using the medium disk of the food grinder; grind half of the ground meat again, using the fine disk. Cut chilled pork fat — about half as much as the total amount of meat — into ¼-inch [6-mm.] cubes. Season the meat and fat.

2 **Stuffing the casing.** Gather a rinsed beef casing about 18 inches [45 cm.] long onto the tube of a sausage funnel, leaving 3 inches [8 cm.] free. Force the meat mixture through the funnel, easing off the casing and filling it tight. When the casing is filled to within 3 inches of the tube end, slide it off the funnel. Tie both ends with string.

Wrapping Crépinettes

Wrapping in caul. Rinse the caul — dry-salted caul must be presoaked as in Step 1, above — and cut it into 8-inch [20-cm.] squares. Place a handful of sausage meat in the center of each square. Pat the meat to flatten it, then wrap the caul around the meat and press it gently into place.

1
Frying
A Versatile Method for Smaller Cuts

Cooking bacon without curling

A tidy way to draw fat from sausages

Making the most of pan juices

Fashioning a sausage coil

Creating sauces from a pan glaze

Deep-fried scallops with a piquant crust

A single length of pork sausage, skewered into a tight coil *(pages 28-29)*, emerges sizzling from the frying pan. Slivers of garlic and a bouquet garni, added partway through the cooking, impart their aromas to the sausage. The juices that remain in the pan after frying will form the basis of an accompanying sauce.

Bacon, sausages and sliced ham, as well as chops and other small, lean cuts of fresh pork, are prime candidates for the frying pan. From the cook's point of view, however, these cuts have little else in common. Their diversity precludes any general rules for frying pork: In each case, the method has to be adapted to the variations in the thickness and the fat content of the cuts.

Because of the need to cook pork thoroughly, rapid sautéing—the technique of frying quickly in a little fat at a high heat—is suitable only for the thinnest, leanest slices of fresh pork. Thicker cuts, such as chops, begin their cooking in hot fat to brown the meat. After the initial searing, however, the heat is reduced so that the meat can cook through without burning. Because thick chops may take up to 30 minutes' cooking, some cooks cover the pan with a lid during the gentle frying phase, as shown on page 27, to prevent evaporation and thus help keep the meat moist.

One result of such long, slow frying is that the meat gives out generous quantities of juices that coagulate on the bottom and sides of the pan. When the pork has cooked, you can create a simple sauce by adding a liquid such as wine or water to the pan, then stirring to incorporate the pan deposits *(page 26)*. To make a sauce with more body, chops or thick, boneless pork slices *(pages 28-29)* may be dredged with a bit of flour before they are fried, and the rich pan sauce that results can then be further thickened with heavy cream.

Bacon, sliced ham and sausages should not be given an initial searing: High heat would rapidly drive out their moisture content, causing the meat to shrink or curl. Ham and Canadian bacon, being relatively lean, are best started in a lightly greased pan. But strips of bacon yield ample fat for their own frying, as do link sausages if the casings are pierced beforehand *(pages 24-25)*.

For small, boneless pieces of pork, deep frying *(pages 30-31)* provides an interesting alternative to the more usual shallow-fat technique. To keep the meat from drying out in the high heat, they are given a protective outer coating of batter, flour or an egg-and-bread-crumb mixture; immersion in hot oil seals the coating almost instantly. Because of the high temperatures involved, only thin slices should be used; the coating on larger pieces would burn before the meat was cooked through.

Applying the Fundamentals to the Meat

The frying of sausage, or of bacon, Canadian bacon and ham slices, is a simple affair, calling for only slight adjustments in technique to suit the characteristics of the different meats.

Bacon and ham slices, for example, may have rinds that should be removed or slit *(Step 1, right, top)* before cooking to keep the meat from curling. The casings of link sausages should be pierced in several places *(Step 1, bottom)* to allow the meat to exude fat during cooking; the holes also vent steam that would build up inside the casings and burst them. Loose sausage meat is simply shaped into patties *(box, opposite, bottom)*.

Bacon strips are well laced with fat and may be fried in an unoiled pan. To prevent them from sticking to the pan before they render their fat, and to counter any tendency to curl, fry the slices very slowly over low heat.

Sausages are similarly well endowed with fat and also should be cooked over low heat. However, because their casings slow the release of fat into the pan, they need initial protection against sticking. Instead of adding extra oil or fat—which would produce too much grease—start by simmering the sausages in a little water. By the time the water evaporates, the sausages will have exuded all the fat that is required for cooking.

When you are cooking lean smoked-ham or Canadian-bacon slices, the pan must be greased; otherwise the meat, lacking fat of its own, would stick. The pan for sausage patties should also be greased—but very lightly—to keep the patties intact in early stages of cooking, before they render their own fat.

Crisping Bacon in Its Own Fat

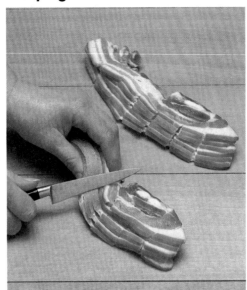

1 **Preparing the bacon.** Hold a handful of bacon slices firmly together and, with a knife, slash across the rind in single strokes, making shallow cuts 1 inch [2½ cm.] apart *(above)*. Or cut the rind from each slice with scissors.

2 **Filling the pan.** Arrange the bacon slices neatly in a cold, heavy skillet. Make sure that the slices do not overlap, since this causes uneven cooking. If the slices are thin and tightly packed together, let them warm to room temperature ahead of time and then heat slightly so you can separate them.

Sausages Browned without Bursting

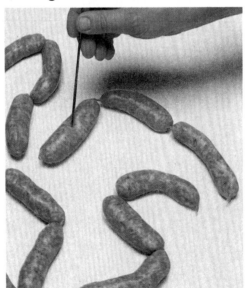

1 **Piercing the sausages.** Separate the sausages, or divide them into linked lengths, as here. Pierce each sausage in two or three places, using any sharp implement, such as a fork, a skewer or a butcher's needle *(above)*.

2 **Adding water.** Place the sausages in a skillet and add ¼ inch [6 mm.] of cold water to the pan. Bring the water to a boil over medium heat and simmer the sausages, rolling them over several times with a slotted spatula for four or five minutes, or until the water evaporates.

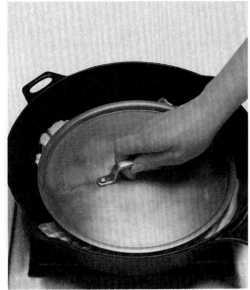

Keeping Lean Slices Moist

3 **Keeping the bacon flat.** Set the skillet over low heat. To ensure that the slices do not curl as they cook, press a lid small enough to fit in the pan over the bacon *(above)*. Pick up the lid from time to time and lift the bacon with a fork to see if it has browned; if it has, turn it and replace the lid.

4 **Cooking and draining.** Depending on the degree of crispness you want, fry bacon slices that are ⅛ to ¼ inch [3 to 6 mm.] thick for five to 10 minutes altogether. Remove the lid and lift the bacon from the pan with a fork or tongs. Drain the bacon on several layers of paper towels or on a cloth *(above)*.

Frying in oil or lard. Lightly grease a skillet with vegetable oil or lard and warm it over medium heat for about two minutes. Cut any rind off the slices, or slash it at 1-inch [2½-cm.] intervals, then lay the slices in the heated pan. Fry for 10 to 12 minutes, turning the slices to brown them evenly.

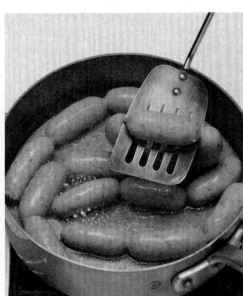

Perfect Sausage Patties

3 **Frying the sausages.** When the water evaporates, the pan should glisten with fat. (If not, add more water to the frying pan and boil it away.) Reduce the heat to low and cook the sausages for about 15 minutes, turning them occasionally to brown them uniformly and to prevent sticking.

4 **Browning and serving.** As soon as the sausages have browned all over, lift them from the pan with the spatula; drain them briefly on paper towels and serve them right away.

Reducing fat. Shape patties of sausage meat ¾ inch [2 cm.] thick and place them in a lightly greased pan set over medium heat. As they cook, gently press the patties several times with a perforated or slotted spatula to squeeze out excess fat. Brown them for five to eight minutes on each side, then drain them on paper towels and serve.

Capitalizing on Natural Juices

A Blueprint for a Pan Fry

Pan frying chops and other fresh pork cuts that are up to 1 inch [2½ cm.] thick requires a relatively long stint at the stove (Steps 1-3, right), but the investment in time yields a delicious dividend. The rich juices drawn from the meat as it cooks coagulate on the bottom of the pan; stirring liquid into these browned deposits—a process known as deglazing—produces a gravy that complements the dish.

The liquid you use for the pan gravy depends on whether you wish to emphasize the pork's natural flavor. In the demonstration at right and below, dry white wine, which is acidic, balances the chops' sweetness; vinegar, beer or hard cider would have a similar effect. To underscore that sweetness, use cream, brandy or fruit juice such as apple or orange.

Alternatively, pans can be deglazed with the moisture exuded by vegetables, whether you are frying chops or more quickly cooked sausages. In the demonstration opposite, below, sweet red, yellow and green peppers are sautéed, then stirred into frying sausages to add their flavor to the cooking residues.

1 **Preparing chops.** With a small paring knife, trim excess fat from the edges of the chops, but leave a thin border of fat to prevent the chops from drying out as they cook. Season the pork chops on both sides with salt and freshly ground pepper (above).

2 **Browning the chops.** Heat a film of oil or lard in a large frying pan. Do not crowd the pan; if the chops are tightly packed, too much moisture will be trapped, and they will stew instead of browning. Brown the chops over medium heat — this takes about five minutes — then turn them to brown the other side.

5 **Deglazing the pan.** Put the pan back on the heat and pour in a generous splash of liquid — here, dry white wine. Stir and scrape vigorously with a wooden spoon to blend the pan deposits into the liquid. Boil the liquid over high heat to reduce it to a syrupy consistency and to concentrate its flavor. Arrange the chops on a dish, and spoon the reduced liquid over them (right). Garnish with finely chopped parsley.

3 **Gentle frying.** Reduce the heat and cover the pan with a lid to hold in the heat and prevent evaporation of the meat juices, thus lessening the risk of the meat's drying out. Cook the chops for 10 to 20 minutes more, turning once.

4 **Pouring off the fat.** To test for doneness, pierce the meat with a sharp implement; the juices will run clear when the chops are cooked through. Remove them to a preheated 200° F. [100° C.] oven. Carefully pour off the hot fat from the pan *(above)*, retaining the meat juices and pan deposits.

Deglazing with Vegetables

1 **Cooking the peppers.** Broil peppers, turning them often, until they blister and char. Cover the peppers with a damp cloth; when they are cool, peel off the skins, then slice the peppers and remove the ribs and seeds. Heat olive oil in a skillet. Add the peppers and finely chopped garlic, and cook them over medium heat for 10 minutes.

2 **Adding the peppers.** In a separate pan, fry sausages *(pages 24-25)* over medium heat until they turn brown. Using a lid to hold in the sausages, pour the fat from the pan. Then add the peppers *(above)*.

3 **Deglazing the pan.** Stir and scrape with a wooden spoon to loosen the pan deposits and blend them with the moisture from the peppers. Add finely chopped parsley and cook for about a minute to release the flavor of the herb. Serve straight from the pan.

Pan Gravies Made Thick and Saucy

Delicious in itself, a thin deglazing gravy *(page 26)* can be transformed into a full-bodied sauce by adding ingredients that thicken it. Among these ingredients are fresh tomatoes: When cooked in a pan deglazed with vinegar, wine or water, they reduce to a rich purée sauce, a fine accompaniment to hearty meats such as coiled sausage *(right; recipe, page 98)*.

Even richer sauces are made with flour and cream. Because flour requires long cooking to eliminate its raw taste, it cannot be added after deglazing. Instead, it is used to coat the meat to be fried *(right, below)*. The flour begins the thickening process as the meat juices are exuded, and is thoroughly cooked at the same time. During the subsequent deglazing, you can create any blend of sauce flavorings you choose. Here, the pan is initially deglazed with wine in which prunes have been marinated and poached *(box, below)*. Heavy cream and currant jelly are then added and reduced to form a luxuriant sauce *(recipe, page 94)*.

A Sausage Coil Smothered with Tomatoes

1 **Preparing the sausage.** On a flat surface, coil a sausage 30 inches [75 cm.] long *(pages 20-21)* into a tight spiral. Select two skewers long enough to pass horizontally through the spiral. Insert one skewer near the loose end of the spiral and push it through. Insert the second skewer to form a cross.

2 **Frying the sausage.** Pierce the sausage and cook it in a pan with a little water *(pages 24-25)*. When the underside browns, lift the sausage from the pan with a spatula. Invert a plate on top of the sausage, then turn the plate and sausage over and gently slide the sausage back into the pan *(above)*.

A Garnish of Prunes

Marinating and cooking. The tart-sweet taste of prunes is a fine complement to the sweet flavor of fresh pork, whether the prunes appear as a stuffing or a garnish. For a garnish, marinate large, firm prunes in white wine overnight. Next day, arrange the prunes in an ovenproof dish and pour in the wine marinade. Cover and poach in a preheated 300° F. [150° C.] oven for one hour. Drain the prunes, reserving the liquid for deglazing.

Lavish Effects with Cream

1 **Preparing the meat.** Ask your butcher for slices about ½ inch [1 cm.] thick cut from a boneless pork loin. Trim all fat from the slices. Turn them in flour to coat them lightly *(above)*; then shake off any excess flour.

2 **Frying in butter.** In a large frying pan, melt butter over medium heat. When the butter starts to sizzle, add the meat. Season it with salt and pepper. Cook the slices on each side until they have browned lightly — about 10 minutes in all. Transfer the slices to a warmed dish and garnish them with marinated, poached prunes *(box, left)*.

3 **Flavoring and deglazing.** Add slivers of garlic and a bouquet garni *(above)*, then cover the pan and cook until the second side browns. Transfer it to a serving dish and keep it warm in a 200° F. [100° C.] oven. Pour off the fat, then deglaze the pan with vinegar.

4 **Making the sauce.** Add ripe tomatoes that have been peeled, seeded and roughly chopped. Cook them for about 10 minutes over medium heat, stirring frequently to help evaporate their juices so that they reduce to a thick purée. Add capers and chopped parsley; cook for one minute more.

5 **Serving.** Remove the sausage from the oven and withdraw the skewers. Loosen the coils to permit the sausage to be evenly sauced. Pour the tomato sauce over the sausage and serve at once. To serve, cut the sausage into lengths and spoon sauce from the serving dish over each portion.

3 **Making the sauce.** Pour the prunes' cooking liquid into the pan and deglaze over high heat. Stir in 1 tablespoon [15 ml.] of currant jelly, until it dissolves. Stir in heavy cream, and simmer until it is reduced to a thick sauce. Strain the sauce onto the meat through a sieve *(right)* and serve at once.

Deep Frying in a Protective Sheath

Small pieces of boneless, lean pork will emerge from deep frying appetizingly crisp on the outside and moist within—so long as a few guidelines are observed.

The first rule is that the pieces must be even thinner than those used for pan frying: Whether you fry boneless loin slices or chunks, or slices of pork scallop cut from the tenderloin, the pieces should be no more than ½ inch [1 cm.] thick. At the high heats used in deep frying, thicker pieces of meat would burn on the outside before the meat cooked through.

To protect the meat, you must coat it with a batter *(recipe, page 97)* or, as in this demonstration, with layers of beaten egg and bread crumbs. When plunged into hot oil or fat, the surface coating hardens to a crisp casing that seals in the meat's moisture and provides an appealing textural contrast to the cooked pork.

Before you coat the meat, you may spread it with a savory mixture for extra flavor. Here, slices of boneless loin are spread with a *tapenade*—a Provençal mixture that derives its flavor and color from olives, capers and anchovies *(recipe, page 167)*. Other possible flavorings are herbed mustard, grated cheese, or green peppers pounded with garlic or onion *(recipe, page 92)*.

To ensure that the coating adheres properly, first dry the meat thoroughly. Then spread it with a flavoring mixture, if you are using one. Apply a preliminary layer of lightly toasted bread crumbs or grated Parmesan cheese before dipping the pork in batter or in beaten egg. Lightly score the finished coating with a crisscross pattern to prevent cracking.

Any heavy pan can be used for frying, provided it is deep enough to allow the meat to float freely when the pan is no more than half full of oil or fat. If you fill a pan to a greater depth, the oil or fat may spatter onto the heat source and ignite.

Choose an oil or fat that can be heated without burning to the high temperature required for deep frying. Most vegetable oils—peanut oil or corn oil, for example—meet this requirement. Olive oil has a relatively low smoking point and is not suitable for deep frying. Of the fats, lard is the logical choice. Butter's smoking point is too low for deep frying.

To ensure that the meat's coating seals immediately when it is placed in the frying pan, the oil or fat should be heated to a temperature of 375° F. [190° C.]. The correct temperature can be gauged with a deep-frying thermometer. Alternatively, drop a cube of bread into the pan; if it sizzles immediately upon contact, the fat is hot enough.

Since only a minute's overcooking may cause the meat to dry out and the coating to char, watch the pieces as they cook and remove them the moment they are golden brown. Then drain the meat on a cloth or paper towels and serve at once, while it is still hot and succulent.

1 Preparing a tapenade. Place the solid ingredients — pitted olives, rinsed capers, anchovy fillets and black pepper — in a mortar and pound them to a paste with a pestle. Add the other ingredients — prepared mustard, lemon juice, olive oil and, if you like, Cognac — stirring constantly so that they are absorbed.

2 Spreading the tapenade. Trim all fat and connective tissue from a lean cut of pork — here, a boneless loin. Cut the pork into slices no more than ½ inch [1 cm.] thick. Spread the *tapenade* sparingly onto one side of each slice with a table knife *(above)*.

3 **Coating the slices.** Coat both sides of the meat with fine, toasted bread crumbs, then dip the slices in egg beaten with a tablespoon [15 ml.] of water. Finally, place the slices on a bed of white bread crumbs and sprinkle on more crumbs to cover. Press the coating lightly with the flat of your hand for an even surface.

4 **Scoring the coatings.** With the dull edge of a heavy knife, score the coating in a crisscross pattern (above). Let the coated slices stand at room temperature for up to one hour so that the coating will dry and adhere better.

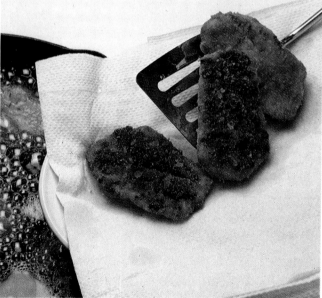

5 **Frying the slices.** In a heavy frying pan, heat enough fat to let the slices float freely. Bring the fat to 375° F. [190° C.]; gently lower the slices into the fat (above) and fry for one and a half to two minutes on each side, until golden brown. Remove the meat with a spatula and drain on paper towels (right). Serve immediately.

2
Grilling, Broiling and Roasting
Sealing in Moistness with Dry Heat

The importance of basting

Treatments for spareribs

Forming a case of crackling

Unexpected stuffings

The benefits of barding

Shaping a crown roast

Cooking and carving a suckling pig

A crown roast of pork, made by joining twin racks of chops *(pages 44-45)*, is carved between the ribs to reveal a center stuffing of sausage meat and spinach. More stuffing surrounds the base of the crown, while an outer ring of new potatoes, sautéed in their jackets, provide a garnish. The roast's own juices accompany it as a sauce.

Grilling, broiling and roasting, the three methods of cooking meat by dry heat, share an ancient origin—the fireplace. The tradition survives in barbecuing, but most cooks now roast meat in the oven or grill it in the broiler. Whatever the equipment, the basic aims remain the same: to produce meat that is deeply colored outside and still succulent within.

Of the various forms of pork, suckling pig—which may be butchered at the age of only six weeks—produces the tenderest results with dry-heat cooking. Other prime candidates for grilling, broiling and roasting are the naturally juicy, less muscular cuts from the loin and hind leg *(diagram, pages 8-9)*. Spareribs and sausages also lend themselves to this kind of cooking: Their abundant fat keeps them moist.

Cured pork has drier, saltier meat than fresh pork. It may certainly be cooked in the oven (the process is called baking rather than roasting in the case of hams), but it requires more preliminary preparation. Country, Smithfield or salt-cured hams and loins must be soaked in cold water, then poached to rid them of excess salt *(chart, pages 10-11);* poaching also partially cooks them, reducing the time these fairly dry meats must spend in the oven. Brine-injected smoked hams need no soaking, but they too benefit from being poached before baking.

Fresh pork, of course, needs no precooking, but it must always be served well done to eliminate the risk of trichinosis. To keep the meat moist during broiling, smear lean cuts with oil or cook them with fatty bacon. Cuts destined for the oven may benefit from barding—covering them with sheets of fat—to shield their exposed flesh. Most hams are at least partly covered with rind, which protects them against drying. For loins, which lack this covering, you can buy rind from a butcher. A rind wrapping offers a bonus: As it cooks, it becomes a crisp, delicious casing of crackling *(pages 40-41)*. Each type of pork must be cooked to a different internal temperature; the temperatures—and the roasting times necessary to achieve them—are specified in the box on page 40. To eliminate guesswork, check the meat's internal temperature with a rapid-response thermometer when you estimate the roast is fully done. Or use a meat-roasting thermometer, inserting it about 30 minutes before the calculated time has elapsed, and putting it deep in the thickest part of the meat—well away from the bones, which could distort the reading.

Tactics That Ensure Succulence

Because pork must always be thoroughly cooked, it needs to be broiled or grilled longer than either beef or lamb—and far enough from the heat to prevent the surface from burning before the meat has cooked through. As a general rule, cook pork 4 to 6 inches [10 to 15 cm.] from the heat source. Allow 15 minutes for each inch [2½ cm.] of thickness, and test carefully for doneness.

Such lengthy times present no problems with sausages, which have enough fat to baste themselves. Among pork sausages, caul-wrapped *crépinettes*, made as described on page 21, seem designed for broiling or grilling. The coating of caul melts as the sausages cook, nourishing the meat and giving the sausages an attractively veined brown glaze.

Leaner pork, however, requires special care to protect it from drying out. Only thin cuts, such as chops, can be broiled or grilled whole; no matter how carefully the heat is regulated, the exterior flesh of meat thicker than 1 inch [2½ cm.] will become dry and burn before the interior cooks. The meat should be smeared with olive or vegetable oil to moisten it during cooking and to help prevent sticking. If you like, you can season the pork ahead of time with herbs: whole or chopped oregano or rosemary leaves, or—used below—whole sage leaves. The strong taste of the herb mellows as it cooks, flavoring the meat delicately.

Larger cuts of lean pork can be cubed for broiling or grilling on skewers. Like chops, cubed pork should be rubbed with oil before cooking. In addition, the cubes can be sandwiched between squares of sliced bacon, which will yield sufficient fat during cooking to keep them basted.

Cubes of dry, crustless bread alternated with the pork will absorb some of the fat and brown to an appetizing crispness. Or the pork and bacon can be strung on skewers along with vegetables—squares of green pepper, wedges of tomato or onion, or whole button mushrooms. Serve the skewered pork with rice or present it on a bed of shredded lettuce *(Step 3, top right; recipe, page 114)*.

Chops Highlighted with Sage

1 **Preparing the chops.** Trim excess fat from the chops, leaving a border up to ½ inch [1 cm.] wide. Rub olive oil into each chop *(left)* and season it. Press fresh herb leaves—in this case, sage—onto each chop *(right)*. Let the chops marinate at room temperature for about one hour to allow the herb flavor to penetrate them. Meanwhile, preheat the broiler for about 15 minutes with the broiler pan and its rack in place, or burn the charcoal in the barbecue-grill pan until a white ash forms on the coals—at least half an hour.

2 **Grilling the chops.** Set the chops on the broiler-pan rack or barbecue-grill rack with the surface of the meat 4 to 6 inches [10 to 15 cm.] from the heat and sear the chops for one minute on each side. Then move the grill rack or broiler pan 1 or 2 inches [2½ or 5 cm.] farther from the heat source to cook the chops through gently. Chops 1 inch thick require about 10 minutes' further cooking. To test for doneness, insert a skewer: The juices should run clear, with no trace of pink. Serve the chops at once.

Cubes Skewered with Bread and Bacon

1 **Preparing the ingredients.** Cut lean pork — here, tenderloin — into 1-inch [2½-cm.] cubes. Cut as many smaller cubes of dry bread, and twice as many bacon squares. Place all the pieces in a bowl. Mix in olive oil, pepper, salt and herbs and marinate for about one hour; preheat the broiler or barbecue.

2 **Assembling the skewers.** Thread the meat and bread onto long skewers, sandwiching the pork between bacon squares and placing a cube of bread between each sandwich. Broil or grill the assemblies 4 to 6 inches [10 to 15 cm.] from the heat for 15 minutes, turning them to ensure even cooking.

3 **Serving.** Rinse lettuce leaves and dry them, then stack them and slice them into thin shreds. Place the lettuce in a serving bowl. Mix lemon juice, salt, a little olive oil and, if you like, sugar in another bowl. Dress the lettuce with the mixture. Arrange the skewers on the lettuce; garnish with lemon wedges.

Crépinettes Crisply Glazed

1 **Preparing the crépinettes.** Make *crépinettes* by wrapping a sausage-meat mixture in caul *(page 21)*. To prevent the *crépinettes* from sticking to the broiler rack, remove the rack before preheating the broiler. Smear a little oil over the *crépinettes* (or oil the cold rack) and place them on the rack.

2 **Broiling the crépinettes.** Position the rack so that the *crépinettes* are 4 to 6 inches [10 to 15 cm.] from the heat source; if they are set closer, the caul fat may flare up. Cook them for about 10 minutes, until the caul melts and browns. Then turn the *crépinettes* and brown the other side for 10 minutes.

3 **Serving.** When they are done, arrange the *crépinettes* on a warmed plate. Here, they are accompanied by apple slices briefly sautéed in butter over high heat. Alternative garnishes include mashed potatoes or raw oysters on the half shell — a specialty of the Bordeaux region of France.

Spareribs: An Invitation to Imaginative Saucing

Spareribs—a thin, fatty cut from the belly—are perfectly suited to cooking in the dry heat of an oven, broiler or grill. When basted liberally with sauce, spareribs gain flavor, remain moist and appear at the table with a crunchy glaze. And the separated ribs are ideally shaped for eating with the fingers.

Like most fresh pork cuts, spareribs will taste better if marinated overnight with salt and herbs *(pages 14-15)*. To prevent them from being excessively salty, they should be wiped dry before cooking, although bits of herbs may be left on. Racks, or sides, of ribs may be left intact to minimize the loss of juices. Or they may be cut apart to maximize the number of surfaces that crispen with glaze.

The ambient heat of an oven produces the moistest meat, whereas the concentrated radiant heat of a broiler or barbecue yields the crunchiest crust. If you choose to roast ribs, prebake them in a hot oven for 10 minutes to draw out excess fat before saucing them. This preliminary cooking has another function: Most sparerib sauces contain sweeteners that would burn in the time it takes to cook raw pork completely. Although the ribs also may be prebaked before broiling or grilling, both of these direct-heat methods melt the fat so quickly that most cooks put the ribs onto the broiler pan or barbecue grill raw.

A tomato sauce such as the one used at right, top *(recipe, page 166)*, is a traditional accompaniment for spareribs in Western cuisines. Such sauces may include spices and herbs, sweeteners such as honey and fruit juice, and acids such as vinegar. Whatever the combination, this type of sauce *(recipe, page 166)* must be simmered to concentrate its flavor and thicken it so that it clings to the meat.

Asian-style sauces like the one used in the demonstration at right, bottom *(recipe, page 115),* are usually thinner mixtures based on soy sauce, although they, too, often include sweet ingredients. Because they do not require thickening, these mixtures are rarely cooked before use. But to ensure their effectiveness as flavorings, you can use Asian sauces first in lieu of a salt mixture to marinate the ribs, and then in their usual role as a basting liquid.

A Tomato Purée Designed for Basting

1 **Starting the sauce.** Place in a mortar all of the solid flavorings — here, a seeded and chopped fresh chili, a garlic clove, dry mustard and herbs. Pound them to a smooth paste with a pestle. Then add the liquid flavorings — in this case, orange juice and equal amounts of wine vinegar and honey.

2 **Straining.** Stir the flavoring mixture together, then pour it into a bowl through a strainer; pick out and discard the remaining whole bits of chili. Use the pestle to press the other ingredients through the strainer.

6 **Coating with sauce.** Remove the pan from the oven. With a spoon or pastry brush, slather enough sauce over the ribs to coat them thickly. Reduce the oven temperature to 350° F. [180° C.] and return the pan to the oven.

7 **Cooking and serving.** Turn the ribs over and baste them at 10-minute intervals. When the sauce has formed a thick, rich brown glaze on the ribs — after about 45 minutes — transfer them to a warmed serving platter. Garnish the ribs with parsley sprigs.

3 **Adding the tomatoes.** Chop an onion into tiny pieces and stew them gently in a little olive oil until soft. Add fresh tomatoes that have been seeded and chopped; alternatively, you may use drained canned tomatoes puréed through a strainer with a pestle *(above)*. Increase the heat slightly.

4 **Cooking the sauce.** Pour the strained flavoring mixture into the pan and blend it with the onion and tomatoes. Bring the sauce to a boil, stirring constantly. Reduce the heat until the sauce barely simmers, then cook it, uncovered, for about 30 minutes to reduce it by half, stirring occasionally.

5 **Precooking the ribs.** If the ribs have been salted, dry them with paper towels. Leave just a sparse coating of herbs and salt on the meat. Divide the ribs into serving portions, if you like. Place them on a rack in a broiling or roasting pan and roast for 10 minutes in a preheated 400° F. [200° C.] oven.

A Tangy Liquid That Doubles as a Marinade

1 **Marinating the spareribs.** In a mortar, pound garlic and spices — here, cloves, cinnamon and allspice — to a paste. Stir in peeled ginger-root slices and the liquid ingredients — in this case, soy sauce, honey and sherry. Rub the mixture into the meat *(above)*; marinate at room temperature for up to four hours, turning the meat now and then.

2 **Grilling the ribs.** Remove the ribs and strain the marinade. Place the ribs on the rack of a preheated broiler pan or grill positioned so that the meat is 4 to 6 inches [10 to 15 cm.] from the heat. Brown both sides, then brush the ribs with the marinade — applied here with rosemary branches. When the basted side has dried, baste the other side.

3 **Carving the ribs.** Turn the ribs several times, basting repeatedly. After about 30 minutes, when both sides have a crisp glaze, transfer the ribs to a carving board. Holding the meat steady with the back of a carving fork *(above)*, cut between the ribs to divide the rack into serving portions.

A Mahogany Sheen for a Roasted Fresh Ham

Most fresh pork roasts, from loins *(pages 42-43)* and crowns *(pages 44-45)* to the ham shown here, are roasted the same way: They begin cooking in a hot oven that sears the meat's surface. Then the temperature is reduced to cook the meat through slowly without drying it. (Roasting times and temperatures are specified in the box on page 40.) Although this basic procedure rarely changes, it can be implemented in various ways to produce different final effects.

Many roasts, for example, come covered at least partly with rind. If you roast the pork British-style, with the rind intact *(pages 40-41)*, you will produce a crisp coat of crackling. If, on the other hand, you adopt the French technique and remove any rind, as demonstrated with this fresh ham, you can build up a rich glaze on the meat by basting it as it roasts. And the rind may be reserved in the refrigerator for as long as four to five days, then used to bard the exposed flesh of lean cuts *(pages 42-43)*.

Whatever technique you choose, the meat will benefit from overnight salting *(Step 3)*. Other flavorings may be added; here, slivers of garlic are inserted in the meat, but leaves of fennel, rosemary or sage could well be substituted.

The prepared pork cooks almost undisturbed for most of its roasting time: You need only baste it occasionally with its own fat and juices. Shortly before roasting is complete, however, fat should be poured from the pan and the pan deposits deglazed with water or wine. The sauce thus formed can then be used to give the meat a dark brown sheen.

The aim in this final basting process is for all of the sauce to evaporate by the end of cooking, leaving the meat encrusted with the pan deposits. If the pan begins to dry out well before the deglazed meat is done, add water or wine each time you baste. If, on the other hand, the sauce remains liquid when the meat is almost done, put it in a small pan and reduce it to a syrup over high heat, then baste until the syrup evaporates.

Roasted ham may be carved by the French method of cutting slices on a bias parallel to the bone. Or, for a more elaborate effect, use the English technique of carving vertical slices *(pages 40-41)*.

1 Removing the rind. Extract the aitch bone from the fresh ham *(pages 12-13)*. Slit the rind lengthwise along the leg, but do not slash the underlying fat. Holding the knife blade flat, insert it under the rind and cut parallel to the surface of the leg, pulling the rind back from the fat as you cut it free.

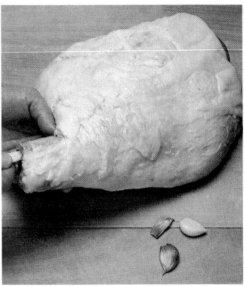

2 Flavoring with garlic. Lightly mash a few garlic cloves with the flat of the knife blade so that the skins will slip off easily. Peel the cloves and slice them lengthwise. Cut slits in the flesh of the butt end of the ham, and between the flesh and bone at the shank end *(above)*. Insert the garlic slices in the slits.

5 Starting the roasting. Put the ham in a preheated 400° F. [200° C.] oven (a rack may be placed in the pan to prevent sticking). After 10 to 20 minutes, reduce the heat to 325° F. [160° C.]. When the meat exudes fat and juices — after about 30 minutes — begin to baste it at 20-minute intervals.

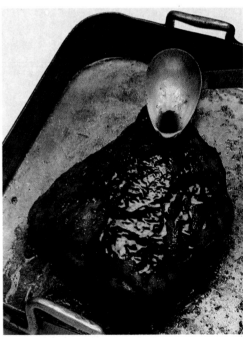

6 Creating the glaze. When the ham is three quarters done — about three and a half hours for a 10-pound [5-kg.] ham — transfer it to a plate. Pour the fat from the pan, add wine or water, and deglaze the pan over medium heat. Replace the ham and return it to the oven. Baste frequently with the deglazing sauce.

3 **Salting the meat.** Put the fresh ham in a dish and sprinkle it with dried herbs — in this case, thyme, oregano and savory — and coarse salt. Rub the salt and herbs into the surface of the entire leg. Cover the dish with foil or plastic wrap and refrigerate overnight.

4 **Drying the meat.** When you are ready to cook the ham, take it out of the dish and discard the juices that the salt has drawn out. Dry the ham thoroughly with a cloth or paper towels. The herbs that cling to the surface may be left to flavor the meat as it roasts.

7 **Carving.** Remove the ham and let it rest for 15 minutes. Carve slices from one side of the fleshy butt end, cutting diagonally *(above)*. At the leg bone, insert the knife at a shallower angle to slice meat from above the bone *(right)*. Carve similar slices from every side.

A Bonus of Crackling for a British-Style Roast

One of the delights of the British method of roasting pork is the golden crust of crackling that forms when the meat is cooked with its rind in place. Roasting melts the fat between the rind and the meat so that the crackling can be split simply down the middle, lifted away, and served in thin, crisp strips.

Before roasting, the pork rind must be scored and smeared with salt and oil. Scoring makes the rind flexible, preventing it from deforming the meat beneath as it shrinks during cooking. The salt and oil help to crisp the crackling.

The roast is cooked like any fresh cut: First briefly seared in high heat to ensure a deep brown exterior, then roasted at gentler heat, as indicated in the box below. A roasted fresh ham, stripped of its crackling, may be carved in vertical slices, as shown opposite, or by the French method demonstrated on page 39. A light gravy can be made by adding some water or wine to the roasting pan to deglaze the deposits, then cleansing the pan juices of fat (Steps 4 and 5, opposite).

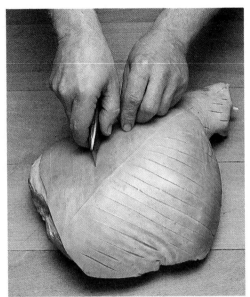

1 **Scoring the rind.** Remove the aitch bone from a fresh ham (pages 12-13). Trim loose fat from the butt end. With a razor-sharp knife or the utility knife shown here, score the rind lengthwise. From this line score a herringbone pattern, cutting only ¼ inch [6 mm.] deep so as not to penetrate the flesh.

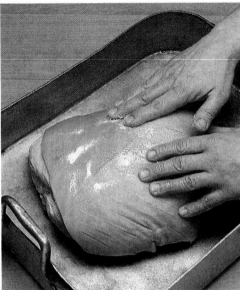

2 **Smearing with oil.** Place the fresh ham in a large roasting pan. If you like, set it on a rack to raise it above the fat and juices it will exude as it cooks. Smear oil liberally all over the ham. Sprinkle salt over it, and rub the salt into the incisions in the rind (above).

Roasting Times and Temperatures

Because pork must be cooked thoroughly but not dried out, the meat should be roasted or baked primarily at moderate temperatures. Some cooks recommend a constant temperature of 325° F. [160° C.] to minimize weight loss. However, for fresh or lightly salted pork a brief spell of high-heat searing at the outset will provide a crisper surface. Start the pork in a preheated 400° F. [200° C.] oven; after 10 minutes, lower the temperature to 325° F.

Large fresh or lightly salted cuts with bones, such as a whole ham or crown roast, need about 25 minutes' cooking time for each pound [½ kg.] to reach a safe internal temperature of 165° to 170° F. [75° C.]. Smaller cuts and boneless roasts require about five minutes more a pound. Weigh stuffed roasts after stuffing to figure the time.

To ensure the correct temperature, use a rapid-response thermometer, or insert a meat thermometer deep into the thickest part of the roast—without touching any bone—about 30 minutes before the estimated time has elapsed.

Exceptions to the searing method are suckling pig (pages 46-49), which colors well at moderate heat, and cured pork. Roast the pig at 325° F. for about 15 minutes a pound, or until a meat thermometer inserted into the largest muscle of a hind leg registers 165° to 170° F. [75° C.].

Cured meats tend to dryness. Poach —do not bake—Smithfield and Virginia hams (pages 10-11). Then glaze them, if you like, with sugar, fruit juice or other sweetener in a 400° F. oven for about 25 to 30 minutes; or braise them as demonstrated on pages 64-65. Bake country and uncooked injection-cured cuts of pork at 325° F. for 20 to 25 minutes a pound until the internal temperature of the meat reaches 160° F. [70° C.]; ready-to-eat hams will reach the requisite temperature of 140° F. [60° C.] after about 15 minutes a pound in a 325° F. oven.

6 **Removing crackling.** Hold the ham steady with the back of a carving fork, and slice down the central line scored along the rind. Slide the knife and fork under each half of the crackling, lift it off and set it aside to serve with the ham.

3 **Roasting.** Place the pan in a preheated 400° F. [200° C.] oven. After 10 minutes, reduce the heat to 325° F. [160° C.]. After one hour, begin basting the ham every 20 minutes with the accumulated fat. If necessary to prevent charring, moisten the bottom of the pan with water or dry white wine.

4 **Removing fat.** Take the pan from the oven and transfer the ham to a warmed plate to rest for about 15 minutes. Tip the pan so that the juices run into one corner, spoon off the fat *(above)*, then pour the juices into a saucepan. Deglaze any meaty deposits in the pan with a little water or wine. Add these juices to the saucepan.

5 **Cleansing the gravy.** Bring the liquid in the saucepan to a boil, then lower the heat and move the pan half off the burner. Spoon off and discard the skin that repeatedly forms on the cooler side of the pan. When no more fat or impurities rise — after 15 to 20 minutes — pour the cleansed juices into a warmed gravy boat.

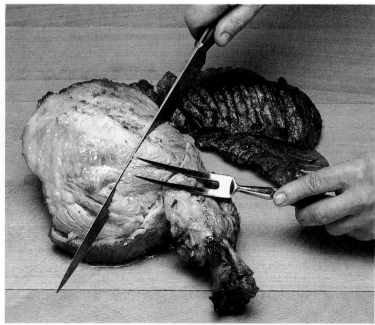

7 **Cutting a notch.** To make vertical slices, first cut into the ham diagonally down to the leg bone at the point where the leg begins to widen. Holding the ham steady with the back of the fork, make a second, vertical cut down to the bone to free a wedge of meat *(above)*. Lift the wedge away, leaving a notch cut out of the roast.

8 **Carving slices.** Carve the ham into slices ¼ to ½ inch [6 mm. to 1 cm.] thick, cutting vertically down to the leg bone. To free the slices, make a horizontal cut along the bone from the notch cut in Step 7. Serve the ham with strips of crackling and the gravy. Accompany the dish, if you like, with applesauce *(recipe, page 167)*.

Two Strategies for Stuffing

Herb-filled Tunnels

Among the pork cuts suitable for stuffing and roasting, boned loins *(pages 12-13)* make particularly handsome presentations. A boned center-loin roast, for example, is a thick cylinder of flesh that can be pierced to provide stuffing space. When it is carved, each loin slice will be decorated with circles of stuffing *(demonstrations, right and below; recipe, page 104)*. A similar effect can be obtained with a blade roast; this cut opens like a book when boned, then is closed around its stuffing *(opposite, bottom)*.

Since the space to be filled is small, these cuts are best stuffed with light ingredients such as herbs or fruit. To perfume the meat strongly, choose sage or rosemary. For a subtler effect, try fennel leaves, as with the center-loin roast here: Their licorice flavor complements the pork's sweetness. Apples, prunes and dried apricots, used here with the blade roast, all have an affinity for pork.

Stuffed and tied in packages, these lean roasts should be barded—covered with fresh pork fat or rind—to keep the flesh from drying out during cooking.

1 Stuffing with herbs. Place a boned center-loin roast on a cutting board, and make several deep cuts in each end of the meat with a long, sharp knife. With your finger or the long handle of a wooden spoon, force coarsely chopped herbs—fennel, here—into the openings, filling them up.

2 Marinating. Lay the roast in a bowl. Sprinkle any remaining herbs over it and pour in enough dry white wine almost to cover it. If you like, add a splash of anise-flavored liqueur to accentuate the fennel's flavor. Cover and marinate the roast in the refrigerator for eight hours or so, turning it two or three times.

6 Serving the roast. When a glaze has formed on the meat and the marinade has evaporated, transfer the loin to a carving board to rest. Spoon excess fat from the roasting vessel, then deglaze the pan juices with white wine or water, boiling the liquid until it reaches the consistency of light syrup. Cut the string from the roast *(above)*, taking care not to damage the glaze. Carve the meat in slices *(right)* and serve with the reduced pan juices.

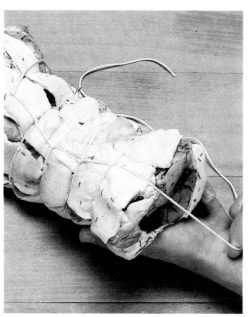

3 **Drying and seasoning.** Lift the roast out of the marinade, place a colander over the bowl, and set the meat in it to drain for a few minutes. Reserve the marinade. Place the meat on a cloth or paper towels and pat it dry. Season with salt and pepper.

4 **Barding and tying.** Cover the meat with fresh pork fat—in this case, scraps from rib chops—rolling and pressing it to make the shape regular. Truss the loin with string looped every 1½ inches [4 cm.] along it. Pass the string around the loin end *(above)* and secure it through the loops on the other side.

5 **Roasting.** Set the loin barded side down in a roasting dish or pan. Roast for 10 minutes in a hot oven, then reduce the heat *(page 40)*. When the meat starts exuding juices, baste it at 10-minute intervals. After 50 minutes, pour off the fat and add the marinade *(above)*. Continue cooking, basting often.

The Sweet Accent of Dried Fruit

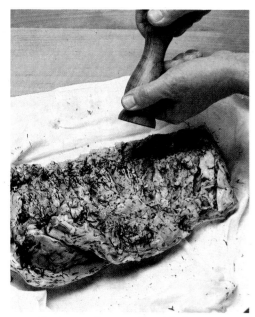

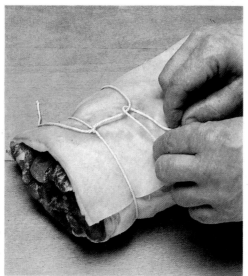

1 **Stuffing.** Soak dried fruit—in this case, apricots—in dry white wine for three hours. Turn a boned blade-roast fleshy side up. Drain the apricots, reserving the liquid, and place them in two rows on each side of the eye muscle that runs down the center of the roast.

2 **Barding and tying.** Fold the edges of the blade over the apricots, rolling the meat into a cylinder. Bard any exposed flesh with a thin layer of fat or, as here, fresh rind. Tie the meat and rind with string *(Step 4, top)*. Place the roast barded side down in a roasting pan.

3 **Cooking and serving.** Roast the blade *(Step 5, top)*, using the wine from the apricots to baste it after 50 minutes. When the roast is done, let it rest while you deglaze the pan *(Step 6, opposite)* for a sauce. Cut away the string, discard the rind and carve the blade *(above)*.

Transforming Rib Racks into a Regal Crown

A crown roast is made by joining two center-rib roasts—racks of rib chops—to form a circle with the bony rib ends standing up like the points of a crown. With stuffing inserted in the crown and more packed around its base, the crown can be carved between the ribs to yield individual servings complete with portions of stuffing.

Ask your butcher for two racks of seven or eight ribs each—from the same animal, if possible, so that they will be of corresponding size. To make the racks flexible enough to bend, you must first cut off the chine and feather bones. Or ask the butcher to remove them, but leave the vertebrae intact, as here, to help preserve the shape of the crown. Then trim off excess fat and cut through the cartilage at the base of the ribs to separate the vertebrae *(Steps 1-3)*. The trimmings may be added to the stuffing—in this case, a sausage-meat-and-spinach mixture *(recipe, page 103)*. The fat in the sausage meat enriches the stuffing as it cooks, creating a crusty, brown accompaniment for the roast.

1 **Chining each rib rack.** With the rib bones facing down, free the chine from the rack by using a boning knife to cut around the knobby vertebrae at the base of the ribs. Bend back the chine and snap it off. Cut along the tops of the feather bones to remove them in one piece. Slice off the layer of fat from the top of the rack *(above)*.

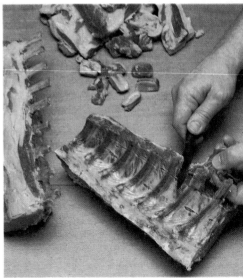

2 **Exposing the rib tips.** With a paring knife, score a line along the length of the rack about 1 inch [2½ cm.] below the rib tips. Cut or scrape out the flesh between the ribs down to this line *(above)*; the exposed tips will form the points of the crown. Reserve the meaty trimmings for the stuffing.

6 **Arranging the stuffing.** Line a roasting pan with foil and place the meat on top, so that you can remove the roast after cooking without dislodging the stuffing. Prepare the stuffing *(pages 18-19)* and pack it inside the crown and around the base *(above)*.

7 **Protecting with foil.** Protect the stuffing at the base of the crown by wrapping it with a folded strip of foil. To keep the rib tips from charring, wrap them in pieces of foil *(above)*. Smear oil over the ribs. Place the meat in a 400° F. [200° C.] oven. After 10 minutes, reduce the heat to 325° F. [160° C.]. For roasting times, see the box on page 40.

8 **Removing the foil.** When the crown is done, remove the foil from the rib tips *(above)* and the base. Wrap the ends of the foil lining the tray over the crown. Slide a broad spatula under the wrapped-up crown and transfer it carefully to a warmed platter. Unwrap the foil and, with the help of the spatula, ease the foil out from under the roast.

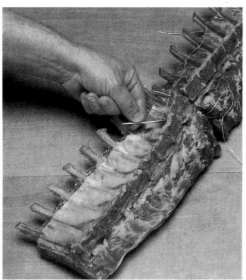

3 **Separating the vertebrae.** Place the racks so that the rib tips are pointing away from you and the vertebrae at the base of the ribs are facing up. With a paring knife, slice around the knob at the base of each rib to sever the thin discs of cartilage between each vertebra *(above)*.

4 **Joining the racks.** Set the racks together, ribs uppermost. With a butcher's needle and cotton string, make a stitch around the two adjacent end ribs halfway down the bones. Cut and knot the string. Make and knot another stitch around the bases of the ribs just above the vertebrae *(above)*. Tie a loop of string around the two end rib tips.

5 **Forming the crown.** Bend the joined racks into a circle with the rib bones facing out. If the ends do not join, trim more fat or flesh from the meaty part of each rack to make room inside the crown. Tie together the tips of the two end ribs and make a single stitch around the bases of the ribs.

9 **Carving the roast.** When the roast has rested for 15 minutes or so, use the back of a large carving fork to steady the crown. With a carving knife, cut between each pair of ribs, starting from the center of the crown and slicing down to the base so that two pieces of stuffing are carved out with each chop. In this demonstration, the roast is garnished with new potatoes that have been sautéed in their skins, then browned under the broiler.

Suckling Pig: The Apotheosis of Pork

Roast suckling pig *(recipes, pages 100-101)* is one of the world's great festive dishes—a lavish centerpiece at banquets and celebrations in almost every country where pork is eaten. Its popularity is not surprising: The six-to-eight-week-old animal has succulent flesh, set off after roasting by a crisp coating of crackling.

Roast pig is anything but a spur-of-the-moment dish. Suckling pigs are available only at butcher shops and ethnic markets, and frequently they must be ordered several weeks in advance. Often the only pigs available are frozen and must be defrosted in the refrigerator, a process that can take up to 48 hours. Fresh or frozen, the pig already will have been cleaned—the belly cut open and the intestines removed. (Ask for the liver and heart, if the butcher does not display them with the pig. Like poultry giblets, these are components you can use in both stuffings and sauces.)

Even if the pig has been cleaned, it may need some extra attention. With a small paring knife, cut away any loose skin, and use tweezers to pluck out hairs remaining in the ears or between the sections of the feet. Any stray body hairs should be removed by singeing them over an open flame.

To heighten the flavor of the meat, salt the pig overnight *(pages 14-15)* before stuffing and cooking it. A variety of stuffings complement roast pig *(recipes, pages 101-102);* in the demonstration here, a sage-and-onion mixture is used.

Traditionally, suckling pig was spit-roasted in front of an aromatic wood fire. An open fire and a rotating spit are still ideal, although the pig can conveniently be roasted in any oven large enough to hold it. The pig need not be seared at the start of roasting; regular basting and its long cooking ensure a crisp, glazed skin.

In the best Dickensian tradition, the roast pig should be presented whole at the dinner table before the intricate business of carving begins *(pages 48-49)*. Carve one side of the pig at a time; first remove the legs, then cut away the loin and belly, and finally divide the stuffing. Take care not to waste any part of the pig; all of the flesh can be eaten, and the bones can be used for stock.

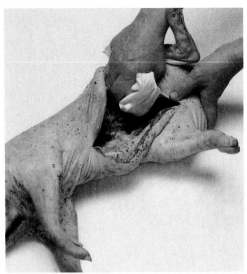

1 Salting and drying. Rub salt and mixed herbs over the pig's skin and inside the body cavity. Wrap the pig loosely in foil and marinate it in the refrigerator for up to 12 hours, or overnight. Unwrap the pig and dry it thoroughly inside and out with a cloth or paper towels.

2 Stuffing the pig. Prepare the stuffing of your choice—in this case, a sage-and-onion mixture *(page 18)*. Stuff the body cavity, pushing the mixture up toward the breast until the entire cavity is filled. Do not pack the stuffing too tight: It will expand during cooking.

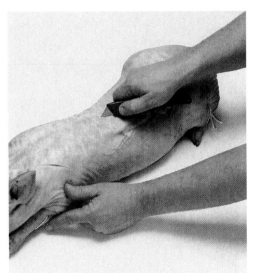

6 Scoring the skin. Turn the pig over. With a sharp knife—a utility knife is used here—make a shallow incision along the backbone, then score each side of the pig diagonally at 1-inch [2½-cm.] intervals from head to tail. Make the cuts no more than ¼ inch [6 mm.] deep—enough for fat to escape but not enough to penetrate the flesh.

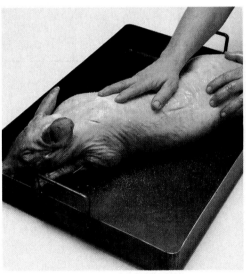

7 Oiling the pig. Place the pig on its belly in a large roasting pan. Smear oil over it, then rub salt into the skin *(above)*. Place small cones of aluminum foil over the pig's ears, and wrap more foil around the tail to protect the thin flesh from burning during roasting.

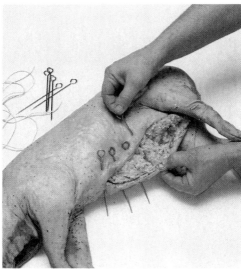

3 **Closing the cavity.** Using trussing skewers about 4 inches [10 cm.] long, fasten together the belly opening at 1-inch [2½-cm.] intervals *(above)*. Insert the skewers about 1 inch [2½ cm.] from the edges of the opening to prevent the skin from tearing during cooking.

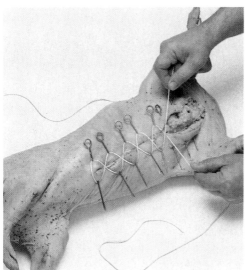

4 **Trussing.** Cut a length of cotton kitchen string at least a yard [90 cm.] long. Loop the string around the skewers in a figure-8 pattern *(above)*. As you pass it around each skewer, pull the string to draw the sides of the opening together. Cut and knot the string behind the final skewer.

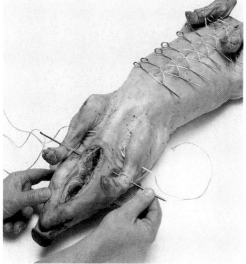

5 **Securing the legs.** Push a butcher's needle threaded with string through the hind thighs and the body between to draw the thighs close to the body. Return the needle through both feet and the flesh between, drawing the feet down. Knot the string. Truss the forelegs by passing the needle twice through the legs and throat *(above)*.

8 **Roasting.** Place the pig in an oven set at 325° F. [160° C.]. After about 30 minutes, baste the pig with the fat it has exuded. If there is no fat, brush the pig with a little warmed oil. Continue to baste the pig every 30 minutes. Allow about 15 minutes' cooking time a pound [½ kg.] for the pig and its stuffing. The pig is ready to eat when the internal temperature reaches 165° to 170° F. [75° C.] and the skin has turned to crisp, brown crackling. ▶

9 **Presenting the roast.** Remove the pig from the oven. Using a cloth to protect your hands, pull out the trussing skewers; the string wrapped around them will fall away. Cut and pull out the strings that hold the legs in place. Remove the foil protecting the ears and tail. Place the pig on a large, warmed serving platter and garnish it; watercress and sautéed apple quarters are used in this case. Let the pig rest 15 minutes before carving it at the table, on its platter or on a large carving board.

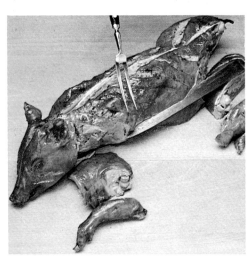

13 **Freeing the loin.** Cut the loin free at the neck. Then cut back from the point where the foreleg was severed (Step 11) to the top of the haunch (above) in order to separate the loin from the belly.

14 **Removing the loin.** With the knife and fork, carefully lift the loin free from the rest of the pig. The rib cage will be exposed. Cut the loin into three equal portions for serving.

15 **Removing the ribs.** Cut away the belly meat to expose the stuffing. With a small paring knife, cut down both sides of each rib to separate the bones from the intervening strips of flesh. Use the knife to lift up each rib (above), then twist the rib free from the spine with your fingers.

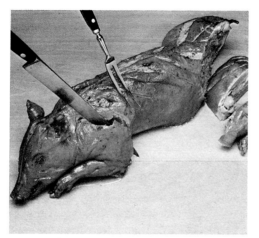

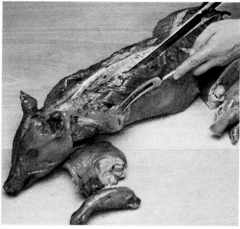

10 **Carving the hind leg.** Holding the meat in place with the back of a carving fork, cut away one hind leg with a carving knife; slice diagonally from the front of the haunch to the tail *(above)*. Then cut through the leg to divide it at the knee joint between the leg bone and the thigh.

11 **Removing the foreleg.** Cut into the shoulder at the point where the leg joins it. Slice behind the shoulder blade to a point about 1 inch [2½ cm.] behind the ear *(above)*. Cut straight down to the throat to separate the leg from the body. Cut the leg into two sections at the knee joint.

12 **Cutting along the spine.** Cut down the length of the shallow incision in the spine, pressing the knife down to the bone. Holding the loin with the back of a carving fork, slice down alongside the ribs, keeping the blade against the bones, to detach the loin in one piece.

16 **Removing the stuffing.** Cut along the top of the rib cage to free the stuffing and the strips of meat left between the ribs *(above)*. Then carve the second side of the pig in the same way as the first. The head can be cut away from the spine with a cleaver and split in two; cut out the meat that it contains and serve this meat with the rest of the pig.

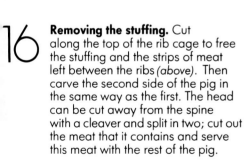

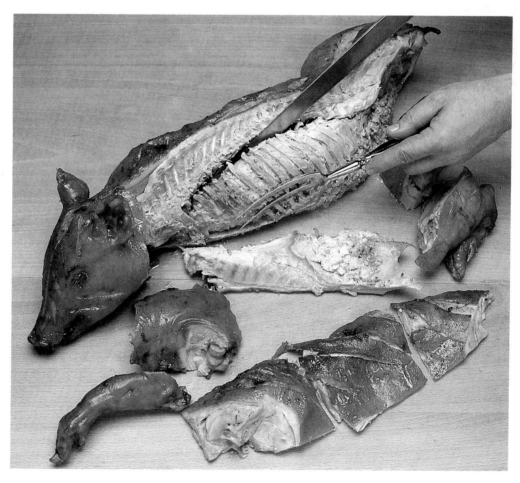

3
Poaching
The Gentlest Cooking Method

The poaching process—cooking meat in barely simmering water, stock or a court bouillon—is kind to all cuts of pork, keeping the meat moist and tender during its necessarily long cooking. Poached pork may be as splendid as the cold dish shown on the opposite page, made by cooking truffle-perfumed loin in stock, then encasing it in a gleaming coat of jelly; or it may be as simple as a farmhouse *potée (pages 58-59),* consisting of smoked or salted meat and vegetables simmered in water and served straight from the pot. And while poaching is fine for the tender cuts used in many dishes, it has special virtue for tough meats such as Boston and picnic shoulders, not to mention gelatinous pig's ears and feet: The slow cooking breaks down tough connective tissues, thus tenderizing them. Finally, poaching is an indispensable method for attenuating the strong flavors of salted or smoked pork cuts, including hams.

Whatever kind of pork you poach, success will depend largely on careful supervision of the temperature at which the meat cooks. If the liquid is allowed to boil, the meat will be tough and stringy, since the high temperature will draw out fat that otherwise would keep the meat tender. It takes practice and experience to recognize when the requisite low, even simmer has been attained. The poaching liquid should be just hot enough for bubbles to form on the bottom and sides of the pan and to drift lazily up, causing the surface to shiver. If you have a deep-frying thermometer, adjust the temperature of the liquid so that the thermometer registers between 175° and 185° F. [80° and 85° C.]. To maintain an even heat, place a lid at an angle over the pan. Partly covering the top in this manner limits evaporation, while preventing steam from building up inside the pan and raising the cooking temperature.

The great bonus of poaching is the enriched stock created as the meat and vegetables in the pan exude their flavors into the cooking liquid. To ensure that a fresh pork stock is not unnecessarily diluted, use just enough liquid to cover the meat. Cured pork, on the other hand, requires additional liquid to draw out and dilute its saltiness. The stock from cured pork can be reused, if not too salty, for poaching other meat. But a little of the stock from fresh pork dishes not only will serve to moisten the meat at the table, but also can be presented as a light broth in its own right, or saved as a base for future soups or sauces.

Spoonfuls of roughly chopped jelly, made by chilling the stock in which the meat was poached, form a glistening garnish for a cold, truffle-studded loin of pork *(pages 56-57).* Jellied stock also covers the loin with a shiny coating, while a strip of chopped parsley set in a glaze of jelly adorns the top.

Salt Pork and Pease Pudding — A Winter Tradition

For centuries, salt pork poached with dried peas, lentils or beans was a staple in cold weather. The combination was a practical one: Salt pork and dried legumes could both be stored through the winter. Although fresh meat and vegetables are always available today, the old combination still makes culinary sense: The pork's saltiness marries well with the dried legumes' earthy flavor.

This classic alliance—here pictured with split peas that have been transformed into a traditional English pease pudding (recipe, page 126)—needs considerable advance preparation. Though fresh pork may be poached in simmering liquid without any preliminaries (pages 56-57), salted pork must first be soaked in cold water, then parboiled to remove excess salt. The duration of these treatments depends on the type and weight of the meat: The Boston shoulder used here, home-salted for three days (page 15), needs overnight soaking and brief parboiling. Soaking times for other home-salted meats are given on pages 14-15; commercially salted cuts must be soaked as explained on pages 10-11.

Dried legumes also require preliminary treatment. Large beans such as red, kidney or lima beans should be soaked in cold water overnight to soften them; if the beans were plunged into hot water without presoaking, their skins would toughen before their interiors were done, and as the interiors expanded in the heat, the beans would explode. As an alternative to overnight soaking, cover the beans with cold water, bring the water to a boil and simmer for a few minutes; then take the beans off the heat, cover the pot, and let the beans soak for one hour.

Tiny lentils or split peas cook through so quickly that they need only brief soaking: One hour in cold water is enough. Split peas intended for a pease pudding must be partially precooked. They are then puréed, blended with egg and butter, and wrapped in cheesecloth to finish cooking in the poaching pot.

The beans are not, of course, the only vegetables in the pot. The poaching liquid always is flavored with aromatic vegetables such as carrots and onions; in addition, garnish vegetables such as potatoes may be included.

1 **Parboiling.** Immerse presoaked salted pork — a Boston shoulder is shown — in water and boil for five minutes. Remove the pork, rinse the pot and return the pork. Add fresh water, a carrot and a clove-studded onion. Simmer for 20 minutes a pound [½ kg.], or until the internal temperature reaches 165° to 170° F. [75° C.].

2 **Cooking the peas.** In another pot, place aromatic vegetables — here, an onion and a carrot — and a bouquet garni of parsley, thyme and a bay leaf. Add presoaked split peas, cover them generously with cold water, bring to a simmer and cook gently for one hour, until the peas are tender.

6 **Poaching the pudding.** An hour before the pork is done, add the pease pudding to the pot. Set the pudding on the meat so that it is submerged in liquid but can easily be lifted out. Replace the lid, setting it slightly ajar, and continue to simmer the pork for the remaining cooking time.

7 **Unmolding the pudding.** Lift the pudding from the pot, supporting it with two large spoons, and place it in a colander to drain for five minutes. Cut the string to untie the cheesecloth. Invert a plate over the pudding and, steadying the pudding with your hand, turn plate and pudding over together. Gently peel off the cheesecloth (above).

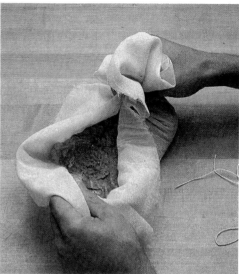

3 **Puréeing the peas.** Drain the split peas and discard the aromatic vegetables and the bouquet garni. Press the peas through a food mill into a large bowl to make a stiff purée, or mash them until smooth with a food masher or electric portable mixer.

4 **Mixing the pudding.** Let the purée cool until the peas are barely warm to the touch. Then add butter and an egg; the peas should be warm enough to melt the butter, but not so hot that the egg begins to cook and separate into lumps. Mix the ingredients together thoroughly.

5 **Molding the pudding.** Spread a doubled layer of dampened cheesecloth on a work surface. Sift flour onto the cloth and rub the flour over the cloth to form a coating that will not leak. Spoon the pease-pudding mixture onto the center of the cloth and smooth its surface. Gather the cloth over the pudding and tie the corners together.

8 **Serving the salted pork.** Remove the pork shoulder from the pot. Steady the meat with a fork and bone it, employing the techniques demonstrated on pages 12-13. Slice the pork ½ inch [1 cm.] thick, and arrange the slices around the pease pudding. Ladle a little of the cooking liquid over the pork to moisten it.

Subtle Marriages of Flavors

One of the advantages of poaching is the range of possibilities it offers for flavoring pork. The poaching water, for example, may be flavored with beer, hard cider or wine, or it may be replaced by stock (*page 16*). Almost any liquid can be enhanced by adding aromatic vegetables.

For poaching cured cuts there is yet another alternative: Recipes from the 17th Century recommend poaching ham in water and hay, on the ground that the hay tenderizes the meat. This claim is questionable, but fresh hay undeniably gives the meat a sweet and appealing fragrance. In this demonstration, hay flavors a lightly smoked ham, but any mild-tasting smoked or salted cut, prepared as described on pages 10-11, may be used (*recipes, pages 118, 124 and 125*).

If you know a farmer, you probably can obtain fragrant hay from him during the summer months; ideally, it will have been recently cut and dried in the sun. Otherwise, buy alfalfa hay—the sweetest kind—at pet shops, where it is sold as fodder. To completely envelop a ham, use about ½ pound [¼ kg.] of hay. Shake out any debris; washing is unnecessary.

To bring out the delicate flavor of lightly cured pork, poach it at just below the simmering point; if you have a deep-frying thermometer, regulate the heat of the liquid until it is between 175° and 185° F. [80° and 85° C.]. After cooking, discard the hay and liquid. The pork can be served hot or—as here—cold, with a crisp coating of bread crumbs.

If you use more conventional flavoring agents for poaching, they may do double duty. On the opposite page, below, sausages (*page 21*) are cooked in a court bouillon and dry white wine (*recipe, page 164*). Some of the poaching liquid, along with the vegetables, is served with the sausages. The rest can be saved for stock.

A Surprising Role for Hay

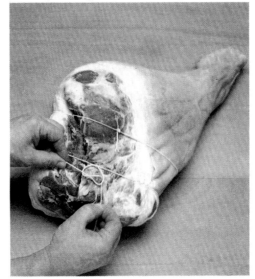

1 **Preparing the ham.** Soak the cured pork—here, a lightly smoked ham—in cold water overnight, then dry it with a towel. Remove the aitch bone (*pages 12-13*), if necessary. To close the gap where the bone was, loop two strings around the broad butt end and knot them across the gap (*above*).

2 **Adding hay.** Put a layer of hay on the bottom of the poaching vessel. Add the ham and cover with more hay (*above*). Pour in enough cold water to cover the ham. Set a lid askew on the pot. Gradually heat the water until its surface starts to tremble. Adjust the heat to just below a simmer.

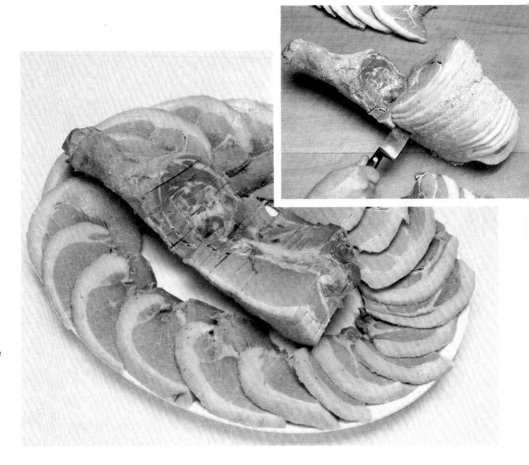

6 **Carving and serving.** Cut two ½-inch [1-cm.] slices from the underside of the leg to make a flat base for the ham to rest on. Then slice the ham vertically, cutting down to the bone. Cut along the bone to free the slices (*inset*). Place the bone, with the remaining meat, on a serving plate; arrange the slices around it.

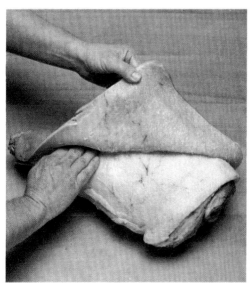

3 **Cooking the ham.** Allow about 20 minutes' cooking time per pound [½ kg.] after the water reaches the simmering point. The ham is done when a rapid-response thermometer shows its internal temperature at 160° F. [70° C.]. Let the ham cool in the pot until it can be handled *(above)*. Pick off loose hay, then sever and remove the strings.

4 **Removing the rind.** With a paring knife, slit the rind along the length of the ham. Push one hand into the slit to separate the rind from the fat beneath it. Use the other hand to peel away the rind *(above)*. Trim off remaining pieces of rind with a knife. If necessary, trim the surface fat to leave a neat, even cover.

5 **Coating with bread crumbs.** Toast fine, fresh bread crumbs in a 300° F. [150° C.] oven for five minutes, or until golden brown, then spread them on a work surface. Lay the ham on the crumbs, and sprinkle more crumbs over the fat *(above)*. Pat the crumbs into the ham with your palm to form a light coating.

A Court-Bouillon Bath

1 **Adding wine.** Prepare the court bouillon by boiling sliced onions and carrots with a bouquet garni in salted water for 10 to 15 minutes. Let the bouillon cool. Prick the casings *(page 24)* of two large sausages, put them in the pot and add about a quarter of a bottle of dry white wine to the mixture *(above)*.

2 **Poaching and serving.** Partly cover the pan, and bring the liquid to a low simmer. Reduce the heat so that the water no longer stirs. After about 45 minutes, transfer the sausages to a warm platter. Slice them thick. Garnish with the aromatics; boiled new potatoes are also used here. Moisten with poaching liquid.

Glistening Films of Aspic

Poached in stock *(page 16)*, lean cuts of fresh pork such as the loin or ham make excellent cold dishes; if the stock is supplied with natural gelatin by the addition of bones or a pig's foot during poaching, it can be turned into a jelly to glaze the meat *(recipe, page 165)*. The boned loin used here is particularly convenient for this treatment: It can be trussed into a cylinder shape for easy glazing and serving. Bone the loin as demonstrated on pages 12-13, reserving the bones to enrich the poaching liquid.

Since the loin usually has little internal fat, it should be larded with strips of fresh pork fat, or lardons, flavored to taste; here the lardons are marinated in a mixture of garlic and Cognac. As the loin cooks, the strips of fat will melt, basting the meat from within.

Additional flavorings can be inserted into shallow slits cut in the loin. A coarsely chopped fresh truffle lends a delectable perfume to the meat; these are available only in winter at specialty food markets in large cities, but chopped pistachio nuts or whole cloves of garlic are good alternatives. To give the prepared loin an appetizing color, dust it lightly with sugar and cook it briefly in a hot oven before poaching.

After cooking, strain the stock, then chill both the meat and stock, which will set to a firm jelly. To give this jelly the syrupy consistency needed to coat the loin, first melt it over gentle heat, then set the liquid over ice and stir it as it cools so that it will thicken evenly.

Because the syrup will adhere to the loin only in thin layers, proper glazing requires several applications. After each layer of syrup is spooned over the meat the loin must be returned to the refrigerator—or more briefly, to the freezer—so that the stock will set to a firm jelly. When the next-to-last layer has partially set, add decorative slices of blanched vegetables, keeping them in place with a final layer of jelly. Or you can decorate the loin by mixing chopped vegetables or herbs, such as the parsley shown here, with the syrup and applying this mixture to the last layer of glaze. Leftover jellied stock may be cut into cubes and used as a garnish for the glazed loin *(Step 10, opposite)*.

1 Cutting lardons. Pound a clove of garlic with salt in a mortar, then moisten it with a little Cognac. If the boned loin has thick surface fat, trim it to within ¼ inch [6 mm.] of the meat. Cut a piece of fat ¼ inch thick into strips ¼ inch wide *(above)* to make lardons. Marinate the lardons in the mortar for an hour.

2 Larding the meat. Place the loin fleshy side uppermost. Clasp the end of each lardon securely in the hinged clip of a larding needle and push the needle under the surface of the meat *(above)*, making one or two stitches, depending on the length of the lardon. Release the clip and snip off surplus fat. Distribute lardons evenly through the meat.

6 Poaching the loin. Add the bones that have been cut from the loin to the poaching vessel. Pour in half a cup [125 ml.] of white wine and ladle in enough hot stock to cover the meat. Bring the liquid slowly to a boil. Reduce the heat until the liquid just simmers, partly cover the pot, and poach the loin; allow 20 minutes per pound [½ kg.].

7 Straining the stock. Let the loin cool for 15 to 20 minutes in the stock, then transfer it to a plate. Strain the stock into a bowl through a sieve lined with wet muslin or cheesecloth. Discard the bones. Cut the string and any rind from the loin, then refrigerate the loin and the stock for several hours, until the loin is chilled and the stock has jellied.

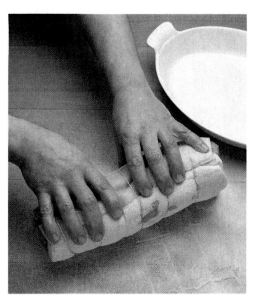

3 **Inserting the truffle.** Scrub a fresh truffle and cut it into thick slices. Avoiding the lardons, make incisions about ½ inch [1 cm.] deep and 1 inch [2½ cm.] long in the loin and insert a piece of truffle *(above)* in each one. Smear the remaining marinade over the meat.

4 **Rolling in sugar.** Roll the loin to form a long cylinder. If the loin is not completely covered with fat, as is the case here, wrap pork rind — available from butchers — over the exposed flesh to protect it during cooking. Truss the loin as shown on page 43. Sprinkle sugar on a work surface. Roll the loin in the sugar *(above)* to coat it lightly.

5 **Browning the meat.** Place the loin, the rind-covered portion down, in a roasting dish. Cook the loin in a preheated 400° F. [200° C.] oven for about 20 minutes, until the surface is a golden brown. Using two wooden spoons or spatulas, transfer the loin to an oblong poaching vessel *(above)*, placing it rind side down to prevent sticking.

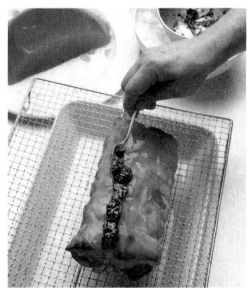

8 **Coating the loin.** Melt the jellied stock over low heat, then thicken some of it in a small metal bowl set over ice. Put the loin on a rack placed over a pan, and spoon the syrupy jelly rapidly over the meat to create a thin glaze. Refrigerate the loin for 10 minutes to set the stock. Thicken more stock, and add one or two layers to the loin in the same way.

9 **Decorating with parsley.** Thicken more melted stock and stir into it some finely chopped fresh parsley. Stir the mixture over ice until it has almost set, then spoon it in a strip along the top of the loin *(above)*. Return the loin to the freezer or refrigerator to firm the jelly.

10 **Serving the loin.** Place the loin on a serving plate. Carve part of the loin into thin slices and glaze the slices with a little thickened stock. Dip a carving knife into hot water. Chop the remaining jelly *(above)* and use it to decorate the loin. Chill the assembly for at least an hour before serving.

A Potful of Mixed Cuts

Poaching offers a prime opportunity for improvisation: Different pork cuts can be simmered together—or with other kinds of meat—to produce a richly varied dish. A classic example is the French farmhouse dish known as *potée*—literally, "potful." *Potées* usually include salt pork and cabbage, plus a wide choice of other meats and vegetables *(recipes, pages 123 and 125)*. Whatever you choose, success depends on timing: Each ingredient goes into the pot at a different time, depending on the amount of cooking it needs.

In the *potée* demonstrated here, the meats are salt pork *(pages 10-11)*, chicken and poaching sausages. The salt pork requires the most advance preparation and cooking: To remove salt, it must be soaked overnight, then parboiled *(Step 1)*. Other cured cuts, such as ham or picnic shoulder, could augment or replace the salt pork; the advance preparation of these cuts is described on pages 10-11.

The chicken is trussed for poaching to keep it in shape: Push a threaded trussing needle into one thigh, through the body, through the other thigh and into one wing. Next, push the needle and string through the wing and the body and out through the other wing. Tie the cut ends of string together. An old stewing chicken may need to poach for two hours or more; a young roaster will poach in an hour. Added last to the pot are quick-cooking poaching sausages.

The vegetables in the *potée* are also cooked in stages. Dried peas or beans such as the lima beans used here must be soaked *(pages 52-53)*. Even then, beans require lengthy cooking: They go into the pot along with the pork. Onions, carrots and turnips need long simmering to render their flavors; if they remain firm, they also can be used as garnishes.

Other vegetables can be added during the last 30 minutes or so of cooking or, if the pot is crowded, cooked separately in poaching liquid. The possibilities include potatoes, boiling onions, and sections of cabbage shaped into balls *(Step 6)*.

For serving, a little poaching liquid always moistens the *potée*. Serve the rest of the broth on its own to precede the main course, or reserve it as stock.

1 **Parboiling the pork.** Cover a piece of presoaked, drained salt pork with cold water and bring the water to a boil over medium heat. Remove and drain the meat. Rinse the pot. Put in presoaked, drained lima beans and cover them with fresh cold water.

2 **Skimming the beans.** Bring the beans slowly to a boil over medium heat, skimming off the starchy scum that rises to the surface. When no more scum appears, reduce the heat so that the liquid just simmers. Add the parboiled pork, and partly cover the pot.

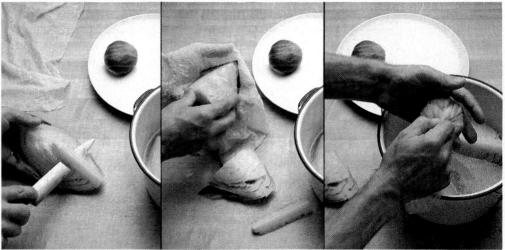

6 **Making a cabbage garnish.** Simmer a quartered green cabbage in the reserved poaching liquid until it is tender — about 30 minutes. Drain each quarter, slice off its tough core *(left)* and cut it in half across its width. Place the cabbage section on a square of cheesecloth *(center)*, gather the edges of the cloth over it and twist the edges tightly together *(right)* to force liquid from the cabbage and shape it into a ball. Remove the cheesecloth and repeat the wrap-and-twist procedure with each cabbage quarter.

3 **Adding aromatics.** After 30 minutes' simmering, put the aromatic vegetables — in this case, whole peeled carrots and quartered peeled turnips — into the pot. Simmer, partly covered, for another 30 minutes.

4 **Adding flavor.** Put a trussed roasting chicken into the *potée*, along with a bouquet garni *(page 16)*. Simmer for 30 minutes, then move the pan half off the heat and spoon off the fat that collects on the cooler side of the liquid.

5 **Cooking sausages.** Remove 2 cups [½ liter] of liquid from the pot to use for cooking the garnish vegetables *(Step 6)*. Add poaching sausages and potatoes to the *potée* and simmer, partly covered, for 30 minutes, or until the meats are tender and the juices run clear.

7 **Serving.** Remove the meats and vegetables from the poaching pot and drain them. Carve the chicken into serving pieces, cut the pork and sausages into neat slices, and arrange all of the meats in the center of a warmed platter. Garnish them with the carrots, turnips, beans and potatoes from the *potée*. Arrange the cabbage balls around the assembly, and ladle on a little of the hot poaching liquid.

4
Braising and Stewing
Slow Cooking
for Rich Results

Separately sautéed button mushrooms are added to an almost complete stew of pork and chestnuts. Glazed white onions, also prepared separately, stud the stew. The cooking liquid has been removed for degreasing; it will be returned to the casserole to simmer briefly before the pork and vegetables are served.

Braising and stewing are two names for a single cooking method. The term braising is most often used to describe cuts of meat cooked whole, sometimes with a stuffing for extra flavor; stewing is used when the meat is cut into pieces. In each case, meat is simmered in a covered pot until it is tender and its juices have blended delectably with the cooking liquid. The method differs from poaching, the other way of cooking pork with moist heat, in that it calls for relatively small quantities of liquid. During cooking, the liquid usually reduces still further to provide a sauce that is the concentrated essence of the entire dish.

Most cuts of pork benefit from a partial cooking before they are braised or stewed. Fresh pork, for example, usually is given a preliminary searing, which provides the meat with an appetizing brown surface, formed as the juices that are drawn out by the heat dry and concentrate into a crust. Large cuts are best seared in a hot oven (400° F. [200° C.]) and can be set on a rack in a roasting pan so that they will brown uniformly without being turned. Small cuts and pork pieces destined for stews can be browned in lard or oil in a skillet. Ham and other salted or smoked cuts, on the other hand, are normally poached before braising to draw out their excess salt.

Although pork can be braised or stewed in water, a full-bodied liquid such as stock or wine will yield a richer sauce. Sometimes fresh pork cuts are first marinated with aromatics in wine or a little vinegar to flavor and tenderize the meat, in which case the strained marinade can then become part of the cooking liquid *(pages 62-63)*. Of the other liquids that complement pork, hard cider contributes a hint of tartness and beer or ale imparts a subtle nutlike taste *(recipe, page 140)*. Small cuts, such as the pork chops shown on page 66, need no additional liquid in most cases; the juices they exude should be sufficient to keep them from drying out during their comparatively brief cooking time.

Braises or stews can be made equally well in an oven or on top of the stove. Ovens provide even heat from all sides, and once the heat is properly adjusted so that the liquid barely trembles, the dish can safely be left to simmer. It is easier to supervise the temperature of the liquid on top of the stove, but uniform cooking demands the use of a heavy pan or casserole that will distribute the heat evenly.

Tender Treatment for a Tough Cut

Any large piece of pork is delicious when braised, but this cooking method has particular value for relatively tough fresh cuts such as the Boston shoulder shown here. The gentle, moist cooking tenderizes the meat and allows it to absorb the flavors of the braising liquid. To make the meat even more succulent, marinate it, using any of the wet marinades described on pages 14-15. If you strain the marinade and add it to the cooking liquid, the dish will take on extra depth.

For even more complex flavoring, you can stuff the meat, using any of the mixtures shown on pages 18-19 and enriching them, if you wish, with the pork trimmings. It is important, however, to coordinate the flavors of the marinade, the stuffing and the cooking liquid. An apple or a prune stuffing, for instance, blends best with meat tenderized in marinade with a wine rather than a vinegar base; the braising liquid could be hard cider or wine, depending on whether you wish to emphasize the fruit in the stuffing or the wine in the marinade.

In this demonstration, the marinade (recipe, page 128) includes white wine, olive oil, garlic, rosemary, bay leaves and—for a pungent touch—juniper berries. The simple egg-and-bread stuffing contains garlic to echo the marinade; the braising liquid is pork stock (page 16).

If you stuff the meat, you must first bone it; boning techniques are described on pages 12-13. The meat can then be butterflied (Step 1), stuffed (in moderation, since starches expand during cooking), and tied in a neat parcel.

Once prepared for braising, fresh pork cuts are seared either in a hot oven or—if they are small enough—in a pan over direct heat to give them a rich, brown crust. They are then simmered at low heat in a small amount of liquid that has been enriched by the deglazed deposits from the searing pan and—in most cases —by the strained marinade. The meat will be ready when it registers 165° to 170° F. [75° C.] on a meat thermometer, or when the juices run clear when a skewer is inserted. After cooking, the braising liquid provides a bonus: Cleansed of fat, it becomes a sauce that unites the flavors of the marinade, meat and liquid.

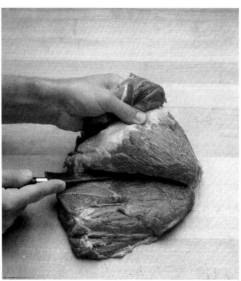

1 Butterflying the cut. Place the boned meat — in this case, a Boston shoulder — fat side down. Slice horizontally through the meat at the thickest edge and stop 1 inch [2½ cm.] from the opposite edge so that you can open the meat like a book. Flatten the opened meat with the side of the knife; slice off protruding pieces and any fat thicker than ¼ inch [6 mm.].

2 Marinating. Place the butterflied pork in a shallow bowl and add the marinade ingredients. Cover the bowl with plastic wrap or foil and let the meat marinate for four hours at room temperature or overnight in the refrigerator, turning it several times.

6 Searing the meat. Place the trussed pork, skin side up, in a roasting pan and put it in a preheated 425° F. [220° C.] oven for 35 to 45 minutes, until the surface browns evenly. Using two wooden spoons to avoid piercing the meat, transfer the pork to a casserole. Spoon the fat out of the pan.

7 Braising. Deglaze the pan (page 26) with the marinade. Pour this liquid over the pork and add hot pork stock until the meat is half-submerged. Cover and place in a 325° F. [160° C.] oven; allow 20 minutes for each pound [½ kg.] of meat. During the last 20 minutes, turn up the heat to 400° F. [200° C.] and remove the lid; baste regularly.

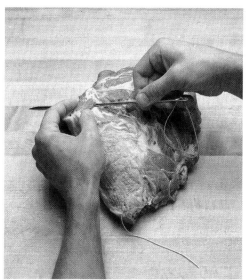

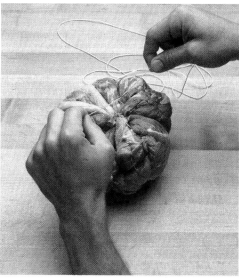

3 **Stuffing.** Lift the pork from the bowl, letting excess marinade drain back into the bowl. Then spread out the meat, cut side up, and pat it dry. Strain the marinade. Prepare the stuffing (a pastelike mixture of chopped parsley, pounded garlic, egg and bread crumbs is used here). Smear the stuffing over the cut side of the pork, leaving a 1-inch [2½-cm.] border all around.

4 **Stitching in the stuffing.** Fold up the butterflied pork as if you were closing a book. Thread a butcher's needle with kitchen string and stitch the three cut edges of the meat back together, leaving 6-inch [15-cm.] tails of string protruding from the first and last stitches. Tie the two ends together.

5 **Tying the meat.** To shape the meat into a compact parcel that will be easy to handle and will cook evenly, pass a length of string around it four or five times in a longitudinal pattern. Gather any loose folds of meat into the parcel as you work. Knot the string tight: The meat will shrink as it cooks.

8 **Preparing the sauce.** Transfer the meat to a warmed plate and let it rest to make carving easier. Meanwhile, strain the braising liquid into a saucepan and bring it to a boil. Reduce the heat to low and move the pan half off the burner. Degrease the simmering sauce by repeatedly spooning off the skin of fat that collects on the cooler side. Season with fresh citrus juice.

9 **Serving.** Cut off the string tied around the meat. Snip loose and remove the stitches. Carve the meat into slices ½ to ¾ inch [1 to 2 cm.] thick, arrange them on a warmed serving platter, and spoon some of the sauce over them. Pass the rest of the sauce separately.

A Sugary Finish for a Whole Ham

The braising of salted or smoked cuts—whether uncooked or labeled ready-to-eat—differs slightly from that for fresh pork. Uncooked ham and other cured cuts need advance soaking and poaching (chart, pages 10-11) to draw out excess salt. Ready-to-eat ham should be poached, but only for about 30 minutes. In either case, poaching softens the rind, making it easy to score or to remove, as shown, so that the fat beneath can be scored to let the flavors of the braising liquid penetrate the flesh. Strong-tasting cured pork is best complemented by a hearty braising liquid—beer, perhaps, or a fortified wine such as the Madeira used here (recipe, page 149).

For most of the cooking time, the cut must be covered to prevent drying and to hold flavor. Toward the end, the meat is lightly coated with white or brown sugar or honey, then cooked uncovered and basted to produce a glaze. Any pan juices may be degreased for a gravy, or they can form the base of a velouté sauce (demonstration, page 17; recipe, page 166).

1 Poaching. Place the meat — here, a smoked, ready-to-eat ham — in a pot and cover it with cold water. Bring the water to a simmer, partly cover and poach for 30 minutes. If the ham is uncooked, allow 15 minutes' poaching per pound [½ kg.]. Drain the ham.

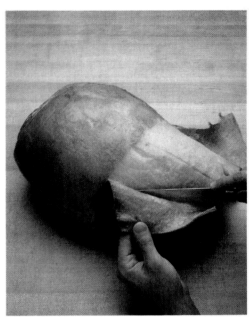

2 Removing rind. Slit the rind along its length. Slicing between the rind and the fat, peel off the rind. Trim the fat to a thickness of ½ inch [1 cm.]; score it in a diamond pattern without cutting the meat. A ready-to-eat ham can now be braised, or set aside for up to two hours.

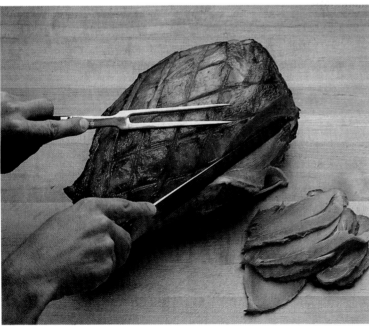

6 Carving a base. Remove the ham from the pan and place it glazed side up on a wooden work surface or cutting board. Let the ham rest for 15 to 20 minutes to firm the meat for carving. Cutting parallel to the bone, remove enough thin, lengthwise slices from the less meaty side to form a flat base on which to rest the ham.

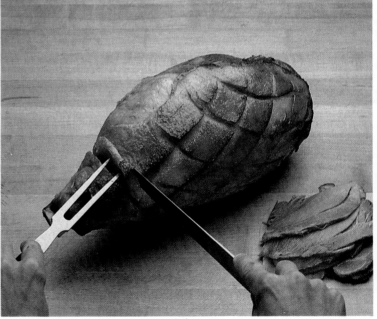

7 Cutting a wedge. Rest the ham on its base and steady it with a carving fork. Using the technique demonstrated on pages 40-41, make two slices down to the bone at the shank end to remove a wedge of meat from the ham. Because cured ham is very firm meat, you should make the wedge — and the succeeding slices — thinner than you would with fresh pork: The two cuts that form the wedge should be no farther than 1 inch [2½ cm.] apart.

3 **Braising.** Place the ham with its meatier side facing up on a rack in a roasting pan or large casserole and pour the braising liquid over it. Cover the pan with a lid or aluminum foil and braise the ham in a preheated 350° F. [180° C.] oven for 45 minutes.

4 **Coating with sugar.** Slide the pan partway out of the oven and remove the lid or foil covering. Dust the ham lightly with confectioners' sugar. Turn up the heat to 425° F. [220° C.] and put the uncovered pan back in the oven.

5 **Basting.** After about 10 minutes, the sugar will begin to form a brown caramel glaze on the ham. Baste the ham with the pan juices every 10 minutes until a meat thermometer indicates 140° F. [60° C.] for ready-to-eat hams, 160° F. [70° C.] for uncooked hams.

8 **Carving.** Cut straight down to the leg bone at about ¼-inch [6-mm.] intervals (left) to carve as many thin slices as you need. Then insert the knife at the shank end and turn the blade to slice horizontally straight along the bone, freeing the slices. For additional servings, turn the ham and slice parallel to the bone.

Packing Extra Flavor into Small Cuts

Small pieces of pork can be stuffed and braised as successfully as the large cuts called for in most recipes. Cutlets, scallops or slices of boned loin can be wrapped around fruit—plums or dried apricots, for example—and braised in stock. Or you can slit a tenderloin lengthwise and fill it with strips of ham and cheese *(recipe, page 130)*.

Among the best small cuts for stuffing are chops cut two ribs thick—double chops. By cutting between the ribs to form a pocket, you can make room for a fruit or vegetable stuffing—sliced apples sautéed in butter, for instance, or the savory onion-and-mushroom mixture used here *(recipe, page 130)*. Do not overfill the pockets: Stuffings that include bread crumbs will swell during cooking and can spill out, even though the pocket is pinched shut with wooden picks. Because they cook fairly fast, stuffed chops usually can be braised in their own juices—with a soupçon of stock, wine or water added only if the pan becomes dry.

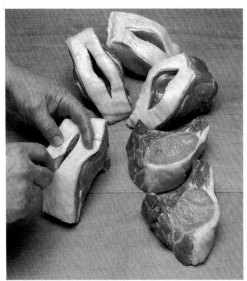

1 **Preparing the chops.** With a small paring knife, trim excess fat from double-thick chops, leaving a border ¼ inch [6 mm.] wide. Cut lengthwise through the fat and the meat beneath it *(above)* to make pockets 2½ to 3 inches [6 to 8 cm.] in length and depth.

2 **Stuffing the chops.** Make the stuffing—in this case, a mushroom-based mixture. Using a teaspoon, fill the pockets loosely. To secure the stuffing, insert two wooden picks diagonally into each chop near the border of fat so that the picks cross at the center of the opening *(above)*.

3 **Cooking the chops.** Heat oil in a deep skillet or sauté pan. Sear the chops briefly on both sides over medium heat. Reduce the heat and cook them for 20 minutes, turning them several times. Cover the chops with a lid *(above)* and braise them for 40 minutes, turning them once and adding a bit of liquid if they look dry.

4 **Serving the chops.** Remove the cooked chops from the pan with a spatula *(above)*. Add a little water or wine to the braising liquid, increase the heat, and stir to deglaze the pan deposits. Strain the liquid through a sieve onto the chops for a smooth sauce. Garnish with chopped parsley *(right)*.

The Quintessential Stew

Pork stews—braises in which pieces of meat are cooked with liquid, aromatic vegetables and flavorings—offer a wide scope for the cook's imagination. The format is broad enough to include such distinctive variations as the wine-based ragouts of France and the beer stews and paprika-spiced goulashes of central Europe (recipes, pages 138, 140 and 154).

Inexpensive cuts such as Boston or picnic shoulder are well suited to stews, since they benefit from slow, moist cooking. The meat acquires more flavor and tenderness if it is marinated overnight.

Before braising, the marinated meat should be dried, then browned over direct heat. Because the meat pieces are small and need frequent turning, the browning is best done in a large skillet or sauté pan. Browning colors the meat and draws out juices that can later be deglazed and incorporated into the stewing liquid. In the stew demonstrated below and overleaf (recipe, page 138), the aromatic vegetables also are browned to draw out their flavor and slightly glaze them.

If you include carrots among the aromatics, they will add a hint of their sweetness—an echo of the pork's flavor—to the pan deposits. This sweetening can be reinforced by sprinkling a little sugar into the pan after the meat and vegetables have been removed. To lend body to the sauce, you can add some flour before deglazing the pan with the principal cooking medium—in this case, the reserved marinade, although dry white wine, beer or pork stock would serve the purpose equally well.

Chestnuts are a welcome addition to pork stews. Shell and peel the chestnuts (Step 6, page 69) after the other ingredients have begun to stew; if added too soon, the nuts may disintegrate during the lengthy cooking.

The taste and appearance of the stew will be greatly improved if you cleanse the liquid of fat and impurities near the end of the cooking time (Step 9, page 68). By then the aromatics will have given up all their flavors. Other vegetables, such as cabbages (page 54) or onions (box, page 69) can be prepared separately to replace the aromatics and added to the stew after the sauce has been cleansed.

1 Marinating the pork. Cut lean, boneless pork into large pieces and trim away any fat. Put the pieces in a deep bowl. Add the marinade—in this case, red wine, sliced onions, parsley, thyme, garlic and a bay leaf. Cover and refrigerate overnight. The next day strain the marinade through a colander (above) and reserve the liquid.

2 Seasoning the pork. Remove the pork pieces from the colander; discard the vegetables and herbs. Dry the meat on a cloth or paper towels and season it with salt and pepper. Melt some lard in a large sauté pan over medium heat. When the fat starts to bubble, put in a batch of meat pieces in one layer. Do not crowd the pan.

3 Adding aromatics. Brown the pork for 15 to 20 minutes, turning the pieces several times. As each batch browns, transfer it to a large casserole. Add a bouquet garni (page 16) to the casserole. When the last batch of meat is in the sauté pan, add the aromatics— here, carrots, peeled garlic cloves and chopped onions—to color briefly. ▶

4 **Deglazing the sauté pan.** Transfer the remaining meat and aromatics to the casserole, then sprinkle a little sugar into the sauté pan *(left)*. When the sugar begins to brown, add flour and stir to form a roux *(center)*. When the roux is lightly colored, pour the strained marinade liquid into the pan *(right)*. Bring it to a boil, stirring and scraping continuously to loosen all of the pan deposits and to blend the flour in thoroughly.

8 **Straining the stew.** When the meat is tender, remove the casserole from the heat. Squeeze the bouquet garni between two spoons, then discard it. Transfer the meat and chestnuts to a dish. Pour the rest of the stew into a strainer set over a saucepan. Return the meat and chestnuts to the casserole; cover it and set it in a warm place.

9 **Cleansing the sauce.** Remove the carrots and discard them. With a pestle, force the onions, garlic and any small chestnut pieces through the mesh into the saucepan *(above)*. Bring the liquid to a simmer, then move the pan half off the heat. Skim off the layer of fat that collects on the cooler side.

10 **Reassembling the stew.** Add the sautéed-mushroom and glazed-onion garnishes to the casserole. When no more impurities rise to the surface of the sauce — this may take 10 to 15 minutes — pour the sauce over the other ingredients in the casserole *(above)*.

5 **Adding the liquid.** Pour the liquid from the pan over the meat and aromatics in the casserole. Add water or more wine — and, if you like, a splash of Cognac — to barely cover the meat and vegetables. Bring to a boil over medium heat, then adjust the heat so that the stew just simmers, and cover.

6 **Preparing the chestnuts.** Cut a cross in the flat side of each chestnut. Boil the nuts in water for about 10 minutes; scoop them out one at a time with a wire skimmer. The shells will have loosened around the crosses. Holding each chestnut with a cloth, peel away the shell and the bitter skin beneath.

7 **Adding the chestnuts.** Put the chestnuts in the stew after it has cooked for about 45 minutes. Replace the lid and cook for about one hour more. Toward the end of cooking, prepare vegetable garnishes for the dish — glazed onions (box, below) and sautéed mushrooms were used here.

11 **Serving the stew.** Cover the casserole and set it over low heat. Simmer for 15 to 20 minutes so that the flavors of the garnish vegetables and the sauce intermingle. Before serving from the casserole (above), sprinkle the stew, if you like, with bread cubes browned in butter, or pounded garlic mixed with chopped parsley.

A Glazed-Onion Garnish

Forming a glaze. Peel small boiling onions and put them in a pan just wide enough to hold them in one layer. Add a knob of butter and a pinch of sugar. Half cover them with water, put the lid on the pan and cook the onions over low heat; shake the pan occasionally to prevent sticking. After about 15 minutes, remove the lid and increase the heat to medium. Cook for five minutes more, or until all of the water has evaporated and the onions have acquired a shiny white glaze.

A Medley
of Methods

How to handle sauerkraut
Two hearty pies
Assembling ham gratins
Crunchy coating for pig's ears
A soufflé made for unmolding
The secret of a delicate mousse
Three ways to use leftovers

The culinary versatility of the pig is renowned: It is edible from head to tail, and, thanks to such processes as sausage making, salting and smoking, the pig provides not one meat but many. As for the options available in preparing this bounty for the table, they are too numerous and diverse to be neatly encompassed by the basic cooking methods of frying, broiling, grilling, roasting, poaching, braising and stewing. You can, for example, create an entirely new repertoire of dishes by combining pork cuts that have been cooked in different ways. This not only provides variety but ensures that each kind of meat receives the most appropriate treatment. Thus, for the pork-and-sauerkraut combination shown opposite and on pages 72-73, fresh pork sausages are braised along with the sauerkraut, while salted and smoked cuts are poached separately so that their pungent flavors do not dominate the dish.

When pork is combined with a starchy element rather than with a vegetable such as sauerkraut, a modest amount of meat can become a generous family meal. You can, for example, cover or enclose sliced, chopped or ground pork with a pastry crust, which helps to keep the meat moist during cooking while the pastry itself turns crisp and golden *(pages 74-75)*. Another approach is to pour a light batter around half-cooked sausages and bake them in the oven, yielding the traditional English dish called toad-in-the-hole *(page 79)*. Or you can poach chopped meat, which has been combined with flour, bread and egg, to make dumplings that serve either as a course on their own or as a garnish for another preparation *(page 84)*.

When the aim is subtlety rather than heartiness, cured ham is a particularly versatile meat. For example, a chilled mousse worthy of any banquet can be made by puréeing ham to absolute smoothness, enriching it with softly whipped heavy cream and lightly setting the mixture in gelatinous stock *(pages 82-83)*. A soufflé-pudding, formed from alternating layers of sauced, puréed ham and spinach, makes a fine, light main-course dish that—unlike airier soufflés—can be unmolded from its cooking vessel for serving *(pages 80-81)*. And countless combinations of ham, vegetables and a coating of sauce can be devised to produce delicious gratins, all of which will emerge crusty and bubbling hot from the broiler or oven *(pages 76-77)*.

Rolled salted pork belly, taken from the pot in which it has poached with smoked hocks, is carved in slices. Both meats will be presented at the table with plump sausages that have been embedded in sauerkraut and braised in wine and stock in a casserole.

Sauerkraut: An Enduring Partner

Sauerkraut—shredded cabbage that is fermented in brine—is a time-honored accompaniment to pork in central Europe. It once served to supplement the salted pork used in winter months, when fresh meat was hard to come by. The natural affinity between the pronounced flavors of the meat and the cabbage has ensured the continuance of the tradition, though now sauerkraut also is frequently served with fresh pork. In this demonstration the sauerkraut accompanies a mixture of cured and fresh meat—salted belly, smoked hocks and fresh sausages—although the cuts used may be varied at will (recipes, pages 152-153).

Whether you buy fresh sauerkraut at a specialty market or use the more readily available canned variety, you will probably wish to attenuate its strong flavor before cooking it: Fermentation gives the cabbage a sharpness that is accentuated by the brine. The sauerkraut should be rinsed and squeezed before cooking to remove some of the salt (Step 3); sauerkraut that tastes too salty after several rinsings should be soaked for half an hour in cold water.

Long, slow braising mellows the flavor of the sauerkraut. Here, it is simmered in stock with a little white wine; some recipes also call for the addition of a glass of flavored brandy, such as kirsch. Apples, onions and juniper berries are traditionally cooked with sauerkraut to give it sweetness and an aromatic edge.

Fresh sausages or fresh pork cuts such as blade, loin, or arm roasts or steaks are best braised along with the sauerkraut to blend their flavors with the cabbage. Because sausages or small cuts need relatively little cooking, they can be added toward the end of the braising time.

Salted pork cuts need soaking (chart, pages 10-11) before they are cooked. The cuts then are usually poached separately from the sauerkraut, so that salt drawn from them during cooking does not overwhelm the finished dish. Mildly flavored smoked sausages, chops or ham can be cooked with the sauerkraut; in the demonstration shown here, however, the belly and the smoked hocks are poached together for convenience.

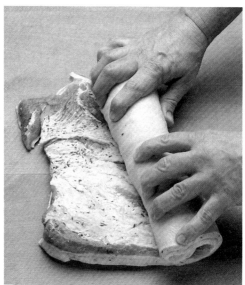

1 **Trussing the salt pork.** Soak salted pork belly (page 14) in cold water for three or four hours. Dry the meat with paper towels, then roll it into a cylinder (above). Tie it with kitchen string, looping the string around the belly at 2-inch [5-cm.] intervals along its length. Knot the string tight.

2 **Poaching the cured cuts.** Place the trussed belly in a large pot. Cover it generously with cold water. Add the smoked cuts—in this case, two hocks. Bring the water just to a simmer, then set a lid ajar over the pot and gently poach the meats until they are tender—about one and a half to two hours from the time the surface of the water starts to shiver.

6 **Adding the stock.** Add juniper berries, tied in a small muslin or cheesecloth bag to facilitate removal after cooking—the berries give the dish a faint, pungent flavor, but they are bitter to eat. Then pour warm stock (page 16) into the casserole until the sauerkraut is almost covered.

7 **Braising the sauerkraut.** Bring the liquid just to a simmer, cover and braise gently for one and a quarter hours. Prick fresh pork sausages in two or three places with a fork and add them to the casserole, pushing them down to embed them in the sauerkraut (above). Cover and braise for 45 minutes more.

3 **Rinsing the sauerkraut.** Rinse the sauerkraut, drain it, then taste it for salt. If necessary, rinse it again. Squeeze the water out with your hands. Set it in a colander to drain further while you prepare the other ingredients.

4 **Starting the braise.** Chop an onion into fine pieces. Melt some lard in a heavy, fireproof casserole. Set the casserole over low heat. Cook the onion gently for about 10 minutes, until it is soft. Add the squeezed-out sauerkraut.

5 **Adding wine.** Pour a generous splash of dry white wine over the sauerkraut and onion. Stir the ingredients together with a spoon. Peel and core an apple and cut it into slices. Add the slices to the casserole.

8 **Assembling the dish.** Remove the casserole from the heat. Set the sausages aside and discard the juniper berries. Heap the sauerkraut on a large, warmed platter, then lay the sausages on top. Remove the poaching pot from the heat, and lift out the belly and the hocks. Cut away the string from the belly and slice the meat. Arrange the slices around the dish. Serve the hocks whole — they can be cut up at the table. The dish may be garnished, if you like, with small potatoes boiled in their skins.

Exploring the Potentials of Pies

Traditional and well loved, pork pies *(recipes, pages 155-158)* invite variation and experiment. They can be made with any fresh or cured lean cut or with leftovers. The meat can be sliced, chopped or ground; it can be used alone or with vegetables or fruits. The ingredients can be baked in a pie dish under a pastry lid or enclosed in a pastry casing.

In the pie demonstrated opposite at top, for example, small pork slices are baked with apples beneath a pastry lid in a deep dish *(recipe, page 156)*. The oblong pie shown below is really a crust-encased meat loaf: A pastry shell is wrapped around ground pork, itself encasing a filling of hard-boiled eggs *(recipe, page 155)*.

Almost any unsweetened, flaky pastry can be used for pork pies, but a short-crust dough *(box, right; recipe, page 167)* bakes to a particularly crisp and appetizing crust. Always check the pastry halfway through the cooking; if it is browning too much, cover it with aluminum foil to prevent burning.

Short-Crust Dough with Lard

Preparing a light pastry for crisp crusts. Sift all-purpose flour and salt into a mixing bowl. Add lard — as here — or butter, cut into small pieces *(left)*. Using two table knives, cut the fat into pea-sized pieces to form a crumbly mixture with the flour *(center)*. Stir a little cold water into the mixture with a fork. Repeat as necessary *(right)* until you can gather the dough into a firm ball. Enclose it in plastic wrap to prevent it from drying out, and chill the pastry in the refrigerator for at least half an hour.

Wrapping Up a Meat-and-Egg Loaf

1 **Preparing the filling.** Mix ground pork with parsley and sautéed, chopped onion. Make short-crust pastry and roll out a third of it into a rectangle. Set this on a baking sheet. Place half of the pork on the pastry, shaping it to leave a 1-inch [2½-cm.] pastry border. Make a trough in the meat; trim the ends of hard-boiled eggs and fit the eggs snugly into the trough *(left)*. Sprinkle with salt and grated nutmeg. Cover with the rest of the pork. Smooth the filling with a knife dipped in hot water to prevent sticking *(right)*.

2 **Covering with pastry.** Place bay leaves on the pork for extra flavor. Roll the rest of the pastry into a rectangle at least 3 inches [8 cm.] longer and wider than the base. Wind it up loosely on the pin and unroll it over the meat *(above)*. Press the pastry cover against the meat, then trim it along the pastry base.

Meat Slices Baked beneath a Pastry Cover

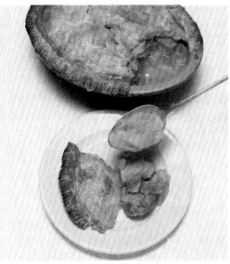

1 **Preparing the filling.** Arrange lean pork slices about ½ inch [1 cm.] thick on the bottom of a deep pie dish, then cover the pork with peeled apple slices. Sprinkle with salt, pepper and a little nutmeg. Add alternating layers of pork and apple until the dish is filled.

2 **Rolling out the pastry.** Add dry white wine to half the depth of the filling, then dot the surface with bits of butter. Roll out the pastry to make a lid slightly larger than the top of the dish and about ⅛ inch [3 mm.] thick. Moisten the rim of the dish with water so the pastry will adhere. Lay the pastry over the dish.

3 **Baking and serving.** Trim the pastry to leave a 1-inch [2½-cm.] overhang. Fold this under the pastry and pinch it firmly to the rim of the dish. Cut a slit in the pastry to allow steam to escape. Glaze the pastry with egg beaten with water. Bake in a 350° F. [180° C.] oven for one and a half hours.

3 **Glazing the pastry.** Use your thumb and forefinger to crimp the two layers of pastry together all around the border. Brush the pastry with beaten egg mixed with a little water. If you like, score the pastry lightly with a fork to make a crisscross pattern. Cut a slit in the center to allow steam to escape.

4 **Baking.** Bake the pie in a preheated 325° F. [160° C.] oven for an hour and a half. From time to time, wipe any fat from the baking sheet. For tidy serving, cut half of the pie into slices on the baking sheet, and transfer the uncut half to a serving platter *(above)*. Arrange the slices on the platter, overlapping them to expose the filling *(right)*.

Sauce-topped Gratins of Sliced Ham

Combined with vegetables, swathed in a creamy sauce, and given a brief spell in a hot oven or under a broiler, slices of cooked pork or ham remain succulent and tender while the sauce acquires the crisp, golden crust characteristic of a gratin. The vegetables, sauce and meat may be varied almost endlessly: The essence of a gratin is improvisation.

For example, thick slices of roasted, poached or braised fresh or cured pork may be placed in a baking dish, then covered with the other ingredients and baked or broiled. The other ingredients may be as simple as a velouté, or white sauce (recipes, page 166), flavored, perhaps, with mustard or puréed tomato. The assembly will be even more inviting if you add vegetables. In the demonstration at right, top (recipe, page 161), ham slices are covered with a sauce containing shallots, tomatoes, mushrooms and heavy cream, and reduced until it is thick enough to coat a spoon.

Slices of meat that are ½ inch [1 cm.] thick or more should be warmed in the oven before the gratin is assembled, because they will not heat through in the short time it takes the crust to form. To keep the meat moist during its preliminary heating, sprinkle it with white wine or stock and cover it (Step 1, right, top).

Paper-thin slices of pork or ham lend themselves to a more intimate partnership with other ingredients: They can be rolled up around a stuffing. In the gratin demonstrated at right, bottom (recipe, page 162), thin slices of ham are wrapped around parboiled leeks and a zucchini stuffing, coated with a simple, cheese-enriched white sauce and baked. Braised Belgian endive or parboiled asparagus could replace the leeks; or instead of using shredded zucchini in the stuffing you might try spinach or chard leaves, parboiled for two minutes and chopped fine.

Most vegetables used in a gratin must first be drained of excess liquid to ensure that the finished dish will be thick and creamy. The zucchini used here are layered with salt to draw off liquid, then are squeezed dry. Mushrooms are sautéed beforehand for the same reason. Spinach or chard should be dipped in cold water after parboiling, then squeezed dry.

A Blanket of Tomato-flavored Cream

1 Warming the ham. Trim excess fat from ½ inch [1 cm.] thick slices of cooked ham, leaving a border of fat no more than ½ inch wide. Put the slices in a gratin dish, sprinkle them with white wine and cover the dish loosely with foil. Warm the ham in a 300° F. [150° C.] oven while you cook the sauce.

2 Preparing the sauce. Put sliced mushrooms in a pan with water, butter, lemon juice and salt. Cover, bring to a boil, then remove the pan from the heat. In a separate pan, cook chopped shallots with dry white wine over high heat. Then strain in the mushroom liquid and bring to a boil.

Ham-wrapped Leeks Baked with Cheese

1 Making stuffing. Stack shredded zucchini in salted layers (above). After 30 minutes squeeze it dry, then sauté it in butter until soft. In separate pans, sauté chopped onion until transparent, and toss grated mushrooms in butter until dry. Mix the vegetables with pepper, chopped parsley and lemon juice.

2 Parboiling leeks. Prepare a white sauce. Slit trimmed leeks lengthwise through the leaves, from the point where they turn green, then soak the leeks in water for 15 minutes and rinse them under running water to remove grit. Cut the leeks to match the size of the thin ham slices (above), tie them in bundles and parboil them in salted water for 10 minutes.

3 **Finishing the sauce.** Stir in peeled, seeded and chopped tomatoes, and cook uncovered over medium heat for 20 minutes to reduce the liquid by one third. Add any juices in the ham dish. Add heavy cream to the sauce and cook it for five to 10 minutes more until it is thick enough to coat a spoon.

4 **Coating the ham slices.** Taste the sauce for seasoning, add a knob of butter and stir in the mushrooms. Take the gratin dish out of the oven and discard the foil. Ladle the sauce over the ham, then put the dish under a broiler or in a 450° F. [230° C.] oven for a few minutes until the surface begins to brown.

5 **Serving the gratin.** Serve the dish immediately, while the sauce is still bubbling. Use a broad spatula to lift out the ham slices with their coating of sauce. Spoon any sauce that remains in the dish over the slices.

3 **Assembling the ham rolls.** Untie the leeks and lay them on a towel to drain. Spread a layer of the vegetable stuffing over the bottom of a buttered gratin dish. On each ham slice, put two leeks and 1 tablespoon [15 ml.] of stuffing. Roll the ham around its filling and, tucking the loose flaps underneath, place the roll in the gratin dish.

4 **Coating the rolls.** Scatter green, brine-packed peppercorns over the ham rolls, if you like. Take the white sauce off the heat, and grate some Parmesan or Gruyère cheese into it. Stir in the cheese with a spoon. Ladle the cheese sauce over the rolls *(above)*.

5 **Cooking the rolls.** Grate a little more cheese over the sauce-covered rolls. Distribute slivers of butter over the sauce, then bake the rolls in a preheated 400° F. [200° C.] oven for 30 minutes. Serve immediately.

Pig's Ears in a Spicy Crumb Crust

Pig's ears and feet, gelatinous cuts valued primarily as stock ingredients, are delicious on their own if slowly cooked to bring out their mild, rather sweet flavors. Cleaning is an important part of their preparation: Surface hair must be singed off over an open flame, and the ears or feet rinsed well in cold water. Long poaching follows. Ears need about two hours of poaching to cook through; feet require at least four hours to make their rinds soft enough to cut.

The poached meats may be served hot with a vinaigrette sauce or, to add textural interest, they can be fried in batter or baked in a bread-crumb coating, as here. To fry or bake the meats, cool them in the poaching liquid, then cut them into slices or strips for even cooking.

In this demonstration, pig's ears are coated with a piquant flavoring—mustard is used in this case—then rolled in bread crumbs and dipped in melted butter. Brief cooking browns the buttery coating to a crisp crust, an admirable contrast to the tender flesh beneath.

1 **Poaching the ears.** Clean the ears and place them in a large pot. Cover with a court bouillon *(recipe, page 164)*. Bring to a boil, skimming off any scum. Simmer the ears, partly covered, for about two hours, until they are tender. Leave the ears in the liquid until cool, then halve them lengthwise and place them in a shallow pan or a tray.

2 **Flattening the ears.** Ladle just enough cooking liquid into the tray to cover the ears; the liquid adds flavor and prevents the ears from discoloring. To flatten the ears for uniform broiling, cover them with a heavy board and weight it. Refrigerate the ears for three to four hours, until the liquid jells.

3 **Coating the ears.** Dip the ears in warm stock to melt off the jelly; any jelly left in the tray can be added to the stock and reused. Using a pastry brush, paint one side of each ear with prepared mustard, then press the ear, coated side down, onto fresh white bread crumbs. Coat the other side of each ear with mustard and bread crumbs in the same way.

4 **Buttering the ears.** Melt some butter in a small saucepan over low heat. Spoon it over one side of each coated ear. Put the ears buttered side down on a baking sheet, and spoon the rest of the melted butter over them.

5 **Cooking the ears.** Put the baking sheet in a preheated 400° F. [200° C.] oven for 10 minutes, turning the ears over once. If the coating does not brown grill the ears under a hot broiler for one to two minutes on each side. Serve immediately. The crisp ears are garnished here with watercress.

Sausages in a Bed of Batter

In one form or another, batter plays an important role in pork cookery. A thin pancake batter, for example, produces ham-filled crepes *(recipe, page 163)*; a more adhesive batter coats small pork pieces for deep frying *(pages 30-31)*.

The most popular of pork-and-batter combinations, however, are batter puddings. These may be made by mixing meat and flavorings with the batter and then putting the mixture in the oven, as in the French farmhouse dish *pounti,* or pork cake *(recipe, page 158)*. Or the batter can be added to fat and meat that are already hot, then baked—exemplified by toad-in-the-hole, the English dish demonstrated here *(recipe, page 158)*.

The sausages, which need longer cooking than the batter, are browned in the fat before the batter is added. Take care that there is only a thin coating of fat in the pan when the batter is poured in, or the final dish may taste greasy. The batter starts to cook on contact with the fat; as it bakes, it rises around the sausages to form a puffy, lightly browned casing.

1 **Preparing the batter.** Sift flour with a pinch of salt into a large mixing bowl. Make a well in the center of the flour and break eggs into the well. Whisk the eggs and flour together, stirring outward from the center to amalgamate the ingredients thoroughly.

2 **Mixing the batter.** As the mixture thickens, add some milk, whisking it with the flour to make a thick paste. Pour in the rest of the milk and whisk until smooth. Melt a knob of lard in a roasting pan. Prick sausages in two or three places, and add them to the pan. Set it in a 400° F. [200° C.] oven.

3 **Cooking the dish.** After about 25 minutes, when the sausages have browned, lift out the pan. Drain off excess fat to leave only a thin layer in the pan. Pour the batter around the sausages *(left)*, and put the pan back in the oven. The dish will be ready to serve after about 35 minutes, when the batter is crisp and brown *(above)*.

A Layered Soufflé Pudding

To make a molded pork dish of airy lightness, you need only mix finely chopped, cooked meat with a base of egg yolks and white sauce, then fold in beaten egg whites. When this blend is baked, the air trapped in the egg whites expands, puffing the mixture up. At the same time, the thick base ingredients give the dish a firmness necessary for unmolding. The result is known—appropriately enough —as a soufflé pudding.

Cooked smoked ham is the best type of pork to use for a soufflé pudding; leftovers from a fresh pork roast can be used instead, but the result will not be as robust in taste. The dish may be flavored by ham alone (recipe, page 159), or you can alternate the ham soufflé pudding mixture with a similar mixture based on a green vegetable to create a dish tiered with contrasting flavors and colors.

In this demonstration, finely chopped spinach alternates with the ham; it has been parboiled to soften it, then squeezed dry (excess moisture would make the soufflé pudding watery). You could substitute chard leaves prepared in the same way, or zucchini that has previously been salted, drained and squeezed, then briefly sautéed to dry it further.

Whatever flavorings you choose, the lightness of the finished pudding will depend largely on the amount of air you beat into the egg whites. Beating is best done by hand with a wire whisk, which allows you to aerate the entire mass of whites. A copper mixing bowl also is useful; it interacts chemically but harmlessly with the egg whites to create more stable air bubbles.

To prevent the whites from deflating when you fold them into the base mixture, lighten the mixture first by stirring a dollop of the whites into it. Then fold in the rest of the whites as gently and quickly as possible. Your hands are the best tools for the job.

As it cooks, a soufflé pudding will not rise as much as a classic soufflé, which has a higher proportion of egg whites. It will fall only slightly as it cools, however, and there is no necessity to rush the soufflé pudding to the table. In fact, the dish should be allowed to rest for a few minutes before you unmold it so that the layers can cool and settle.

1 Advance preparation. Trim the spinach, removing the stems and discolored leaves, and rinse it well. Plunge the spinach into boiling water for one minute; drain it, squeeze it dry, and chop it fine. Cut up the ham and purée it in a food processor, or grind it in a food mill. Put the ham and the spinach into separate large bowls.

2 Adding the egg yolks. Make a white sauce (recipe, page 166). Cool the cooked sauce to lukewarm. Crack the eggs, dropping the whites into a large bowl and the yolks into the cooled sauce. Stir each yolk thoroughly into the sauce (above) before you add the next.

5 Layering the mixtures. Butter a deep baking dish. Cut wax paper to the size of the bottom of the dish, butter it, and press it into the dish buttered side up. Spread a layer of the ham mixture in the dish, then a layer of the spinach mixture. Add alternating layers of ham and spinach until the dish is filled to within 1 inch [2½ cm.] of the rim.

6 Baking the pudding. Put the baking dish in a preheated 350° F. [180° C.] oven. Reduce the heat immediately to 300° F. [150° C.] and bake for about 40 minutes, until the pudding has swelled and is springy to the touch. Remove the pudding and let it settle for two or three minutes.

3 **Stirring in the sauce.** Add half of the sauce-and-yolk mixture to the bowl of puréed ham and the other half to the bowl of chopped spinach. Stir the sauce thoroughly into each ingredient.

4 **Adding the egg whites.** Using a wire whisk and a circular motion that lifts the whites and incorporates air, beat the egg whites until they stand in soft peaks. Add a dollop of egg white to each of the two mixtures and fold it in by hand. Gently fold half of the remaining white into each mixture.

7 **Serving the pudding.** Run a knife blade around the inside of the baking dish to loosen the soufflé. Place an inverted, warmed serving plate over the top. Grip the dish and plate firmly and turn them over to reverse the pudding onto the plate *(above)*. Peel off the wax paper and serve the soufflé at once, spooning or slicing it cleanly in order to display the different layers *(right)*.

Ham Reincarnated as a Satiny Mousse

One of the most attractive ways of using pork leftovers is to transform them into a cold mousse. Smoked ham most often serves this purpose *(recipe, page 160)*, although you could substitute roasted fresh pork—or even poached or braised pork, as long as it is not coated with a sauce of contrasting flavor.

The ingredients of a mousse are not elaborate. In addition to the meat, you will need some sauce for richness, a little jellied stock *(pages 56-57)* to set the ingredients, and freshly whipped cream, which gives the mousse its lightness. The meat is first puréed, then combined with the sauce; a velouté is used here, although a white sauce *(recipe, page 166)* would serve equally well. Thus moistened, the meat is passed through a sieve to ensure its smoothness.

Some of the jellied stock serves to line the mold, preventing the mousse from sticking, and giving it a glistening coat when it is unmolded. The remainder of the stock is combined with the sieved meat in order to set it. Finally, the cream is blended into the still-liquid mixture. The cream should be whipped only until it forms soft, slightly drooping peaks; if it is beaten until stiff, the texture of the finished dish will be dry and cottony.

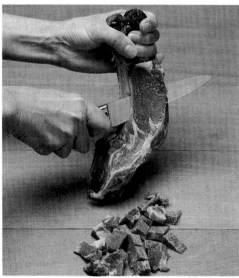

1 **Puréeing the meat.** Cut cooked meat—in this case, braised smoked ham—off the bone and trim off any fat. Chop the meat into small pieces, then purée it, using a food processor or a food mill. Put the meat in a large bowl.

2 **Blending in the sauce.** Prepare a thick velouté sauce *(recipe, page 166)*. Pour the sauce into a bowl set in a larger bowl of ice. To prevent a skin from forming, stir the sauce occasionally as it cools. Add the cold sauce to the ham in spoonfuls, blending in each one with the spoon or a pestle.

6 **Folding in the cream.** Pour the cream into the purée before the stock sets. With the wooden spoon, fold the cream into the other ingredients gently but thoroughly until the mixture becomes absolutely smooth.

7 **Filling the mold.** Pour the mixture into the coated mold. Lift the mold from the bowl of ice and tap it gently on the table to settle its contents. Cover the mold with plastic wrap or foil and refrigerate it for about four hours, or until the mousse has set firm.

3 **Puréeing the mixture.** With the pestle or a scraper *(above)*, press the meat mixture, a spoonful at a time, through a fine sieve — a drum sieve is shown — set over a plate. Transfer the sieved mixture to a bowl set over ice. Clean the underside of the sieve mesh and add the scrapings to the bowl.

4 **Coating the mold.** Melt jellied pork stock over gentle heat. Set a metal mold in a bowl of crushed ice and pour in a ladleful of stock. Rotate the bowl and mold to swirl the stock around the sides of the mold *(above)*; continue until a thin, even layer of jelly has set firm. Leave the mold in the ice.

5 **Adding the stock.** Whip heavy cream lightly until it forms soft peaks. Ladle the rest of the stock into the meat-and-velouté purée *(above)*. Stir with a wooden spoon to cool the stock and incorporate it into the mixture.

8 **Unmolding the mousse.** To loosen the mousse for unmolding, dip the mold briefly in hot water almost up to the rim, then rapidly dry the outside with a towel. Invert a chilled serving plate over the top of the mold. Turn plate and mold over together and lift the mold away *(above)*. Serve at once *(right)*.

Turning Leftovers into Dumplings

Often served as a garnish, dumplings become hearty meals if made with a generous proportion of meat. On this page, cooked smoked ham is used *(recipe, page 163)*, but leftover fresh pork can be substituted. Chop the meat by hand to give the dumplings a rough texture.

All dumplings include a starchy element to give them body, a liquid or fat to moisten the ingredients, eggs to bind them, and flavorings. In this demonstration, the ham is mixed with flour and crisp, sautéed bread cubes. Milk is the moistener, and parsley and onion add flavor. Cooked potatoes or rice, however, could provide the starch; stock, water, oil or melted butter could serve as the moistening agent; and the herbs and seasonings can be varied to taste.

The dumplings are poached in stock or water kept at a gentle simmer; a rolling boil might break them. Serve the dumplings as they are, or cover them with a white sauce *(recipe, page 166)*—flavored, if you like, with parsley or puréed tomato—and brown them in the oven.

1 **Preparing the ingredients.** Sauté ¼-inch [5-mm.] bread cubes in butter until golden, and stew chopped onions in butter until transparent. Chop the herb — in this case, parsley — dice the meat, and set out some flour. Then whisk an egg with milk in a mixing bowl; if you like, add an extra yolk for richness.

2 **Molding the dumplings.** Stir the bread cubes, onion, ham and parsley into the egg and milk. Let the bread soak briefly, then stir in flour until the mixture is a stiff paste. Dip two spoons in cold water to prevent sticking; scoop up a spoonful of the mixture with one, and form it into an egg shape with the other.

3 **Immersing the dumplings.** With the second spoon, push the dumpling into a pan of simmering salted water. Dip both spoons in cold water again and mold the next dumpling. Repeat until all of the mixture is used. Do not crowd the pan: Dumplings expand as they cook.

4 **Poaching and serving.** Cover the pan and adjust the heat so that the water continues to simmer. Poach the dumplings for 15 to 20 minutes. They will rise to the surface when they are cooked through. Lift them out with a perforated spoon. Place them on a warmed dish and serve them immediately. Alternatively, put them in a heatproof dish, cover them with a white sauce, sprinkle the top with bread crumbs, and bake in a preheated 425° F. [220° C.] oven for five to 10 minutes to brown them.

Anthology of Recipes

Drawing upon the cooking traditions and literature of more than 33 countries, the editors and consultants for this volume have selected 212 published pork recipes for the Anthology that follows. The selections range from the simple to the elaborate—from barbecued spareribs to fresh ham, marinated in spiced red wine, roasted to succulence, then crusted with rye-bread crumbs to produce a spectacular main dish with the taste of wild boar.

Many of the recipes were written by world-renowned exponents of the culinary art, but the Anthology, spanning nearly 300 years, also includes selections from now rare and out-of-print books and from works never published in English. Whatever the sources, the emphasis is always on careful preparation of fresh, natural ingredients that blend harmoniously.

Since many early recipe writers did not specify amounts of ingredients, the missing information has been judiciously added. Where appropriate, clarifying introductory notes have also been supplied; they are printed in italics. Modern terms have been substituted for archaic language, but to preserve the character of the original recipes, and to create a true anthology, the authors' texts have been changed as little as possible. For this reason, cooking times, especially in older recipes, may seem overlong by today's standards—and you may want to shorten them. Some instructions have necessarily been expanded, but where the directions still seem abrupt, the reader need only refer to the appropriate demonstrations in the front of the book.

For ease of use, the recipes are organized by cooking methods. Recipes for standard preparations—stock, velouté sauce and pastry, for example—appear at the end of the Anthology. Cooking terms and ingredients that may be unfamiliar—including Oriental flavorings and sauces—are explained in the combined General Index and Glossary at the end of the book.

Apart from the primary components, all recipe ingredients are listed in order of use, with the customary U.S. measurements and the new metric measurements provided in separate columns. The metric quantities given here reflect the American practice of measuring such solid ingredients as flour or sugar by volume rather than by weighing them, as European cooks do.

To make the quantities simpler to measure, many of the figures have been rounded off to correspond to the gradations that are now standard on metric spoons and cups. (One cup, for example, equals 237 milliliters; wherever practicable in these recipes, however, a cup appears as a more readily measurable 250 milliliters—¼ liter.) Similarly, weight, temperature and linear metric equivalents are rounded off slightly. For these reasons, the American and metric figures are not equivalent, but using one set or the other will produce equally good results.

Sausage Making

The techniques of filling sausage casing are demonstrated on pages 20-21.

English Country Pork Sausages

To serve 6

1 lb.	boneless lean pork shoulder, ground or finely chopped	½ kg.
½ lb.	fresh pork fat back, ground or finely chopped	¼ kg.
1 tbsp.	salt	15 ml.
	freshly ground pepper	
1 tbsp.	chopped fresh parsley or 1 tsp. [5 ml.] thyme and 2 or 3 finely chopped sage leaves	15 ml.
about 2 yards	sausage casings, washed and drained	about 2 meters

Mix the meat and fat well with the salt, a little pepper and the parsley or thyme and sage. Fill the casings with this mixture. The sausages may be fried, grilled or baked.

ANTONY AND ARAMINTA HIPPISLEY COXE
THE BOOK OF THE SAUSAGE

Oxford Sausages

To serve 8

2 lb.	boneless pork, coarsely chopped or ground	1 kg.
2 lb.	beef suet, finely chopped or ground	1 kg.
1 tbsp.	grated lemon peel	15 ml.
8 cups	fresh bread crumbs	2 liters
1 tbsp.	salt	15 ml.
1 tbsp.	finely chopped mixed herbs	15 ml.
2 tsp.	chopped, mixed fresh sage and thyme	10 ml.
2 tsp.	pepper	10 ml.
2 tsp.	grated nutmeg	10 ml.

Combine all of the ingredients thoroughly and shape into sausage patties, then broil or fry to preference.

JOAN POULSON
OLD THAMES VALLEY RECIPES

Pork Sausages in Lace

To serve 5

1¾ lb.	ground pork	850 g.
1 tsp.	salt	5 ml.
⅓ tsp.	Hungarian paprika	1½ ml.
	black and white pepper	
1	hard roll, soaked in ⅔ cup [150 ml.] milk	1
1 or 2	garlic cloves, crushed	1 or 2
10 oz.	pork caul fat	300 g.
1 tsp.	lard	5 ml.

Put the pork into a dish and add the salt, paprika and a pinch each of black and white pepper. Then add the roll, together with the milk and the garlic. Mix this sausage stuffing and put it in a cool place or in the refrigerator for one hour.

Wash the caul fat in several changes of water, and then spread it out and cut it into 10 pieces of equal size. Divide the stuffing into 10 equal parts, lay each on a piece of caul fat and roll the fat tightly around the stuffing to form a sausage.

Grease the inside of a pan of suitable size with the lard, place the sausages in it in neat rows, and bake them in a preheated 425° F. [220° C.] oven for about 20 minutes, or until they are well browned.

JÓZSEF VENESZ
HUNGARIAN CUISINE

Sausages Greek-Style

Loukanika

To make twenty 4-inch [10-cm.] sausages

1 lb.	boneless lean pork, cut into pieces	½ kg.
½ lb.	fresh pork rind, boiled in water for 2 hours, drained and cut into pieces	¼ kg.
½ lb.	fresh pork fat, cut into pieces	¼ kg.
1 tsp.	salt	5 ml.
1 tsp.	grated fresh orange peel	5 ml.
1 tsp.	crushed dried marjoram or thyme	5 ml.
1	bay leaf, ground in a mortar	1
⅓ cup	dry red wine	75 ml.
1 tsp.	ground allspice or coriander or a mixture of both	5 ml.
	freshly ground pepper	
2	garlic cloves, crushed (optional)	2
2 yards	sausage casing, washed and drained	2 meters

Finely mince the pork, rind and fat together, then combine them with all of the seasonings in a bowl. Knead thoroughly.

Use a pastry bag to force the meat mixture into the casings, tying the casing at 4-inch [10-cm.] intervals.

To cook, poach the sausages in water for one hour, then drain. Fry the sausages in a skillet over medium heat, or use as suggested in any recipe. Drain and serve hot.

To store, freeze uncooked in meal-sized batches. The sausages should be used within a day or two if not frozen.

VILMA LIACOURAS CHANTILES
THE FOOD OF GREECE

Spicy Creole Sausage

Chaurice

The high seasoning distinguishes this Creole sausage from all others. *Chaurice* must be seasoned very hot, so do not fear to have too much red pepper. It can be fried in boiling lard (sufficient to have the sausage swim in it) for breakfast, and served, after draining of all grease, on a hot dish with minced parsley thrown over as a garnish. It is used in making jambalaya; and a few *chaurice*, thrown into the pot of boiling cabbage or beans, add greatly to the flavor.

To make 35 to 40 sausages

4 lb.	boneless lean pork, finely chopped	2 kg.
2 lb.	boneless fatty pork, finely chopped	1 kg.
3 tsp.	salt	15 ml.
2 tsp.	freshly ground pepper	10 ml.
1 tsp.	cayenne pepper	5 ml.
1 tsp.	crushed dried red chili	5 ml.
1 tsp.	paprika	5 ml.
2	large onions, finely chopped	2
1	garlic clove, finely chopped	1
1	sprig thyme, finely chopped	1
3	sprigs parsley, finely chopped	3
2	bay leaves, finely chopped or crumbled	2
½ tsp.	ground allspice	2 ml.
about 5 yards	sausage casings (preferably sheep casings), washed and drained	about 5 meters

Combine the lean and fatty pork, then season highly with the salt, pepper, cayenne, chili and paprika. Add the onions and garlic, and the herbs and allspice, mixing thoroughly. When well mixed, fill the sausage casings with the mixture, tying them in the lengths you desire.

THE PICAYUNE CREOLE COOK BOOK

Polish Sausage

Kielbasa

Well known in Central Europe and parts of the Soviet Union, this sausage has become associated most often with Poland (several versions hail from that country) and is therefore referred to in market nomenclature as "Polish sausage." The ingredients of kielbasa (as of practically all sausages) are remarkably variable, changing from town to town and even from house to house, but garlic does appear to be a constant. Hearty and rustic, this sausage can be used in all recipes that call for garlic sausage.

To make about 2 ¾ pounds [1.3 kg.] sausage

1 ¼ lb.	lean, trimmed pork, cut into 1-inch [2½-cm.] dice and chilled	⅔ kg.
14 to 16 oz.	fresh pork fat, cut into ½-inch [1-cm.] dice and chilled	420 to 500 g.
10 oz.	trimmed beef shin, cut into ½-inch [1-cm.] dice and chilled	300 g.
4 tsp.	coarse (kosher) salt	20 ml.
1 ¾ tsp.	ground black pepper	9 ml.
3 tbsp.	sweet Hungarian paprika	45 ml.
1 tsp.	dried marjoram, crumbled	5 ml.
½ tsp.	dried savory, crumbled	2 ml.
2 tsp.	finely minced garlic	10 ml.
⅓ cup	ice water	75 ml.
about 2 yards	hog casing, washed and drained	about 2 meters

Mix together in a small bowl the salt, pepper, paprika, marjoram, savory and garlic. In the container of a food processor combine the beef, half of the pork fat, half of the ice water, and half of the mixed seasonings and process to a very fine grind. Scrape into a mixing bowl.

In a bowl combine the remaining seasonings, the pork, the remaining pork fat and the rest of the water. Process half of the mixture at a time to a coarse grind and add it to the beef mixture. Mix together very thoroughly, cover and chill for 24 hours.

Stuff the sausage into casings, tying links from 10 to 30 inches [25 to 75 cm.] long, depending upon your preference. Both sizes (and everything in between) are considered traditional. Hang the sausages in a cool, airy place for several hours, or until the skin is smooth, dry and crackly. If it's too hot or humid to hang the sausages, refrigerate them, uncovered, for at least 12 hours. They may be stored in the refrigerator for up to three days.

HELEN WITTY AND ELIZABETH SCHNEIDER COLCHIE
BETTER THAN STORE-BOUGHT

Oxford Skinless Sausages

The amount of nutmeg in this recipe, once traditional, may not please modern tastes. You may wish to reduce it.

To serve 8

1 lb.	slab bacon with the rind removed, finely chopped	½ kg.
1 lb.	lean veal, finely chopped	½ kg.
1 lb.	beef suet, finely chopped	½ kg.
2 cups	dry bread crumbs	½ liter
1 tsp.	finely grated fresh lemon peel	5 ml.
1	nutmeg, grated	1
6	fresh sage leaves, very finely chopped	6
2 tsp.	salt	10 ml.
1 tsp.	pepper	5 ml.
1 tbsp.	chopped, mixed fresh thyme, savory and marjoram leaves	15 ml.

Mix the meats, suet, bread, lemon peel, seasonings and herbs well all together, and press down in a pan. Set aside till you want to use it. Then, with floured hands, roll portions of the sausage meat into the size and shape of link sausages, and fry in fat or broil a fine golden brown.

FLORENCE WHITE
GOOD THINGS IN ENGLAND

❧

Large Country Sausage

Saucisson à Cuire

For a more delicate and fancier sausage (what is called *cervelas* in French), the meat has to be chopped finer—about ⅛ inch [3 mm.] thick. Omit the garlic and add a large black truffle and 2 tablespoons [30 ml.] pistachios, both chopped.

To make 3 or 4 large sausages

2½ lb.	boned pork shoulder, chopped coarsely or put through the large-hole disk of a food grinder	1 kg.
1½ tbsp.	salt	22 ml.
¾ tsp.	freshly ground white pepper	4 ml.
½ cup	dry white wine	125 ml.
1	small garlic clove, chopped (optional)	1
2 yards	sausage casing, washed and drained	2 meters

Mix all of the ingredients together thoroughly and stuff the casing. Keep the sausages for at least two days in the refrigerator before using.

JACQUES PÉPIN
A FRENCH CHEF COOKS AT HOME

Truffled Sausages

Saucisses aux Truffes

For modern tastes, the amounts of nutmeg and mace in this recipe might be drastically reduced.

The substitution of a clove of garlic for the truffles will convert these into *saucisses à l'ail*, or garlic sausages.

To serve 8 to 10

2 to 2½ lb.	boneless lean pork, finely chopped	1 kg.
1 lb.	fresh pork fat, finely chopped	½ kg.
1	fresh truffle, finely chopped	1
3 tbsp.	salt	45 ml.
2 tbsp.	white pepper, or a pinch of cayenne pepper	30 ml.
1	nutmeg, grated	1
1 tsp.	freshly pounded mace	5 ml.
1 tbsp.	dried powdered mixed herbs	15 ml.
about 2 yards	sausage casings, washed and drained	about 2 meters
¾ cup	Madeira (optional)	175 ml.

Mix the pork, fat and truffles with all the seasonings. Fry a morsel of the mixture, taste, and heighten any of the seasonings if desired. If the sausages are for immediate use, and the addition is liked, moisten the mixture with the Madeira. Put the mixture into delicately clean skins, using a sausage-making machine or a pastry bag.

ELIZA ACTON
MODERN COOKERY

❧

Fennel and Paprika Sausage

To serve 8

3 lb.	lean pork butt, cut into thin strips, then into the smallest pieces possible	1½ kg.
1 tsp.	fennel seeds	5 ml.
1½ tbsp.	paprika	22 ml.
½ cup	strained fresh orange juice	125 ml.
1½ tbsp.	salt	22 ml.
½ tsp.	pepper	2 ml.
2 yards	sausage casing, washed and drained	2 meters

Soak the sausage casing in the orange juice for several hours or overnight. Put the cut meat into a large bowl. Add the salt, pepper, fennel seeds and paprika, and mix well. Refrigerate the mixture and keep it cold for ease in handling.

Wash the casing thoroughly in lukewarm water, and stuff it with the meat mixture, packing it firmly. Tie the casing with string about every 5 inches [12½ cm.] to form the sausages.

JOE FAMULARO AND LOUISE IMPERIALE
THE FESTIVE FAMULARO KITCHEN

Burgundian Sausage

Le Judru

To serve 6 to 8

3½ lb.	boneless pork Boston shoulder, diced	1¾ kg.
½ lb.	fresh pork fat back, coarsely chopped with knives	¼ kg.
¼ lb.	pork trimmings, coarsely chopped with the fat	100 g.
3 tbsp.	salt	45 ml.
	freshly ground pepper	
	grated nutmeg	
¾ cup	Cognac	175 ml.
2	medium-sized truffles, diced	2
4 yards	large hog or beef sausage casing, washed and drained	4 meters
½ cup	peeled pistachios (optional), coarsely chopped	125 ml.

Mix the pork, fat back and trimmings with the salt, pepper and nutmeg. Add ½ cup [125 ml.] of the Cognac, mix well, and let marinate, covered, in a cool place for 24 hours. Marinate the diced truffles and the pork or beef intestine, separately, each in half of the remaining Cognac. The next day mix the truffles into the pork, adding the pistachios if you wish. Fill the casing with the stuffing mixture, being careful not to pierce it. Press the sausage lightly to be sure that no air pockets are left. Tie the two ends with string.

Place the sausage in a large pan, preferably a fish poacher, of cold water and bring gently to 160° to 170° F. [70° to 75° C.], or just below the simmering point. Poach for one and a half hours, then allow the sausage to cool in its cooking liquid. Set the sausage, still in the pan, in a cool place. The next day, return the pan to the heat and bring slowly to a temperature of 170° to 180° F. [75° to 80° C.]. Poach the sausage for a further one and a half hours. The sausage may be served hot, accompanied by boiled potatoes and butter, or cooled in its cooking liquid and served cold.

ALEXANDRE DUMAINE
MA CUISINE

Fresh Hot Spanish Sausages

Chorizos

To make 1 ¾ to 2 pounds [875 g. to 1 kg.] sausages

1¼ lb.	lean pork, cut into 1-inch [2½-cm.] dice and chilled	⅔ kg.
10 oz.	fresh pork fat, cut into ½-inch [1-cm.] dice and chilled	300 g.
¾ tsp.	cumin seeds	3 ml.
5 to 8	small dried red chilies, seeded, or 1½ tsp. [7 ml.] dried hot red-pepper flakes	5 to 8
1½ tsp.	coriander seeds	7 ml.
3 or 4	whole cloves	3 or 4
½ tsp.	sugar	2 ml.
2½ tsp.	coarse (kosher) salt	12 ml.
4 tsp.	paprika (medium hot, if available)	20 ml.
¼ tsp.	whole black peppercorns	1 ml.
½ tsp.	finely chopped garlic	2 ml.
⅓ cup	red wine	75 ml.
2 yards	hog casings, washed and drained	2 meters

Combine the cumin seeds, chilies or red-pepper flakes, coriander and cloves in a small pan and shake over medium heat until the chilies or flakes are slightly toasted and the seeds start to crackle—about one minute. Combine the toasted seasonings with the sugar, salt, paprika, and peppercorns in a spice mill or mortar and grind to a coarse texture. Mix with the garlic in a bowl.

Combine the pork, fat and seasonings in a large bowl. Put half of the mixture in the container of a food processor, add half the wine, and process to a fairly coarse grind. Scrape into a bowl and repeat with the remaining meat mixture and wine, then combine the batches. Chill thoroughly.

Stuff the sausage casings, tying off the links at 3 to 4 inches [8 to 10 cm.]. Hang the *chorizos* in a cool, airy place for eight to 12 hours, or until they are firm, smooth and dry to the touch. If the weather is hot or very humid, instead of hanging the sausages, refrigerate them, uncovered, for at least 12 hours. To store, refrigerate for up to three days.

HELEN WITTY AND ELIZABETH SCHNEIDER COLCHIE
BETTER THAN STORE-BOUGHT

Fried Pork Sausages

To serve 5

2 to 2½ lb.	boneless fatty pork, coarsely chopped or ground	1 kg.
1 tsp.	salt	5 ml.
¼ tsp.	Hungarian paprika	1 ml.
	black pepper	
	white pepper	
1 or 2	garlic cloves, crushed, boiled in 2 tbsp. [30 ml.] water for 5 minutes and puréed	1 or 2
2 to 3 yards	sausage casings, washed and drained	2 to 3 meters
2 tbsp.	lard	30 ml.

Place the meat in a dish, salt it and spice it with the paprika and a pinch each of black and white pepper. Add the puréed garlic and mix the whole thoroughly. Fill the sausage skins with the stuffing, twisting and tying to separate sausages. Grease a pan with the lard and place the sausages in it. Roast in a preheated 425° F. [220° C.] oven for 20 minutes or until done. Serve with mashed potatoes and braised cabbage or with pickled cucumbers.

JÓZSEF VENESZ
HUNGARIAN CUISINE

Breaded Pork Chops

Kotlety Schabowe Panierowane

To serve 6

6	pork loin chops	6
	salt	
⅓ cup	flour	75 ml.
2	eggs, lightly beaten	2
½ cup	fine dry bread crumbs, sieved	125 ml.
4 tbsp.	lard	60 ml.

Chop off the tips of the rib bones of the chops, leaving the ribs 1½ inches [4 cm.] long. Cut off any excess fat, leaving a rim about ½ inch [1 cm.] wide. Make shallow cuts around the edges to prevent the chops from curling up, and pound the chops lightly to make pear-shaped cutlets.

Salt the cutlets lightly on both sides, and dip them first into the flour, then into eggs, and finally into the bread crumbs, pressing with your hands to make the crumbs adhere. Heat the lard in a frying pan over high heat and brown the cutlets on both sides. When they are brown, reduce the heat and cook for about 15 minutes until done.

Arrange the cutlets in a row on a warmed, oblong platter, overlapping them. Serve with potatoes, sauerkraut or cabbage, tomatoes or salad, or cooked and grated beets mixed with horseradish sauce.

Z CZERNY, KIERST, STRASBURGER AND KAPUŚCIŃKA
ZDROWO I SMACZNIE

Pork Chops with Mustard Sauce

To serve 4

4	pork loin chops, cut ¾ to 1 inch [2 to 2½ cm.] thick	4
4 tbsp.	butter	60 ml.
	salt and pepper	
1	egg yolk	1
1 tbsp.	prepared mustard	15 ml.
¼ cup	heavy cream	50 ml.
½ cup	dry white wine	125 ml.
2 tbsp.	water	30 ml.
1	garlic clove, mashed	1
1 tsp.	tarragon	5 ml.
½ tsp.	brandy	2 ml.
2 tsp.	chopped fresh tarragon, optional	10 ml.

In a heavy skillet, melt 2 tablespoons [30 ml.] of the butter until foamy and hot, then add the pork chops and brown them well on both sides. Sprinkle the chops with salt and pepper. Cover the skillet, reduce the heat, and simmer for 15 minutes. (If the butter in the pan has burned while the chops were browning, remove the chops, pour out the fat, and wipe the skillet; melt 2 tablespoons of fresh butter, return the chops and proceed as above.)

While the chops are cooking, prepare the sauce flavorings. In a small bowl, beat together the egg yolk and mustard. Stir in the cream and put aside.

Remove the chops to a warmed serving platter and keep warm. Turn up the heat under the skillet, pour in the wine and water, scraping all the juices from the bottom. Add the garlic, tarragon, and a little salt and pepper; boil for one minute. Remove the skillet from the heat, add the mustard-cream, and stir for a few seconds. Return the skillet to the heat, stirring until the sauce thickens. Do not allow it to boil.

Add the brandy. Taste for salt and pepper; correct the seasonings if necessary.

Spoon the sauce liberally over the cooked pork chops. If fresh tarragon is in season, chop a little and sprinkle it over the sauce. Serve at once.

CAROL CUTLER
THE SIX-MINUTE SOUFFLÉ AND OTHER CULINARY DELIGHTS

Pork Chops with Caper Sauce

Chuletas de Cerdo Empanadas con Salsa de Alcaparras

To serve 6

6	pork loin chops	6
	salt and pepper	
½ cup	flour	125 ml.
2	eggs, beaten with 1 tbsp. [15 ml.] olive oil	2
1 cup	bread crumbs	250 ml.
¾ cup	olive oil	200 ml.
1 tbsp.	chopped onion	15 ml.
½ cup	dry white wine	125 ml.
½ cup	puréed tomato	125 ml.
2 tbsp.	capers, rinsed and drained well	30 ml.
2 tbsp.	chopped sour gherkins	30 ml.
1 tbsp.	chopped fresh parsley	15 ml.
1	hard-boiled egg, chopped	1
1	lemon, cut into 6 wedges	1
6	sprigs parsley	6

Prepare the chops by cutting the meat away from the end of each bone to leave about 1 inch [2½ cm.] of bone bare. Beat the chops slightly to flatten them out. Season them with a little salt and pepper and pass them first through the flour, then through the beaten eggs and lastly through the bread crumbs, pressing the chops lightly with a knife so that the crumbs adhere thoroughly. Heat the oil in a large frying pan, and fry the chops over medium heat until they are golden, seven or eight minutes on each side. Remove the chops from the pan and cover to keep them warm.

Strain the cooking oil through a fine sieve into a saucepan. Over medium heat, cook the chopped onion in the oil for a minute or two, then add the wine, puréed tomato, capers, gherkins, chopped parsley and a pinch of salt. Cook the mixture slowly for 20 minutes. Taste for seasoning.

Arrange the chops in a circle on a warmed serving dish and pour the sauce into the center. Sprinkle the sauce with the chopped egg. Decorate each chop with a lemon wedge and a sprig of parsley.

MANUAL DE COCINA

Pork Chops Seasoned with Adobo

Chuletas de Puerco Adobadas

The mild, brick-red ancho chilies called for in this recipe are the most widely used chili in Mexico; they can be bought dried in Latin American markets throughout the United States.

Adobo, a paste made of ground chilies, spices, herbs and vinegar, was originally used for pickling meat. In this recipe, the pork chops are marinated in an *adobo* and then cooked very slowly. You can keep the seasoned pork for several days in the refrigerator before cooking; the meat becomes drier, but the flavor improves daily.

To serve 6

6	thick pork shoulder chops, pounded flat	6
4	large *ancho* chilies, lightly toasted on a dry griddle, slit, stemmed and seeded	4
⅛ tsp.	cumin seeds	½ ml.
⅛ tsp.	oregano	½ ml.
⅛ tsp.	thyme	½ ml.
1 tbsp.	salt	15 ml.
2	garlic cloves	2
½ cup	mild white vinegar or strained Seville orange juice	125 ml.
2 tbsp.	lard	30 ml.
	sliced onion	
	shredded lettuce	
	sliced radishes	

At least one day ahead, put the chilies in a bowl and cover them with hot water. Let them soak for about 20 minutes, then transfer them with a slotted spoon to a blender. Add the cumin, oregano, thyme, salt, garlic and vinegar, and blend into a fairly smooth paste. Do not overblend.

Spread both sides of the chops with the paste and set in the refrigerator to season overnight.

On serving day, melt the lard in a skillet and fry the chops very slowly on both sides until they are well cooked—about 20 minutes, depending on the thickness of the meat. When they have cooked through, increase the heat and brown them quickly.

Serve the chops immediately, garnished with the onion slices, and decorate the plate with the lettuce and radishes.

DIANA KENNEDY
THE CUISINES OF MEXICO

Minute Chops

Cotolette alla Minuta

	To serve 4	
4	pork loin chops	4
1	egg, lightly beaten	1
2 cups	bread crumbs	½ liter
½ cup	olive oil	125 ml.
1	lemon	1
	Giblet sauce	
½ lb.	chicken hearts and gizzard lobes, finely chopped	¼ kg.
1	onion, finely chopped	1
1 tbsp.	butter	15 ml.
1	small carrot, finely chopped	1
1	rib celery, finely chopped	1
1	sprig fresh parsley, finely chopped	1
1	sprig fresh rosemary, finely chopped	1
1	garlic clove, finely chopped	1
½ oz.	dried mushrooms, soaked in water for 30 minutes, stems trimmed, finely chopped	15 g.
1 cup	stock *(recipe, page 165)*	¼ liter
3	tomatoes, peeled, seeded and chopped	3
3½ oz.	lean fresh pork sausage, sliced	125 g.

To make the sauce, cook the onion in the butter over medium heat until lightly colored. Stir in the chicken giblets, carrot, celery, parsley, rosemary, garlic and mushrooms. Cook until the giblets are slightly softened, then add the stock and the tomatoes. Cook for 10 minutes. Finally, add the sausage slices and cook until the sausage is done and the sauce reduced—about 30 minutes.

Meanwhile, prepare the chops by dipping them first in the egg and then in the bread crumbs. Fry them in the olive oil over medium heat until browned on both sides and cooked through—about 15 minutes. Arrange the chops side by side in a heated serving dish, squeeze the lemon over them, and pour on the sauce.

CARMEN ARTOCCHINI
400 RICETTE DELLA CUCINA PIACENTINA

Pork Cutlets from Alentejo with Green-Pepper Paste

Costeletas de Porco a Alentejana

To make green-pepper paste, pound 1 seeded and deribbed pepper with 1 teaspoon [5 ml.] of chopped fresh ginger root, 1 teaspoon of chopped onion and 1 teaspoon of salt—or purée the mixture in a blender. If put in a jar and covered with oil, the paste will keep in a refrigerator for up to two weeks.

	To serve 4	
8	pork cutlets, trimmed of all fat	8
2 tsp.	green-pepper paste, or substitute puréed green-pepper pulp	10 ml.
	salt and pepper	
2	garlic cloves, finely chopped	2
3 tbsp.	dry white wine	45 ml.
2	eggs, lightly beaten	2
1 cup	bread crumbs	¼ liter
	fat for deep frying	
	orange slices	

Season the cutlets with salt, pepper and the garlic; coat them with the green-pepper paste mixed with the white wine. Refrigerate for 24 hours. Dip the cutlets in the eggs and then the bread crumbs, and deep fry them in fat. Serve the cutlets with slices of orange.

CAROL WRIGHT
PORTUGUESE FOOD

Villager's Pork Cutlets

Tranches de Porc Villageoise

	To serve 4	
4	pork cutlets (about 4 oz. [125 g.] each), pounded flat	4
2 tbsp.	lard	30 ml.
½	garlic clove	½
3 tbsp.	olive oil	45 ml.
1 tsp.	prepared mustard	5 ml.
1 tbsp.	chopped fresh parsley	15 ml.
	salt and pepper	
2 or 3 tbsp.	hot water	30 or 45 ml.
	deep-fried potato quarters	

Heat the lard in a heavy skillet until it is very hot. Arrange the cutlets in the pan, one beside the other. Do not cover the pan. Let the cutlets cook for five or six minutes until they have browned. Then turn them over to let them brown on the other side. Turn down the heat and cook them for another 12 to 15 minutes.

Rub a warmed serving platter with the garlic. Mix the olive oil, mustard, parsley, salt and pepper on the platter. Put the cutlets on the platter and turn them in the seasoning. Keep them hot.

Drain off the fat from the skillet. Pour the hot water into the pan and, over high heat, scrape the bottom of the pan to dissolve the meat drippings. Pour these juices over the cutlets. Surround them with the potatoes and serve very hot.

MADAME SAINT-ANGE
LA BONNE CUISINE DE MADAME SAINT-ANGE

Deep-fried Pork Cutlets

Tonkatsu

To serve 2

2	pork cutlets (5 oz. [150 g.] each), pounded flat and edges slit	2
	salt and pepper	
½ cup	flour	125 ml.
1	egg, lightly beaten	1
½ cup	dry bread crumbs	125 ml.
	oil for deep frying	
Tomato-pineapple garnish		
4 to 6	small tomatoes	4 to 6
2	slices pineapple, halved	2
2 tbsp.	butter	30 ml.
3 to 4	leaves cabbage, shredded	3 to 4
Hot tomato sauce		
3 tbsp.	tomato sauce	45 ml.
1 tbsp.	Worcestershire sauce	15 ml.
1 tsp.	mustard	5 ml.

Season the cutlets with salt and pepper, and coat them thinly and evenly with the flour, shaking off any excess. Dip the meat in the egg, then in the bread crumbs, coating the surfaces evenly. Heat the oil to 325° to 335° F. [160° to 170° C.] and fry the meat, turning once, for five to six minutes. Raise the temperature just before removing the meat, to crisp it.

Meanwhile, for the garnish, cut a deep cross in each tomato, put in a piece of butter, and arrange on a baking sheet with the pineapple. Bake in a 400° F. [200° C.] oven for five minutes. Arrange the baked tomatoes and pineapple slices with the shredded cabbage upon the fried cutlets.

Blend all of the sauce ingredients together in a bowl and pass it separately.

MINEKO ASADA
120 PORK SIDE DISHES

Pork Scallops, Hunter-Style

Costolettine di Maiale alla Cacciatora

To serve 6

12	pork scallops (1½ to 2 lb. [¾ to 1 kg.]), pounded flat	12
7 tbsp.	butter	105 ml.
1 tsp.	flour	5 ml.
¼ cup	white wine vinegar	50 ml.
3	salt anchovies, filleted, soaked in cold water for 10 minutes, dried and chopped	3
1	thick slice salt pork without the rind, blanched in boiling water for 10 minutes, drained and chopped	1
	salt	

In a large skillet, fry the scallops a few at a time, adding the butter as needed. Drain off the butter; sprinkle the scallops with the flour, turning them so that the flour absorbs any remaining fat. Add the vinegar, bring to a boil and remove the pork from the skillet. Put the anchovies and salt pork into the skillet. Boil for a few minutes, add the pork and, when hot, sprinkle with salt to taste and serve at once.

OTTORINA PERNA BOZZI
VECCHIA BRIANZA IN CUCINA

Mock Eel

Falscher Aal

To serve 2

4	pork scallops (about ¼ lb. [125 g.] each), pounded flat	4
	salt and pepper	
8	fresh sage leaves	8
3 tbsp.	butter	45 ml.
	lemon slices	
	small potatoes, boiled	

Slit the edges of the scallops to keep them flat. Rub salt and pepper into the scallops. Roll each scallop up tightly, press two sage leaves against each roll, and tie it up with string.

Fry the rolls in half of the butter over medium heat for about 10 minutes, or until all sides are golden. Then arrange the rolls on a platter. Melt the remaining butter until it foams, and pour it over the scallops. Serve with lemon slices and small boiled potatoes.

HERMINE KIEHNLE AND MARIA HÄDECKE
DAS NEUE KIEHNLE-KOCHBUCH

Minute Pork Slices

Émincé de Porc Frais à la Minute

This is one of the dishes that demand the least preparation time when one has nothing ready in advance and must hastily improvise a quick dinner or lunch.

	To serve 4	
8	thinly sliced pork scallops (about 1 lb. [½ kg.])	8
7 tbsp.	butter	105 ml.
¼ cup	fine dry bread crumbs	50 ml.
1 tbsp.	fines herbes	15 ml.
	salt and pepper	
2 tbsp.	water	30 ml.
5 or 6	shallots, chopped fine	5 or 6
1 tsp.	flour	5 ml.
1 tbsp.	prepared mustard	15 ml.

Mix the bread crumbs, herbs, salt and pepper together. In a skillet, melt 4 tablespoons [60 ml.] of the butter and lightly brown the pork slices. Sprinkle the slices with the breadcrumb mixture and turn them to coat both sides. When the pork slices are well browned, after about 10 minutes, put them in a serving dish and keep them warm.

Deglaze the skillet with the water. In another pan, sauté the shallots in 1 tablespoon [15 ml.] of the remaining butter without permitting them to brown. After about five minutes, add the deglazed juices from the skillet. Knead together the flour and the remaining 1 tablespoon of butter to form a *beurre manié* and stir this mixture into the shallot mixture to thicken it. Stir in the mustard, and pour this sauce over the pork slices.

JULES BRETEUIL
LE CUISINIER EUROPÉEN

Leeks Wrapped in Pork

	To serve 4 to 6	
1¼ lb.	boneless lean pork, cut into 12 thin slices	⅔ kg.
12	leeks, thoroughly rinsed and cut into 4-inch [12-cm.] lengths	12
2 tbsp.	oil	30 ml.
½ cup	soy sauce	125 ml.
1 tbsp.	sugar	15 ml.
¼ cup	sake	50 ml.

Wrap each leek in a slice of pork and secure with a wooden pick or two. Heat the oil in a frying pan over medium heat and add the wrapped leeks, frying and turning until they are browned on all sides (about 10 minutes). Add the soy sauce, sugar and *sake*, reduce the heat and cover the pan. Simmer for three or four minutes, until the leeks are tender. Remove the lid and shake the frying pan vigorously, turning the leeks so that they become coated with the sauce. Transfer the leeks to a warmed serving dish and remove the picks. Pour over the leeks the remaining sauce and serve.

PETER AND JOAN MARTIN
JAPANESE COOKING

Pork Slices with Prunes

Noisettes de Porc aux Pruneaux

	To serve 8	
2½ lb.	pork tenderloin or boneless pork loin, trimmed of all fat, cut into 8 slices	1¼ kg.
3 cups	dried prunes (about 1¼ lb. [⅔ kg.])	¾ liter
1¼ cups	Vouvray or other semidry wine	300 ml.
	flour	
4 tbsp.	butter	60 ml.
	salt and pepper	
1 tbsp.	currant jelly	15 ml.
2 cups	heavy cream	½ liter

Soak the prunes overnight in the wine.

The next day, bring the prunes and wine to a simmer and cook them gently for 30 minutes. Alternatively, poach the prunes in the wine in a 300° F. [150° C.] oven in a covered baking dish for one hour or until they are plump and tender.

Coat the pork slices lightly with flour, heat the butter in a skillet and sauté the pork until it is golden brown on both sides. Season the slices with salt and pepper as they cook. When the pork is tender, in about five or six minutes, transfer it to a warmed serving dish.

Arrange the prunes around the pork and pour the prune cooking liquid into the skillet. Stir to deglaze, and reduce the liquid until it is syrupy. Stir in the currant jelly, then add the cream, bring to a boil and reduce this sauce, if necessary, until it thickens slightly. Correct the seasoning, pour the sauce over the pork and serve hot.

CURNONSKY
RECETTES DES PROVINCES DE FRANCE

Pork Pieces with Chili Sauce

To serve 4

½ lb.	pork tenderloin, sliced very thin	¼ kg.
¼ cup	peanut oil	50 ml.
1	small green pepper, halved, seeded, deribbed and cut into small triangular pieces	1
½ cup	bamboo shoots, sliced	125 ml.
2 tbsp.	thinly sliced fresh ginger root	30 ml.
4	scallions or small leeks, sliced	4
1½ tbsp.	soybean paste	22 ml.
1	fresh red chili, stemmed, seeded and chopped	1

Soy seasoning

2 tbsp.	light soy sauce	30 ml.
1 tbsp.	cornstarch	15 ml.
¼ tsp.	pepper	1 ml.
¼ tsp.	sesame-seed oil	1 ml.
1 tsp.	sugar	5 ml.
1 tbsp.	water	15 ml.
1 tbsp.	peanut oil	15 ml.

Chili-garlic sauce

1 tsp.	Shanghai chili sauce	5 ml.
1 tsp.	finely chopped garlic	5 ml.
1 tbsp.	soybean paste, fried in 1 tbsp. [15 ml.] peanut oil	15 ml.
1 tbsp.	Chinese rice wine, or substitute dry sherry	15 ml.
1 tbsp.	light soy sauce	15 ml.
1 tbsp.	sugar	15 ml.
½ tsp.	sesame-seed oil	2 ml.
¼ cup	water	50 ml.
1 tsp.	cornstarch	5 ml.

Mix the pork slices with the soy seasoning ingredients and let them stand for 10 minutes. Combine all of the chili-garlic sauce ingredients in a bowl.

Heat 2 tablespoons [30 ml.] of the oil in a skillet or wok. When it is very hot, add the green pepper and the bamboo shoots and quickly stir fry over high heat. Remove the mixture to a warmed plate.

Heat the remaining oil in the same pan and add the ginger, scallions or leeks, and soybean paste. Stir fry for a minute or two, add the pork slices and cook for three minutes.

Add the chili-garlic sauce, red chili, and the fried green pepper and bamboo shoots. Mix until well combined and serve.

LUCY LO
CHINESE COOKING WITH LUCY LO

Diced Pork with Cucumber

To serve 4

¾ lb.	pork tenderloin or boneless loin, cut into ¾-inch [2-cm.] cubes	⅓ kg.
1½ tbsp.	soy sauce	22 ml.
1½ tsp.	cornstarch	7 ml.
5 tbsp.	peanut oil	75 ml.
2	small cucumbers, diced	2
2	scallions, sliced lengthwise into shreds	2
1	small piece fresh ginger, shredded	1
2	fresh red chilies, stemmed, seeded and sliced lengthwise into shreds	2
1 tbsp.	hot soybean paste	15 ml.

Vinegar sauce

2 tsp.	brown Chinese vinegar or red wine vinegar	10 ml.
1 tsp.	salt	5 ml.
1 tsp.	sugar	5 ml.
1 tbsp.	soy sauce	15 ml.
½ tsp.	cornstarch	2 ml.
2 tbsp.	water	30 ml.
1 tbsp.	sesame-seed oil	15 ml.

Mix the pork with the soy sauce and cornstarch. In a skillet or wok, heat 3 tablespoons [45 ml.] of the peanut oil and stir fry the pork and cucumber in it for about 30 seconds. Remove from the pan and set the pork and cucumber aside.

Combine the sauce ingredients in a bowl, stirring to blend. Heat 1 tablespoon [15 ml.] of the peanut oil in the pan, add the scallions, ginger and chilies, and stir fry over high heat for one or two minutes. Add the hot soybean paste, then the pork and cucumber, and stir fry for a couple of minutes. Add the vinegar sauce and the remaining peanut oil. Serve.

THE TECHNIQUE OF CHINESE COOKING

Pork with Clams

Lombo de Porco com Amêijoas à Alentejana

To serve 6

2 to 2½ lb.	boned pork loin roast	1 kg.
24	small live hard-shell clams (about 1 quart [1 liter]), well scrubbed	24
4	garlic cloves, crushed	4
	salt and pepper	
6 tbsp.	lard	90 ml.
2	onions, sliced	2
3 tbsp.	chopped fresh parsley	45 ml.
1 tsp.	paprika	5 ml.
1	fresh red chili, seeded and chopped	1

Rub the pork with three of the crushed garlic cloves and a little salt and pepper. Leave at room temperature for several hours, then cut the pork into thick slices. Heat the lard in a skillet over high heat and sauté the pork slices for about five or six minutes, or until brown on both sides. Remove the slices from the skillet and keep them warm.

Pour off most of the fat from the skillet and lightly brown the remaining garlic clove. Add the onion, parsley, paprika, chili and, finally, the clams. Cover the skillet and cook the clams over high heat, shaking the skillet from time to time, for five to 10 minutes or until the clam shells open. (Remove and discard any clams that remain shut.) Add the pork, stir to mix the pork and clams, heat thoroughly, and serve.

MARIA ODETTE CORTES VALENTE
COZINHA REGIONAL PORTUGUESA

Latvian Pork Stroganoff

Lettischer Kursemes "Stroganoff"

To serve 4

1½ lb.	pork scallops, thinly sliced, pounded flat and cut into strips 1 inch [2½ cm.] wide	¾ kg.
4 oz.	fresh pork fat, cubed	125 g.
2 or 3	medium-sized onions, chopped	2 or 3
1 tbsp.	flour	15 ml.
2	sour gherkins, finely chopped	2
½ cup	stock *(recipe, page 165)* or water	125 ml.
½ cup	sour cream	125 ml.
	salt	
1 tsp.	paprika	5 ml.

Fry the pork for 10 minutes over medium heat with the fat and the onion, turning the strips frequently. Sprinkle with

the flour and continue cooking for two or three minutes. Add the gherkins, stock, sour cream, salt and paprika. Bring to a boil, stirring, and then remove the pan from the heat. Serve the stroganoff with boiled potatoes.

KULINARISCHE GERICHTE

Stir-fried Pork Strings with Hot Sauce

To serve 4

½ lb.	pork tenderloin, cut into fine julienne	¼ kg.
1 tbsp.	soy sauce	15 ml.
1 tbsp.	cold water	15 ml.
1 tbsp.	cornstarch	15 ml.
3 cups	peanut oil	¾ liter
1 tsp.	chopped garlic	5 ml.
2 tsp.	chopped fresh ginger	10 ml.
6	water chestnuts, sliced thin	6
2 tbsp.	dried black wood-ear Chinese mushrooms, soaked in warm water for 15 minutes, stems discarded, sliced into thin strips	30 ml.

Vinegar and bean-paste sauce

1 tbsp.	brown vinegar or wine vinegar	15 ml.
1 tbsp.	hot bean paste	15 ml.
1 tbsp.	soy sauce	15 ml.
2 tsp.	Chinese wine or substitute dry sherry	10 ml.
1 tsp.	sugar	5 ml.
½ tsp.	salt	2 ml.
1 tsp.	cornstarch	5 ml.
1 tsp.	sesame-seed oil	5 ml.
¼ tsp.	black pepper	1 ml.
1 tbsp.	finely sliced scallions	15 ml.

Mix the pork with the soy sauce, cold water and cornstarch, and leave to marinate for about 15 minutes.

Combine the sauce ingredients in a bowl and stir to blend. Heat the oil in a skillet or wok. When the oil is very hot, add the pork and stir fry for 30 seconds, then remove and set aside. Drain all but 3 tablespoons [45 ml.] of oil from the pan. Over high heat, quickly stir fry the garlic and ginger. Add the water chestnuts, wood ears and pork strings, and stir thoroughly. Add the sauce, stir to mix evenly, and serve.

FU PEI MEI
PEI MEI'S CHINESE COOKBOOK

Sweet-and-Sour Pork

To serve 2 to 4

1 lb.	boneless lean pork, preferably fresh ham butt end	½ kg.
3 cups	peanut oil or flavorless vegetable oil for deep frying	¾ liter
	Cornstarch batter	
¼ cup	cornstarch	50 ml.
¼ cup	flour	50 ml.
¼ cup	chicken stock *(recipe, page 165)*	50 ml.
1	egg, lightly beaten	1
1 tsp.	salt	5 ml.
	Sweet-and-sour sauce	
¼ cup	sugar	50 ml.
¼ cup	red wine vinegar	50 ml.
1 tbsp.	peanut oil or flavorless vegetable oil	15 ml.
1 tsp.	garlic, finely chopped	5 ml.
1	large green pepper, seeded, deribbed and cut into ½-inch [1-cm.] squares	1
1	medium-sized carrot, sliced into 2-inch [5-cm.] strips ¼ [6 mm.] inch wide and ¼ inch [6 mm.] thick	1
½ cup	chicken stock *(recipe, page 165)*	125 ml.
1 tsp.	soy sauce	5 ml.
1 tbsp.	cornstarch, dissolved in 2 tbsp. [30 ml.] cold water	15 ml.

Trim the pork of any excess fat and, with a cleaver or sharp knife, cut the meat into 1-inch [2½-cm.] cubes.

To make the batter, mix together the cornstarch, flour, stock, egg and salt in a large bowl. Set aside.

Just before cooking, add the pork cubes to the batter and stir until each piece of meat is well coated. Preheat the oven to 250° F. [120° C.]. Pour the 3 cups [¾ liter] of oil into a wok and set it over high heat. When the oil almost begins to smoke or reaches 375° F. [190° C.] on a deep-frying thermometer, drop in half of the coated pork cubes one by one. Fry for five to six minutes, regulating the heat so that the pork turns a crisp, golden brown without burning. Remove the pork with a strainer or slotted spoon to a small baking dish and keep it warm in the oven. Fry the other half and add to the first batch.

To make the sauce, pour off any oil remaining in the wok or use a 10-inch [25-cm.] skillet. Set the pan over high heat for about 30 seconds. Pour in the tablespoon [15 ml.] of oil, swirl it about in the pan and heat for another 30 seconds, turning the heat down to moderate if the oil begins to smoke.

Add the garlic, then the green pepper and carrot, and stir fry for two to three minutes until the pepper and carrot darken somewhat in color. Be careful not to let them burn. Pour in the stock, sugar, vinegar and soy sauce, and bring to a boil. Boil rapidly for about one minute, or until the sugar has thoroughly dissolved. Immediately give the cornstarch mixture a quick stir to recombine it and add it to the pan. Cook a moment longer, stirring constantly. When the sauce is thick and clear, pour the entire contents of the pan over the fried pork and serve at once.

FOODS OF THE WORLD
THE COOKING OF CHINA

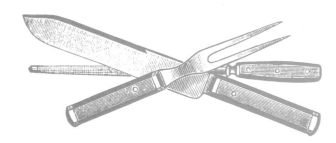

Fried Pork Flavored with Lime Juice and Soy Sauce

Babi Tembra

The four chilies called for in this recipe will produce an extremely hot, but typically Szechwan, dish. You may prefer to use only one or two chilies, and to moderate their pungency by twisting and pulling out their stems to remove the seeds —the hottest parts of the chilies.

To serve 4

1¼ lb.	boneless pork, cut into julienne	⅔ kg.
6 tbsp.	oil	90 ml.
4	onions, thinly sliced	4
4	fresh red hot chilies, sliced thinly crosswise	4
¼ cup	sugar	50 ml.
¼ cup	dark soy sauce	50 ml.
¼ cup	strained fresh lime juice	50 ml.
½ tsp.	salt	2 ml.

Heat a heavy frying pan or wok over high heat until very hot, add the oil and stir fry the onions until limp. Add the chilies immediately and then the pork. Stir fry and, when the pork is half cooked, after four or five minutes, add the sugar, reduce the heat to medium, then add the soy sauce, lime juice and salt. Simmer for two minutes.

MRS. LEE CHIN KOON
MRS. LEE'S COOKBOOK

Italian Sausages with Peppers

The polenta suggested as an accompaniment to this dish is an Italian version of cornmeal mush, made by stirring cornmeal in water over heat until the mixture becomes a thick porridge.

Although it is not necessary, this dish is far better if you take the trouble to peel your peppers. Either stick them on a fork and turn them over a flame, or place them under the broiler until they char and the skin blackens and bursts. They may then be peeled with ease.

To serve 6

12 to 18	Italian sausages (about 1½ to 2 lb. [¾ to 1 kg.]), pricked with a fork on all sides	12 to 18
4 to 5	red or green peppers, halved, seeded, deribbed and cut into strips	4 to 5
about ⅓ cup	olive oil	about 75 ml.
2	garlic cloves, finely chopped	2
	salt	
1 tbsp.	red wine vinegar	15 ml.
2 tbsp.	chopped fresh flat-leafed parsley	30 ml.

Blanch the sausages in simmering water for six or seven minutes. Drain, and then brown them in 2 to 3 tablespoons [30 to 45 ml.] of the olive oil. Cook slowly until they are done, about 10 minutes.

Pour enough olive oil in a heavy skillet to cover the bottom of the pan. Heat the oil and add the garlic and the pepper strips. Sauté gently for about 10 minutes, until the peppers are just tender. If you have broiled and peeled them, they will take less cooking. You may cover the pan for part of the time to tenderize the peppers. Add salt to taste and, just before the peppers are done, add the vinegar. Combine the peppers, sausage and parsley and serve with polenta or rice.

EDITORS OF HOUSE & GARDEN
HOUSE & GARDEN'S NEW COOK BOOK

Sausages Languedoc-Style

Saucisses à la Languedocienne

Toulouse sausages are long pork sausages made from coarsely chopped meat flavored with mace and nutmeg; they are obtainable from French butchers. Any pork poaching sausage may be substituted. If you do not have meat stock on hand, it may be omitted and the quantity of puréed tomato increased.

To serve 4

2 lb.	Toulouse sausage, pricked with a fork	1 kg.
3 tbsp.	lard or rendered goose fat	45 ml.
4	garlic cloves, chopped	4
1	bouquet garni	1
2 tbsp.	vinegar	30 ml.
1½ cups	reduced meat stock, made by boiling down 3 cups [600 ml.] beef or veal stock (recipe, page 165)	300 ml.
½ cup	puréed tomato	100 ml.
3 tbsp.	pickled capers, rinsed and drained well	45 ml.
1 tbsp.	chopped fresh parsley	15 ml.

Twist the sausage into a coil and secure the coil with two crossed skewers. Heat the lard or goose fat in a large sauté pan and put in the sausage. Add the garlic and the bouquet garni. Cook with a lid on for 18 minutes, turning the sausage after 10 minutes. Drain the sausage and put it on a round dish. Dilute the pan juices with the vinegar. Moisten with the reduced stock and the puréed tomato. Boil for a few moments. Add the capers and the chopped parsley and pour the sauce over the sausage.

PROSPER MONTAGNÉ
THE NEW LAROUSSE GASTRONOMIQUE

Sausages with Beans and Basil

To serve 2 or 3

¾ lb.	fresh Italian, large-link pork sausages or any fresh, mildly spiced garlic sausage, pricked with a fork	⅓ kg.
1 lb.	fresh green beans, preferably Italian Romano beans, cut diagonally into 2-inch [5-cm.] lengths	½ kg.
2 tbsp.	butter	30 ml.
1 tbsp.	dry white wine	15 ml.
2 to 3	large garlic cloves, crushed	2 to 3
	salt and freshly ground pepper	
⅓ to ½ cup	finely chopped fresh basil leaves	75 to 125 ml.

Cover the bottom of a large heavy frying pan with cold water to a depth of ⅛ inch [3 mm.]. Add the sausages, cover the pan tightly and simmer for 15 minutes, turning the sausages once. Pour off into a bowl all except ⅓ cup [75 ml.] of the cooking liquid in the pan. In the remaining liquid, cook the sausages uncovered, over medium heat for a further 15 minutes until they brown well on all sides. Add a little of the reserved liquid as necessary.

Meanwhile, cook the beans, uncovered, over the highest heat in boiling salted water until tender-crisp, three to four minutes, then drain them well. Remove the sausages from the frying pan and discard all except 2 tablespoons [30 ml.] of the drippings. Slice the sausage diagonally into 1½-inch [3½-cm.] pieces and return them to the frying pan. Add the butter, wine, garlic, beans and a little salt and pepper. Sauté, turning, until the beans are heated through and the flavors are blended. Sprinkle with basil and serve.

SHIRLEY SARVIS
WOMAN'S DAY HOME COOKING AROUND THE WORLD

Skewers of Meat, Sicilian-Style

Spiedini di Carne alla Siciliana

To serve 4

1 lb.	ground pork	½ kg.
	salt and pepper	
¼ cup	finely chopped fresh parsley	50 ml.
1 tbsp.	finely chopped fresh basil	15 ml.
1 lb.	mozzarella cheese, sliced	½ kg.
1	loaf Italian bread with crust removed, sliced	1
3	eggs, well beaten in a flat bowl	3
2 cups	fine bread crumbs	½ liter
	oil or lard, for deep frying	

Salt and pepper the meat; add the parsley and basil. Mix well and form into 1½-inch [4-cm.] round patties. Cut the cheese and the bread into round slices, or medallions, of the same size. On skewers, place in turn a medallion of bread and one of cheese, and a meat patty, repeating until each skewer is full, with bread at each end. Roll the skewers in the eggs, then in the bread crumbs, and deep fry in oil or lard. Slide the contents of the skewers off onto a large platter for serving.

WILMA REIVA LASASSO
REGIONAL ITALIAN COOKING

Ham Croquettes with Egg Sauce

To serve 6

2½ cups	finely ground cooked country-style ham	625 ml.
18 tbsp.	butter	270 ml.
¾ cup	flour	175 ml.
3½ cups	milk or light cream	875 ml.
	salt and freshly ground black pepper	
½ tsp.	Worcestershire sauce	2 ml.
½ tsp.	dry mustard	2 ml.
4	eggs	4
	dry bread crumbs	
	fat or oil for deep frying	
½ cup	finely chopped onion	125 ml.
1 cup	sliced fresh mushrooms	¼ liter
1	green pepper, finely chopped	1
½ tsp.	sage	2 ml.
¼ tsp.	marjoram	1 ml.
	light cream	
6	hard-boiled eggs, chopped	6

To make the cream sauce, melt 12 tablespoons [180 ml.] of the butter and blend in the flour. Gradually stir in the milk or cream. Season with a little salt and pepper, and bring to a boil, stirring. Still stirring, cook for three minutes.

Place the ham in a bowl and add the Worcestershire sauce, mustard and 1½ cups [375 ml.] of the sauce mixed with two of the eggs, lightly beaten. Set the remaining sauce over hot water.

Mix the ham and sauce and set aside to cool. Chill until the mixture is firm, about three hours. Beat the two remaining eggs. Shape the mixture into croquettes, dip in the eggs and then in the bread crumbs—two times if necessary to coat the croquettes well.

Using a basket, deep fry a few croquettes at a time in fat or oil heated to 365° F. [185° C.]. When golden—after about three minutes—drain the croquettes on paper towels.

Heat the remaining 6 tablespoons [90 ml.] of butter in a skillet and sauté the onion in it until tender. Add the mushrooms, green pepper, sage and marjoram, and cook until the vegetables are tender.

Add enough light cream to the reserved sauce to make it a pouring consistency. Stir in the cooked vegetables and the chopped eggs. Season to taste with salt and pepper. Serve this sauce separately with the croquettes.

JEAN HEWITT
THE NEW YORK TIMES SOUTHERN HERITAGE COOKBOOK

Smoked Chops, Bachelor-Style

To serve 4

4	smoked pork chops	4
½ cup	dark brown sugar	125 ml.
2 tbsp.	prepared mustard	30 ml.
2 tbsp.	butter	30 ml.
¼ cup	port	50 ml.

Rub the sugar into both sides of the chops, then coat them with mustard. Melt the butter in a heavy skillet and, when hot, put in the chops and brown them on both sides. Cover the skillet, reduce the heat, and cook for 15 minutes, turning once. Remove the chops to a warmed platter. Skim off any fat from the juices in the pan, pour in the port and heat. When hot, pour over the chops.

LOUISE SHERMAN SCHOON AND CORRINNE HARDESTY
THE COMPLETE PORK COOKBOOK

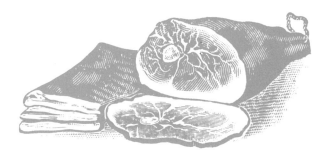

Ham with Red-eye Gravy

To serve 4

4	slices country-style ham, cut ¼ inch [6 mm.] thick	4
1 cup	freshly brewed coffee	¼ kg.

With a sharp knife, trim the excess fat from the ham slices and cut the fat into small bits. Place the fat in a heavy, ungreased 12-inch [30-cm.] skillet and, stirring frequently, fry over medium heat until the bits are crisp and have rendered all their fat. Discard the bits of fat. Fry the ham in the rendered fat, turning the slices so that they color evenly.

Transfer the fried ham to a warmed platter and pour the coffee into the skillet. Bring to a boil over high heat, meanwhile scraping in the brown bits that cling to the bottom of the pan. Boil briskly, uncovered, until the gravy turns red, then pour it over the ham and serve at once.

Ham with red-eye gravy is a favorite breakfast dish, traditionally served with boiled grits or hot biscuits—or both.

FOODS OF THE WORLD
AMERICAN COOKING: SOUTHERN STYLE

Roasting, Grilling and Broiling

Stuffed Roast Suckling Pig

Cochon de Lait, Farci, Rôti au Four

The techniques of preparing and serving a suckling pig are demonstrated on pages 46-49.

To serve 8 to 12

1	suckling pig (12 lb. [5 kg.]), prepared for roasting	1
	olive oil	
Sage and onion stuffing		
7 tbsp.	finely chopped, blanched fresh sage leaves	105 ml.
5	large onions (about 2 lb. [1 kg.])	5
1 lb.	beef suet, finely chopped	½ kg.
3	eggs, beaten	3
4 cups	slices firm, white homemade-type bread, crusts removed, soaked in milk or water and squeezed	1 liter
½ cup	flour	125 ml.
	salt and freshly ground pepper	
	mixed spice	
	grated nutmeg	

In a preheated 325° F. [170° C.] oven, bake the onions in their skins for one hour, or until they are soft. Cool, peel and finely chop them. Make the stuffing by mixing the chopped onions with the suet, sage, eggs, bread and, finally, the flour. Season to taste with salt, pepper, mixed spice and nutmeg.

Stuff the pig and sew up the opening. Press the pig's body into shape, truss the pig, and place it in a large roasting pan. Roast in a preheated 350° F. [180° C.] oven for about two hours, basting frequently with the olive oil to ensure that the skin will be crisp and crackling.

P. E. LALOUE
LE GUIDE DE LA CHARCUTERIE

Brazilian Roast Stuffed Suckling Pig

Leitão Recheado

The manioc meal called for in this recipe is a fine, flourlike meal made from the dried pulp of the bitter cassava or manioc root. Like semolina, it is obtainable wherever Latin American foods are sold.

To serve 8

1	suckling pig (12 lb. [6 kg.]), prepared for roasting with the heart, kidneys and liver reserved	1
6 or 7	slices bacon	6 or 7
Vinegar-and-wine marinade		
2 cups	vinegar	½ liter
2 cups	dry red wine	½ liter
1	garlic clove, pounded to a paste	1
1½ tbsp.	salt	22 ml.
1½ tsp.	pepper	7 ml.
1 tbsp.	whole cloves	15 ml.
2	bay leaves	2
1 tsp.	cumin seeds	5 ml.
Ham-and-sausage stuffing		
1 cup	chopped smoked ham	¼ liter
1 cup	chopped smoked sausage	¼ liter
2 or 3	slices bacon, chopped	2 or 3
½	garlic clove, pounded to a paste	½
	reserved pig's liver, kidneys and heart, washed, trimmed and finely chopped	
1	onion, chopped	1
1 tbsp.	chopped fresh parsley	15 ml.
2 tbsp.	chopped scallion	30 ml.
1 cup	manioc meal or semolina, cooked in 2 cups [½ liter] boiling water for 8 to 10 minutes	¼ liter
2	hard-boiled eggs, chopped	2
1 cup	pitted ripe or green olives	¼ liter
	salt and pepper	

Mix together the ingredients for the marinade. Pour over the pig, cover and marinate in the refrigerator for 24 hours, turning the pig over occasionally in order to let the marinade soak in thoroughly.

To make the stuffing, fry the bacon, ham and sausages with the garlic paste and the pig's liver, kidneys and heart. Brown, stirring continuously and adding small amounts of water each time the pan gets dry, until all of the meats are cooked and tender, about 30 minutes. Add the onion, parsley and scallions and fry until the mixture is well browned. Gradually add the cooked manioc meal or semolina, stirring constantly until the mixture is thoroughly blended. Remove from the heat and add the eggs and olives. Taste the stuffing and season accordingly.

Remove the pig from the marinade and pat it dry. Strain and reserve the marinade. Stuff the pig with the ham-and-sausage mixture and lace it up. Preheat the oven to 400° F. [200° C.]. Place the pig in a roasting pan, cover with the bacon slices and roast in the oven for 20 minutes. Reduce the heat to 350° F. [180° C.] and continue to roast for a total of 35 minutes to the pound [½ kg.]. Baste several times with the strained marinade.

MARGARETTE DE ANDRADE
BRAZILIAN COOKERY

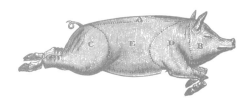

Buckwheat Groats Stuffing for Suckling Pig

Farsz z Kaszy

To cook the buckwheat groats, sauté about ½ cup [125 ml.] of groats in 1 tablespoon [15 ml.] of butter for one minute; pour on 2 cups [½ liter] of boiling stock or water, cover, and cook over low heat for one hour or until fluffy and tender.

To make enough stuffing for a 12- to 15-pound [6- to 7½-kg.] pig

1½ cups	cooked buckwheat groats	375 ml.
	suckling pig liver, lungs, heart and kidneys, chopped fine	
¼ lb.	salt pork with the rind removed, chopped fine	125 g.
2	medium-sized onions, finely chopped and sautéed in butter until soft but not brown	2
1	egg	1
	salt and pepper	
	grated nutmeg	
¼ tsp.	marjoram	1 ml.
½ cup	stock (recipe, page 165)	125 ml.

Combine the meats and salt pork with the sautéed onions, egg, seasoning and spices. Add this mixture to the groats and mix thoroughly. Moisten with stock.

MARJA OCHOROWICZ-MONATOWA
POLISH COOKERY

Raisin Stuffing for Suckling Pig

Farsz z Rodzynkami

To make enough stuffing for a 12- to 15-pound [6- to 7½-kg.] pig

1 cup	raisins, soaked in warm water for 10 or 15 minutes and drained	¼ liter
	suckling pig liver, lungs, heart and kidneys, cut into pieces	
¼ lb.	salt pork with the rind removed, cut into pieces	125 g.
1	large onion, coarsely chopped	1
1	carrot, coarsely chopped	1
1 or 2	ribs celery, coarsely chopped	1 or 2
½	celeriac, coarsely chopped	½
½	Hamburg parsley root, coarsely chopped	½
1	parsnip, coarsely chopped	1
2 tbsp.	chopped fresh parsley	30 ml.
	salt	
½ cup	water	125 ml.
4 tbsp.	butter	60 ml.
1	large stale roll or 4 slices stale homemade-style bread, moistened in milk	1
3	eggs, the yolks separated from the whites, the yolks lightly beaten, the whites stiffly beaten	3
¼ cup	bread crumbs	50 ml.
	pepper	
	grated nutmeg	
½ tsp.	sugar	2 ml.

Place the prepared vegetables and parsley with the pig giblets and salt pork in a pan. Season with a little salt, add the water and half of the butter, bring to a simmer and cover tightly. Remove the liver after about 15 minutes and reserve it; the other meats will take about 15 minutes longer. When done, put everything—including the liver—through the fine blade of a food grinder together with the roll or bread.

Melt the remaining butter, combine with the egg yolks, and add the bread crumbs, pepper, nutmeg, sugar and raisins. Combine with the meat mixture and mix thoroughly. Finally fold in the beaten egg whites and mix lightly.

MARJA OCHOROWICZ-MONATOWA
POLISH COOKERY

Crown Roast of Pork with Sausage-Apple Stuffing

To serve 10 to 12

8 to 9 lb.	crown roast of pork, consisting of 22 chops	4 to 4½ kg.
3 tbsp.	butter	45 ml.
¾ cup	finely chopped onion	175 ml.
¼ cup	finely chopped celery	50 ml.
½ cup	tart apples, peeled, cored and coarsely diced	125 ml.
½ cup	fresh bread crumbs	125 ml.
1 lb.	ground pork (the crown roast trimmings plus extra pork, if necessary)	½ kg.
½ lb.	well-seasoned sausage meat	¼ kg.
½ cup	finely chopped parsley	125 ml.
½ tsp.	sage	2 ml.
1½ tsp.	salt	7 ml.
	freshly ground black pepper	

Preheat the oven to 350° F. [180° C.]. For the stuffing, melt the butter over medium heat in an 8- to 10-inch [20- to 25-cm.] skillet. When the foam subsides, add the onion and cook, stirring frequently, for about five minutes, then add the celery and apples. Cook without browning for about five minutes. Scrape the contents of the pan into a large mixing bowl. Add the bread crumbs, ground pork, sausage meat, parsley, sage, salt and a few grindings of black pepper. With a large spoon, mix all of the ingredients gently but thoroughly together. To taste the stuffing, fry a small ball of it in the skillet. Then season the rest of the mixture with more salt and pepper if necessary.

Fill the center of the crown with the stuffing, mounding it slightly. Cover it with a round of foil and wrap the ends of the chop bones in strips of foil to prevent them from charring and snapping off. Place the crown in a shallow roasting pan just about large enough to hold it easily, and roast it in the center of the oven, undisturbed, for about three hours, or until a meat thermometer, if you have used one, reads 170°-175° F. [77°-79° C.]. One half hour before the pork is done, remove the circle of foil from the top of the stuffing to allow the top to brown.

Carefully transfer the crown to a large, heated, circular platter, strip the foil from the ends of the chops and replace it with paper frills. Let the crown rest for about 10 minutes before carving and serving.

To carve the pork, insert a large fork in the side of the crown to steady it and, with a large, sharp knife, cut down through each rib to detach the chops. Two chops for each person is a customary portion, accompanied by a generous serving of the stuffing.

FOODS OF THE WORLD
AMERICAN COOKING

Spinach and Sausage-Meat Stuffing

Farce aux Épinards

This recipe makes enough stuffing to fill the center of a crown roast as well as to form a base for the crown, as shown on pages 44-45.

To make 3 pounds [1 ½ kg.] of stuffing

2 lb.	spinach	1 kg.
2 lb.	lean pork belly, coarsely chopped	1 kg.
2 lb.	chard greens	1 kg.
2 or 3	onions, chopped	2 or 3
2	eggs	2
2 tbsp.	chopped fresh parsley	30 ml.
	salt and pepper	
1 tbsp.	chopped fresh thyme	15 ml.
	dry bread crumbs (optional)	

Bring a large saucepan of water to a boil, plunge in the spinach and chard, and blanch them for two minutes. Drain them well, then press out all of the water with your hands. Chop them. Add the onions, the pork, eggs, parsley, a little salt and pepper, and the thyme, and mix well. If the mixture does not have a firm consistency, add bread crumbs by spoonfuls until it does.

HUGUETTE COUFFIGNAL
LA CUISINE PAYSANNE

Florentine Pork Roast

Arista alla Fiorentina

To serve 6

2 lb.	boneless pork loin roast, trimmed of excess fat, rolled and tied	1 kg.
1	sprig fresh rosemary	1
1	garlic clove, slivered	1
3	whole cloves	3
	salt and pepper	
½ cup	water	125 ml.

With a sharp knife, make slits in the meat and insert small tufts of rosemary and slivers of garlic. Stick the cloves into the meat, season it with salt and pepper, and place it in a roasting pan with the water. Roast in a preheated 350° F. [180° C.] oven, basting occasionally, until the water has almost disappeared and the meat is done, about one hour. Remove the meat from the pan and serve hot or cold.

IL RE DEI CUOCHI

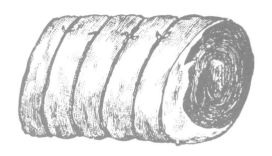

Pork Roast

Puerco Horneado

In this Latin American dish, the pork is equally good when served cold.

To serve 8

4 lb.	boned pork loin roast, or 6 lb. [3 kg.] unboned loin roast	2 kg.
1 tsp.	salt	5 ml.
1 tsp.	pepper	5 ml.
1 tsp.	ground saffron or crushed saffron threads	5 ml.
½ tsp.	marjoram	2 ml.
½ tsp.	basil	2 ml.
½ tsp.	ground cumin	2 ml.
3	garlic cloves, finely chopped	3
1 cup	boiling water	¼ liter
3 tbsp.	grated onion	45 ml.
2 tbsp.	wine vinegar	30 ml.
¼ tsp.	cayenne pepper	1 ml.
2 tbsp.	finely chopped fresh parsley	30 ml.
½ cup	cold water	125 ml.

Combine the salt, pepper, saffron, marjoram, basil, cumin and garlic. Mix into a paste and rub into the pork. Wrap the roast in wax paper and refrigerate it overnight.

Place the pork in a roasting pan and roast in a preheated 400° F. [200° C.] oven for 30 minutes. Reduce the heat to 350° F. [180° C.], then pour the boiling water over the pork and continue to roast for a total of 25 minutes a pound [½ kg.]. Baste frequently with the pan juices.

Transfer the roast pork to a warmed platter. Degrease the roasting juices, and combine ¼ cup [50 ml.] of this pan gravy in a saucepan with the onion, vinegar, cayenne pepper, parsley and cold water. Bring to a boil and cook over low heat for two minutes. Carve the pork and serve the sauce in a separate gravy boat.

MYRA WALDO
THE COMPLETE ROUND-THE-WORLD COOKBOOK

Fennel-marinated Roast Pork

Porc Rôti au Fenouil

The technique of stuffing a pork loin with fennel is demonstrated on pages 42-43.

Wild fennel is much more richly perfumed than the bulb fennel found in the market, but if the former is unavailable, the feathery leaves of bulb fennel may be substituted—the *pastis* will reinforce their somewhat attenuated accent. Potatoes and large sweet onions, both baked in their skins, the skins of the latter removed before serving, a chunk of butter placed on each, are a good accompaniment . . . or little new potatoes cooked gently in butter, sautéed, with a handful of unpeeled garlic cloves.

To serve 4		
2 to 2½ lb.	pork loin roast, boned but not tied up, pared of all but a thin sheet of surface fat	1 kg.
about 24	tender sprigs fresh fennel, chopped	about 24
1 to 2 tbsp.	*pastis*	15 to 30 ml.
1 cup	dry white wine	¼ liter
	salt and pepper	

With a sharp knife, pierce the meat six or eight times, forcing generous pinches of chopped fennel into these slits in sufficient quantity so that, when the roast is carved, the cross section will present a pattern of green spots.

Place the meat in a large mixing bowl, sprinkle over the remaining fennel, add the *pastis* (using the larger quantity if you have cultivated fennel), and pour on two thirds of the wine. Marinate, unrefrigerated, with a plate covering the bowl, for four to five hours, turning the meat several times.

Lift the meat out, leave it to drain for a few minutes in a sieve placed over the marinade and sponge it dry with absorbent paper. Salt and pepper the interior lightly and roll the roast up into its original form, the apron (the thinner side of the meat) wrapped around the outside as far as it will go. Tie it up, sprinkle with salt, and roast it, using a small skillet or heavy gratin dish as a roasting pan, for about one hour and 10 minutes in all, beginning at 400° F. [200° C.] and turning the oven down to 325° F. [160° C.] after 10 to 15 minutes.

After the first 30 minutes, begin to baste regularly with the fat in the pan. Twenty minutes before the end of the cooking time, drain the fat from the pan, pour in the marinade, and continue basting regularly. By the end, the liquid should be completely evaporated, the bottom of the pan containing only caramelized juices, the roast itself handsomely glazed from repeated basting.

Transfer the roast to a heated serving platter, remove the strings, discard the fat from the pan and—over high heat—deglaze the pan with the remaining wine, reducing it by about two thirds. Pour the juice over the roast and, when carving, serve a spoonful of the mingled deglazing liquid and the juices that escape from within the meat over each slice.

RICHARD OLNEY
SIMPLE FRENCH FOOD

Roast Pork, Puerto Rican-Style

Cerdo Asado

To serve 8		
6 lb.	pork loin roast	3 kg.
2 tbsp.	lard or butter	30 ml.
2 cups	fresh orange juice	½ liter
1 tbsp.	finely grated fresh orange peel	15 ml.
2	garlic cloves, finely chopped	2
1 tbsp.	salt	15 ml.
1 tsp.	pepper	5 ml.
	cayenne pepper	
⅛ tsp.	oregano	½ ml.

Melt the fat in a saucepan. Add the orange juice and peel, the garlic, 1 teaspoon [5 ml.] of salt, ½ teaspoon [2 ml.] of pepper, a dash of cayenne pepper and the oregano, and mix together. Rub the remaining salt and pepper into the pork.

Place the pork roast in a roasting pan and pour the orange mixture over it. Baste several times. Roast in a preheated 350° F. [180° C.] oven for two to three hours, or until the pork is well browned. Baste frequently during the roasting period. Serve the pork thickly sliced. Any juice remaining in the pan may be served with the meat.

MYRA WALDO
THE COMPLETE ROUND-THE-WORLD COOKBOOK

Garlic Roasted Pork

Arrosta di Maiale all'Aglio

To serve 4		
2 to 2½ lb.	pork loin roast or fresh ham	1 kg.
2	garlic cloves, slivered	2
1 tsp.	mixed, crumbled oregano, thyme and rosemary	5 ml.
2 tsp.	prepared mustard	10 ml.
3 tbsp.	olive oil	45 ml.
	salt and pepper	

Sprinkle the slivers of garlic with the herbs, pressing to make them adhere. Make a few cuts in the surface of the meat, and insert the herb-coated garlic. Mix together the mustard and oil and brush it well over the meat. Let it rest for an hour. Then wrap the roast in aluminum foil, and cook in a preheated 350° F. [180° C.] oven for about one and a half hours. Turn off the oven and let the meat rest for about 15 minutes before removing it and unwrapping the foil. Slice the meat quite thinly. This roast is also magnificent cold.

PIER ANTONIO SPIZZOTIN (EDITOR)
I QUADERNI DEL CUCCHIAIO D'ARGENTO—GLI ARROSTI

Pork Roast with Lemon Glaze

To serve 4 to 6

4 lb.	boned, but not rolled, pork loin roast	2 kg.
¼ cup	rosemary	50 ml.
1 cup	white wine	¼ liter
½ cup	sugar	125 ml.
½ cup	strained, fresh lemon juice	125 ml.
3 tbsp.	Cognac	45 ml.

Slash the meat with the grain at various intervals and stuff these cuts liberally with about 3 tablespoons [45 ml.] of the rosemary. Place the meat in a dish. Pour the wine over the meat and sprinkle the remaining rosemary over the top. Marinate the meat at room temperature for one and a half hours, turning it a couple of times. Remove the meat from the marinade, pat it dry and roll it into a cylindrical shape. Tie it with string and put it into a roasting pan.

Place the meat in a preheated 450° F. [230° C.] oven for 15 minutes, then reduce the heat to 350° F. [180° C.]. After 30 minutes, baste the roast with the fat in the pan.

Mix the sugar, lemon juice and Cognac, and stir until the sugar is dissolved. When the meat has roasted for one hour, remove the pan from the oven and pour off the fat. Spoon the lemon-and-Cognac mixture over the roast and return it to the oven. Cook for 30 minutes, basting the roast with the glaze every five to 10 minutes. The glaze should become thick and the roast a glossy brown. Remove the roast from the oven and let it sit for a few minutes before slicing it.

DORIS TOBIAS AND MARY MERRIS
THE GOLDEN LEMON

To Dress a Pork Loin with Onions

The 18th Century cookery book from which this recipe comes was signed only "By a Lady"; the anonymous author was Hannah Glasse.

To serve 6

4 lb.	pork loin roast	2 kg.
8	medium-sized onions (about 2 lb. [1 kg.]), thinly sliced	8
1 tbsp.	flour	15 ml.
1 tbsp.	vinegar	15 ml.
1 tbsp.	prepared mustard	15 ml.

Place the meat in a roasting pan and surround it with the onions. Pour on ½ cup [125 ml.] of water. Roast for one and a half hours in a preheated 350° F. [180° C.] oven.

When the pork is nearly done, move the onions to a saucepan and let them simmer over low heat for a quarter of an hour, shaking them well. Then pour out all of the fat as well as you can, shake in a very little flour and the vinegar, shake all well together and stir in the mustard. Set this sauce over the heat for four or five minutes.

Lay the pork in a dish, and serve the onion sauce separately. This is an admirable dish to those who love onions.

THE ART OF COOKERY MADE PLAIN AND EASY

Roast Pork with Corn-Bread Stuffing

To serve 4 to 6

4 to 5 lb.	pork loin roast, the chops cut apart between the ribs almost to the backbone	2 kg.
4 cups	corn-bread crumbs	1 liter
1 cup	biscuit or stale bread crumbs	¼ liter
1 tsp.	sage	5 ml.
	salt	
¼ tsp.	pepper	1 ml.
1 tbsp.	chopped fresh parsley	15 ml.
2 tbsp.	oil or roast drippings	30 ml.
1	large onion, chopped	1
1 cup	diced celery	¼ liter
1½ cups	beef stock *(recipe, page 165)*	375 ml.

Preheat the oven to 325° F. [160° C.]. Put the pork in a shallow pan that is just large enough to hold it easily, and roast it for one hour.

Meanwhile, mix the corn-bread and biscuit crumbs, sage, salt to taste, pepper and parsley. Heat the oil or drippings from the roast in a skillet. Add the onion and celery and cook until tender but not browned. Add the vegetables to the crumb mixture along with the broth. Mix lightly.

Remove the roast from the oven and drain off the fat from the pan. Gently push the chops apart with the handle of a wooden spoon and fill the spaces between them with the stuffing mixture. Spread the remaining stuffing in the pan. Place the pork on the stuffing and roast it for one and a half to two hours, until a meat thermometer inserted in the center chop registers 165° F. [74° C.]. Place the roast on a warmed platter and the stuffing in a serving bowl. Let the roast stand for 20 to 30 minutes before serving.

JEANNE A. VOLTZ
THE FLAVOR OF THE SOUTH

Pork Loin Roast with Gratin of Turnips

La Longe de Porc Niçoise au Gratin de Navets

To serve 4 to 6

4 lb.	pork loin roast	2 kg.
6 to 8	medium-sized young turnips, peeled and thinly sliced (about 1½ lb. [¾ kg.])	6 to 8
2	garlic cloves, slivered	2
	fresh sage (optional)	
	salt and pepper	
	sliced homemade-type, firm white bread	
	freshly grated cheese (preferably Gruyère)	

With the point of a knife, make small incisions in the meat and insert the garlic slivers, adding a few leaves of sage, if desired. Put into a preheated 325° F. [170° C.] oven, and roast for one and a half to two hours, or until done.

Meanwhile, boil the sliced turnips in salted water until they are just tender, a few minutes only. Drain them. In a deep gratin dish, put first a layer of bread slices, then a layer of turnips. Season with salt and pepper and sprinkle with grated cheese. Continue the layers until all of the turnips have been used and the dish is full, finishing with a layer of cheese. Put the dish in the top of the oven for 20 to 30 minutes, or until a gratin has formed on the surface. The bread will absorb the remaining water from the vegetables.

Serve the gratin, sprinkled with the roasting juices, as an accompaniment to the meat.

JOSÉPHINE BESSON
LA MÈRE BESSON: MA CUISINE PROVENÇALE

Pork Loin with Cheese Sauce

Varkenshaasjes met Kaassaus

To serve 4

2 lb.	boned, rolled pork loin roast	1 kg.
	salt and pepper	
½ tsp.	ground cumin	2 ml.
4 tbsp.	butter	60 ml.
2½ cups	grated mild Gouda cheese (about 10 oz. [300 g.])	625 ml.
¼ cup	prepared mustard	50 ml.
⅓ cup	heavy cream	75 ml.
2 tbsp.	Calvados (apple brandy)	30 ml.

Season the pork loin with the salt, pepper and cumin. Melt the butter in a heavy casserole and brown the meat on all sides. Mix the cheese with the mustard and ¼ cup [50 ml.] of the cream, and spoon the mixture over the meat. Roast under the broiler or in a preheated 425° F. [220° C.] oven, until brown, about 30 to 40 minutes. Place the meat on a warmed dish, deglaze the casserole with the Calvados, and stir in the remaining cream. Cook over high heat, stirring all the time, until the sauce thickens slightly, then pour the sauce over the meat. Serve accompanied by boiled new potatoes and buttered green beans.

HUGH JANS
VRIJ NEDERLAND

Loin of Pork with Pistachios on Apple Brown Betty

To serve 6 to 8

4 lb.	boned pork loin roast, trimmed of all excess fat	2 kg.
2 tsp.	salt	10 ml.
1 tsp.	pepper	5 ml.
1 tsp.	ground ginger	5 ml.
1 cup	finely chopped onions	¼ liter
1 cup	dry white wine	¼ liter
3	apples, peeled, cored and diced	3
4 cups	stale white bread, diced	1 liter
4	eggs	4
1 cup	milk	¼ liter
2 tbsp.	finely chopped pistachio nuts	30 ml.

Remove the pork from the refrigerator one hour before you are ready to roast it. Preheat the oven to 450° F. [230° C.].

Rub the surface of the pork with the salt, pepper and ginger. Place the pork in a shallow roasting pan, without a rack, and roast it for 25 minutes. Add the chopped onions and roast for five to 10 minutes more, until the onions are lightly browned. Stir the white wine, diced apple and bread cubes into the pan and roast for another 25 minutes. Beat the eggs and milk together and stir into the roasting-pan mixture. Sprinkle the chopped pistachio nuts all around and stir them lightly into the mixture. Roast for an additional 25 minutes, or until the pork is golden and tender.

Slice the pork and arrange it on a heated platter over the pistachio and apple brown-Betty mixture.

ALBERT STOCKLI
SPLENDID FARE—THE ALBERT STOCKLI COOKBOOK

Rumanian Marinated Loin of Pork

Mariana Nasta, a Rumanian living in London, won a newspaper cookery contest with this recipe. The technique of boning a pork loin is demonstrated on pages 12-13.

	To serve 6 to 8	
3 to 4 lb.	pork loin roast, boned and rolled	1½ to 2 kg.
	salt and freshly ground pepper	
	ground cumin	
	beef stock (optional)	
3 tbsp.	sour cream	45 ml.
½ tbsp.	cornstarch	7 ml.
	watercress	
	Wine-and-vinegar marinade	
1 cup	dry white wine	250 ml.
½ cup	wine vinegar	125 ml.
1	large onion, coarsely chopped	1
2	carrots, coarsely chopped	2
2	celery ribs, coarsely chopped	2
2	garlic cloves, coarsely chopped	2
1	bay leaf	1
½ tsp.	thyme	2 ml.
	salt	
6 to 8	peppercorns	6 to 8

Rub the meat with salt, pepper and a generous pinch of cumin. Place in a large earthenware dish and let it stay for three to four hours in a cool place.

For the marinade, combine all of the ingredients and simmer them for about 15 minutes in a covered pan. Let the marinade cool. Pour the cooled marinade over the meat. Turning the meat from time to time, let it marinate for two hours. Preheat the oven to 375° F. [190° C.].

Remove the meat from the marinade, place it in an ovenproof casserole and roast it for 25 minutes, turning it once. Now pour over the marinade liquid and vegetables, cover the casserole and cook the meat for about one hour. Baste from time to time and add stock if the juice reduces too much.

When ready, place the meat on a hot serving plate. Degrease the cooking juices and strain them through a fine sieve into a small saucepan. Mix the sour cream with the cornstarch and stir it into the juices. Simmer over low heat, stirring the gravy until it is smooth and thick. Correct the seasoning. Serve the roasted loin sliced, pouring the gravy over the meat. Garnish with watercress.

MICHAEL BATEMAN AND CAROLINE CONRAN (EDITORS)
THE SUNDAY TIMES BEST BRITISH MEAT DISHES

Roast Pork with Potatoes and Onions

Carré de Porc à la Boulangère

	To serve 4 to 6	
1½ lb.	boned, rolled pork loin roast	¾ kg.
	salt and pepper	
4 tbsp.	butter or lard, melted	60 ml.
3	medium-sized potatoes, thinly sliced	3
1	large onion, thinly sliced and sautéed in butter until soft but not colored	1
1	bouquet garni	1
	chopped fresh parsley	

Season the pork with salt and pepper, and put it into a large, oval ovenproof dish. Brush the meat with a little of the melted butter or lard and put it in a preheated 400° F. [200° C.] oven for 15 minutes. When the meat is browned all over, surround it with the potatoes and the sautéed onion. Season the potatoes and onion with salt and pepper. Put into the dish, buried in the potatoes, the bouquet garni. Sprinkle the potatoes with the remaining butter or lard. Cover the dish and put it in a 325° F. [170° C.] oven to bake for 50 minutes.

Take out the bouquet garni, sprinkle the potatoes with chopped parsley, and serve from the cooking dish.

PROSPER MONTAGNÉ AND A. GOTTSCHALK
MON MENU

Roast Pork Loin, Monção-Style

Lombo de Porco à Moda de Monção

Monção is a town in northernmost Portugal.

	To serve 6	
2 to 2½ lb.	pork loin roast	1 kg.
4 tbsp.	butter	60 ml.
½ cup	dry white wine	100 ml.
4	whole cloves	4
4	peppercorns	4
	salt	
1	bay leaf	1

Place the pork in a baking dish. Spread the butter on top of the loin, and surround it with the wine, cloves, peppercorns, salt and bay leaf. Put the dish into a preheated 350° F. [180° C.] oven and roast the pork for about one to one and a half hours, or until it is done and well browned. Baste the pork occasionally during cooking with the liquid from the dish.

MARIA ODETTE CORTES VALENTE
COZINHA REGIONAL PORTUGUESA

Marinated Roast Pork

Porc Mariné

To serve 8 to 10

5 lb.	boned pork loin or Boston shoulder roast	2½ kg.
2 tbsp.	butter	30 ml.
2	onions, sliced	2
2	carrots, sliced	2
2 or 3	sprigs parsley	2 or 3
1	bay leaf	1
1	sprig thyme	1
1	sprig basil	1
1	garlic clove	1
¾ cup	vinegar	175 ml.
2 cups	boiling water	½ liter
	salt and pepper	
2	whole cloves	2
	grated nutmeg	

Shallot and wine sauce

2	shallots, chopped	2
½ cup	dry white wine	125 ml.
2 tbsp.	flour	30 ml.
2 tbsp.	butter	30 ml.
1	garlic clove, chopped	1
1	sprig parsley	1
¾ cup	beef stock *(recipe, page 165)*	175 ml.
	salt and pepper	
	grated nutmeg	
1	sprig thyme	1
1	whole clove	1
½	bay leaf	½
1 tbsp.	capers, rinsed and drained well	15 ml.

In the butter, gently sauté the onions, carrots, parsley, bay leaf, thyme, basil and garlic. Moisten with the vinegar and boiling water; add a little salt and pepper with the cloves and nutmeg. Cover and simmer for one hour. Strain this marinade. When the marinade has cooled completely, put in the pork and marinate it in the refrigerator for 24 hours.

Take the pork out of the marinade and drain it, saving the marinade. Wipe the pork dry; roll and tie it. Put the pork in a roasting pan with a few spoonfuls of water and roast for about two and a half hours at 350° F. [180° C.], turning and basting occasionally.

Meanwhile, make the sauce. Brown the flour in the butter, add the shallots, garlic and parsley, and cook for two minutes. Add the white wine, the stock and 1¼ cups [300 ml.] of the marinade. Add some salt and pepper, the nutmeg, thyme, clove and bay leaf. Simmer very gently for 45 minutes, uncovered, skimming occasionally.

When the meat is cooked, pour the fat out of the roasting pan. Deglaze the pan with a little water, and pour the juices into the sauce. Strain the sauce into a warmed gravy boat containing the capers.

MADAME SAINT-ANGE
LA BONNE CUISINE DE MADAME SAINT-ANGE

Sage-roasted Pork

Rôti de Porc à la Sauge

In the Provence Alps, it is customary to marinate pork before roasting it.

To serve 6

3 lb.	boned pork loin roast	1½ kg.
2 cups	dry white wine	½ liter
¼ cup	olive oil	50 ml.
1	large onion, sliced	1
3	sprigs thyme	3
1	bay leaf	1
4	whole cloves	4
4	sprigs fresh sage	4
	salt and pepper	

Into a deep dish, put the pork roast with the wine, 2 tablespoons [30 ml.] of the olive oil, the onion, thyme, bay leaf and cloves. Turn the meat several times (four times in two hours) while it marinates.

Take the pork out of the dish and set it into another so that the marinade can drain off. Meanwhile, preheat the oven to 375° F. [190° C.].

Lard the pork roast with the sage by making small slits with a knife and inserting the leaves. Pour the remaining oil into a roasting pan and put in the pork. Roast it for about one and a half hours, turning it and basting from time to time with the pan juices. When it is cooked, season the pork roast with salt and pepper.

HENRI PHILLIPON
CUISINE DE PROVENCE

Roast Pork with Fruit Stuffing

The technique of boning a pork loin is shown on pages 12-13.

To serve 10

5 lb.	pork loin roast, boned	2½ kg.
1 cup	dried apricots (about ¼ lb. [125 g.]), cooked in water to cover until soft	¼ liter
1	orange, the peel grated and the juice strained	1
1	lemon, the peel grated and the juice strained	1
4 tbsp.	butter, melted	60 ml.
4 cups	soft bread crumbs	1 liter
½ cup	walnuts, coarsely chopped	125 ml.
1½ tsp.	salt	7 ml.
½ tsp.	pepper	2 ml.

To make the dressing, drain and dice the apricots, and mix them with fruit peels and juices. Pour melted butter over the bread crumbs, add the nuts and seasonings, and blend the two mixtures, adding, if necessary, additional fruit juices. Spread the stuffing on the pork and roll up the loin, fastening it securely with skewers. Put the loin into a preheated 400° F. [200° C.] oven and brown it on all sides, then reduce the temperature to 325° F. [170° C.] and roast, allowing a total cooking time of 25 minutes for each pound [¼ kg.].

THE DAILY TELEGRAPH
FOUR HUNDRED PRIZE RECIPES

Pork Roasted in Milk

Arrosta di Maiale al Latte

To serve 6

3 lb.	boned pork loin roast, rolled and tied	1½ kg.
1 quart	milk	1 liter
	Juniper marinade	
1 tbsp.	juniper berries	15 ml.
⅔ cup	olive oil	150 ml.
1 tbsp.	vinegar	15 ml.
2	garlic cloves, lightly crushed	2
1	sprig fresh rosemary	1
	salt and pepper	

Put the marinade ingredients into the pot that will be used for cooking the meat. Put in the meat, cover and let marinate for 24 hours at room temperature, turning the meat often.

The next day, pour in the milk and roast the meat, uncovered, in a preheated 350° F. [180° C.] oven. After about one hour, increase the heat to 400° F. [200° C.] and continue to roast, basting regularly, for another 20 minutes or until the meat is browned. At the end of roasting, the milk will be almost evaporated, transformed into an exquisite sauce to serve on the sliced meat.

PIER ANTONIO SPIZZOTIN (EDITOR)
I QUADERNI DEL CUCCHIAIO D'ARGENTO—GLI ARROSTI

Roast Pork with Eggplant and Tomatoes

Filet de Porc à la Provençale

To serve 6 to 8

2 to 2½ lb.	boneless pork loin roast	1 kg.
12	fresh sage leaves	12
1	garlic clove, slivered	1
¼ cup	coarse salt	50 ml.
1 tsp.	thyme	5 ml.
1	bay leaf, crumbled	1
1 tbsp.	lard, melted, or 1 tbsp. [15 ml.] olive oil	15 ml.
2	eggplants, peeled and cut into large cubes	2
4	tomatoes, quartered	4
¼ cup	olive oil	50 ml.

With a small, sharp knife, make incisions in the meat and insert the sage leaves and garlic slivers. Mix the salt with the thyme and bay leaf, and coat the pork with this seasoning. Cover and allow to marinate for several hours or overnight in the refrigerator.

Discard the liquid that has been drawn from the meat, wipe off the excess salt, tie up the roast and put it in an oval earthenware gratin dish. Brush with the lard or oil and put in a preheated 350° F. [180° C.] oven. Roast for 20 minutes.

Meanwhile, sauté the eggplant and the tomatoes separately in the oil for a couple of minutes each. Arrange the vegetables in alternating mounds around the pork, and continue to roast for 45 minutes, basting occasionally.

PROSPER MONTAGNÉ AND A. GOTTSCHALK
MON MENU

Roast Pork Loin, Old Polish-Style

Schab po Staropolsku

To serve 6

3 lb.	pork loin roast	1½ kg.
7 tbsp.	lard	105 ml.
	salt	
1 cup	pitted, dried prunes, parboiled for 5 minutes and drained	¼ liter
2 cups	stock (recipe, page 165), heated to boiling	½ liter
½ cup	raisins, soaked in warm water for 15 minutes and drained	125 ml.
1 tbsp.	honey	15 ml.
1 tbsp.	butter	15 ml.
½ tsp.	marjoram	2 ml.

Brown the meat on all sides in the lard. Transfer the meat to a roasting pan, and sprinkle it with salt. Add the prunes, pour the boiling stock over the meat, and roast in a preheated 375° F. [190° C.] oven for about an hour, basting regularly. Remove the meat to a warmed platter. Purée the prunes and degreased pan juices through a strainer or food mill into a saucepan, and add the raisins, honey, butter and marjoram. Cover and simmer this sauce for a few minutes. Slice the meat, pour the sauce over it, and serve with buckwheat groats or potatoes and seasonal salads such as apples with horseradish sauce.

B. MARKUZA-BIENIECKA AND J. P. DEKOWSKI
KUCHNIA REGIONALNA WCZORAJ I DZIŚ

Roast Pork Loin with Wine and Herbs

Carré de Porc Provençale

To serve 4 to 6

3 lb.	rack of pork loin chops	1½ kg.
1	garlic clove, slivered	1
	salt	
1 cup	dry white or red wine	¼ liter
2 or 3	sprigs thyme	2 or 3
	fresh pork rind in 1 piece, as long and as wide as the rack of pork	
1 tbsp.	chopped fresh parsley	15 ml.
½ cup	fine bread crumbs	125 ml.

Insert a few little slivers of garlic close to the bones in the pork loin. Rub the meat well with salt. Pour the wine over the meat, add the thyme and leave the meat to steep for a couple of hours.

Put the rind into a baking pan and on it place the meat, fat side up. Pour the marinade over the meat. Cover the pan with greased paper or foil and cook in a preheated 350° F. [180° C.] oven for approximately one and a quarter hours. If the liquid dries up, add a little water.

Mix the parsley and the bread crumbs. Remove the paper or foil from the meat and spread the parsley mixture over the fat side, pressing it gently down with a knife. Reduce the oven heat to 300° F. [150° C.] and cook the meat, uncovered, for another 35 to 50 minutes, basting now and again with the pan juices so that the parsley and the bread crumbs form a nice golden coating.

ELIZABETH DAVID
FRENCH PROVINCIAL COOKING

Roast Pork with Oregano and Wine, Cretan-Style

Hirino Riganato

The sauce left over from this dish, chilled and degreased, may be used to flavor a gravy, a pilaf or a pasta dish.

To serve 6 to 8

5 lb.	pork roast, preferably the shank half of the leg	2½ kg.
2	garlic cloves, slivered	2
	salt	
2 tsp.	dried oregano	10 ml.
½ cup	dry red wine	125 ml.
½ cup	tomato juice or peeled, seeded and chopped tomatoes	125 ml.
3 tbsp.	strained fresh lemon juice	45 ml.

Wipe the pork with damp paper towels. With the tip of a sharp knife, pierce the meat on all sides and insert the garlic slivers. Rub the meat all over with salt and oregano, then place in a shallow roasting pan in a preheated 325° to 350° F. [170° to 180° C.] oven, and roast uncovered for two and a half hours or until thoroughly cooked.

After the first 30 minutes of cooking, pour the wine over the meat and pour the tomato juice or chopped tomatoes around the meat. Baste the roast occasionally with the liquid in the pan. When done, remove from the oven and pour the lemon juice over the meat. Cool thoroughly, then carve the meat into very thin slices and serve cold.

VILMA LIACOURAS CHANTILES
THE FOOD OF GREECE

Leg of Pork Cooked like Wild Boar

Schweineschlegel nach Schwarzwildart

To serve 4 to 6

3 lb.	fresh ham roast, rind and most outer fat removed	1½ kg.
½ cup	dry red wine	125 ml.
1 cup	dark rye bread, grated	¼ liter
	salt	
8 tbsp.	butter	120 ml.

Red wine marinade

1 cup	dry red wine	¼ liter
½ cup	vinegar	125 ml.
½ cup	water	125 ml.
1 tbsp.	juniper berries	15 ml.
2	bay leaves	2
2	sprigs parsley	2
1 tsp.	thyme	5 ml.
1 tsp.	marjoram	5 ml.
1 tsp.	peppercorns	5 ml.
4	whole cloves	4
2	slices lemon	2
1	onion, halved	1
1	carrot, sliced	1
1	leek, sliced	1
1	rib celery, sliced	1

Combine all of the marinade ingredients in a bowl, put in the pork, cover, refrigerate and marinate the pork for five days, turning it occasionally. Dry the pork well and brown it in a roasting pan in 4 tablespoons [60 ml.] of the butter. Add the wine and about half of the strained marinade. Roast in a preheated 350° F. [180° C.] oven, basting frequently.

After two hours, cover the upper side of the meat thickly with the grated bread mixed with a little salt. Melt the remaining 4 tablespoons of butter and pour it over the crumbs, or cover the bread coating with thin slices of the butter. Turn up the heat to 425° F. [220° C.], and continue to roast for 10 to 15 minutes or until the coating is crisp.

Serve the roast hot with a mixed salad, or cold with a mayonnaise mixed with chopped green herbs.

HERMINE KIEHNLE AND MARIA HÄDECKE
DAS NEUE KIEHNLE KOCHBUCH

Leg of Pork Cooked like Game

Schweinskeule nach Jägerart

To serve 6

2 to 2½ lb.	boned fresh ham, rind removed	1 kg.
	salt	
2 cups	water	½ liter
2 tbsp.	vinegar	30 ml.
3	peppercorns	3
2	allspice berries	2
2	carrots, sliced	2
1	bay leaf	1
1	Hamburg parsley root, sliced	1
1	turnip, sliced	1
2	onions, sliced	2
8 tbsp.	butter	120 ml.
⅓ cup	flour	75 ml.
½ cup	dry white wine	125 ml.
2 to 3 tbsp.	strained fresh lemon juice	30 to 45 ml.
⅓ cup	currant or rose-hip jelly	75 ml.

Trim all fat from the meat and season the meat with salt. Bring the water and vinegar to a boil with the peppercorns, allspice berries, carrots, bay leaf, parsley root, turnip and onions. Boil this marinade for five minutes, then let it cool before pouring it over the meat. Cover and refrigerate for one to two days, turning the meat occasionally.

Remove the meat from the marinade and tie it up. Strain out the vegetables, reserving the liquid. In a heavy casserole brown the marinade vegetables in the butter, then add the meat and brown it on all sides. Put the casserole into a preheated 350° F. [180° C.] oven, and roast for one and a half hours, basting often with the marinade.

When the meat is done, remove it to a warmed serving platter. Degrease the pan juices. Add the flour to the pan juices and stir over medium heat until blended. Stir in the wine and lemon juice and cook until the sauce is thickened. Stir in the jelly and cook until it dissolves into the sauce. Add salt if necessary, then strain the sauce over the meat. Serve with dumplings.

JOZA BŘÍZOVÁ AND MARYNA KLIMENTOVÁ
TSCHECHISCHE KÜCHE

Mock Goose

*This recipe takes its title from the stuffing used for the pork —
a mixture traditionally used to stuff goose.*

The main feature of this dish from old English cookery is
the goose stuffing: this and the fact that the cheaper cuts of
pork—Boston shoulder or picnic shoulder—may be used,
make it a useful economy dish.

	To serve 6	
4 lb.	pork picnic shoulder roast, boned	2 kg.
2 tbsp.	butter	30 ml.
1 tbsp.	flour	15 ml.
6	small potatoes	6
6	small onions	6
2	eggs, lightly beaten	2
2 bunches	watercress	2 bunches
1 tbsp.	chopped fresh parsley	15 ml.
	Dry stuffing	
1½ cups	bread crumbs	375 ml.
3 tbsp.	chopped fresh sage	45 ml.
⅔ cup	chopped onion	150 ml.
4 oz.	beef suet, chopped	125 g.
1	apple, peeled and grated	1
	salt and freshly ground pepper	

Score the fat of the shoulder in a diamond pattern. Prepare
the dry stuffing by mixing together all of its ingredients and
place one third of the mixture into the cavity where the
shoulder bone has been removed; then tie the meat with
string. Mix the butter and flour together and rub all over the
shoulder, then roast in a preheated 325° F. [170° C.] oven for
25 minutes to each pound [50 minutes to each kg.].

Place the potatoes and onions around the shoulder one
and a quarter hours before the roast is ready. Mix the eggs
with half of the remaining dry stuffing, form the mixture
into balls and pan fry them or cook them in the pan with the
roast. When the roast is almost cooked, sprinkle the rest of
the dry stuffing all over the surface. When nicely colored,
place the roast on a serving dish together with any stuffing
that may have fallen into the pan.

To serve, carve the required number of portions of meat
on the dish, then garnish with the potatoes, onions and fried
balls of stuffing. If you want to be the good old English cook,
place a fine bouquet of watercress at each end of the dish.
Finally, glaze the roast and onions with a little of the rich
gravy left in the roasting pan after the excess fat has been
removed. Sprinkle with chopped parsley and serve very hot,
with a sauceboat of the gravy.

STANLEY FORTIN
THE WORLD BOOK OF PORK DISHES

Stuffed Shoulder of Pork

L'Épaule de Porc Fourrée

	To serve 6	
4 lb.	boneless pork picnic shoulder arm roast, with the rind left on and scored at regular intervals	2 kg.
¾ cup	dark rum	175 ml.
2½ cups	dry bread crumbs	625 ml.
1 cup	milk	¼ liter
½ tsp.	sage	2 ml.
½ tsp.	thyme	2 ml.
1 tbsp.	finely cut fresh chives	15 ml.
½	small fresh hot chili, stemmed, seeded and finely chopped	½
1	bay leaf, finely crushed	1
1 tbsp.	chopped fresh parsley	15 ml.
2	large garlic cloves, chopped	2
	salt and freshly ground pepper	
6	*melegueta* peppercorns or allspice berries, finely crushed	6
1 cup	chicken stock *(recipe, page 165)*	¼ liter

Pour ½ cup [125 ml.] of the rum over the meat and let it
stand while the stuffing is being prepared. Soak the bread
crumbs in the milk, then squeeze them dry. Mix the crumbs
with the sage, thyme, chives, chili, bay leaf, parsley, garlic, a
little salt and pepper, and the crushed *melegueta* peppercorns or allspice berries. Drain the rum from the meat and
pour it over the stuffing, mixing lightly.

Stuff the shoulder and sew it up. Place on a rack in a
roasting pan and roast in a preheated 325° F. [170° C.] oven
for two hours and 45 minutes. Remove the meat to a warmed
serving platter and set it aside to rest.

Pour off the fat from the pan, add the remaining rum to
the juices in the pan and deglaze it, stirring and scraping up
all of the brown bits. Pour in the chicken stock and simmer
until the sauce is reduced to about 1 cup [¼ liter]. Serve the
sauce in a sauceboat separately. The skin of the shoulder
should be crisp and crunchy.

ELISABETH LAMBERT ORTIZ
THE COMPLETE BOOK OF CARIBBEAN COOKERY

Breaded Chops

To serve 6

6	pork chops, cut 1 inch [2½ cm.] thick	6
1¼ cups	dry bread crumbs	300 ml.
3 to 4 tbsp.	fresh lemon juice	45 to 60 ml.
½ cup	olive oil	125 ml.
	salt and pepper	
1	egg, lightly beaten	1
1 tbsp.	water	15 ml.
⅓ cup	freshly grated Parmesan cheese	75 ml.
2 tbsp.	chopped fresh parsley	30 ml.
2 tbsp.	butter	30 ml.

Combine the lemon juice, ⅓ cup [75 ml.] of olive oil, the salt and pepper. Marinate the chops in this mixture for two hours. Drain the chops and pat them dry on paper towels. Mix the egg and water. Dip the chops in this mixture. Combine the bread crumbs, cheese and parsley. Coat both sides of the chops with the crumb mixture.

In an ovenproof skillet, brown the chops in the remaining olive oil mixed with the butter. Cover, and bake the chops in a preheated 350° F. [180° C.] oven for 45 minutes to one hour.

LOUISE SHERMAN SCHOON AND CORRINNE HARDESTY
THE COMPLETE PORK COOK BOOK

Pork Chops Baked with Aromatic Herbs

This dish is a good example of one in which the scent of aromatic herbs makes the whole difference; it should provide ideas for many others of the same sort.

To serve 2

2	thick pork chops, the meat lightly scored on each side	2
1	garlic clove, halved	1
	salt and pepper	
2 tbsp.	olive oil	30 ml.
6	sprigs thyme	6
4	bay leaves	4
12	sprigs fennel	12

Rub the meat with the cut surfaces of the garlic clove. Press in some salt and a little freshly milled black pepper. Coat each side of both chops with olive oil. In an ovenproof baking dish arrange the thyme, bay leaves and fennel. On top put the chops. If you have time, make these preparations an hour or so in advance, or in the morning for the evening, so that the herbs and seasonings have already scented the meat before cooking starts. Put the dish under the broiler, and let the chops brown lightly on each side. Now cover the dish with oiled paper or foil, transfer it to a preheated 325° F. [170° C.] oven, and leave for 40 to 50 minutes. Finally, pour off into a bowl any excess fat that has come from the meat during cooking. Serve the chops as they are, in their cooking dish, herbs and all. It is a simple enough dish, deliciously flavored and needing no accompaniment other than a green salad or a few sliced tomatoes dressed with oil and sprinkled with onion and parsley.

ELIZABETH DAVID
DRIED HERBS, AROMATICS AND CONDIMENTS

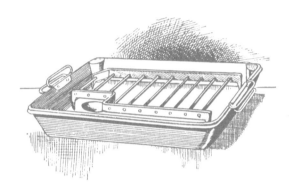

Grilled Skewered Pork Loin

"Lombello" Arrosto

To serve 6

2 to 2½ lb.	boned pork loin roast, fat removed, cut into 18 slices ½ inch [1 cm.] thick	1 kg.
24	slices Italian or French bread, from a long thin loaf	24
24	slices prosciutto ham, cut to the same dimensions as the pork slices	24
8 tbsp.	lard	120 ml.
	salt and pepper	

Take one large skewer (or six small ones) and thread onto it a slice of bread, one each of ham and pork, another slice of ham and one of bread. Repeat until all of the ingredients are used up. Melt the lard and pour 4 tablespoons [60 ml.] of it over the meat and the bread. Season with salt and pepper, and grill over charcoal embers or beneath an oven broiler, turning the skewer frequently and basting the meat from time to time with the remaining melted lard. The cooking time will be from 20 to 30 minutes; the bread should be crisp and golden, and the meat cooked through. Serve immediately.

ADA BONI
ITALIAN REGIONAL COOKING

Pork Tenderloin Grilled on the Skewer

This is an ingenious little recipe adapted from one well known in Italian household cookery. The simplicity of the ingredients makes the charm of this little dish, as indeed it does of most skewer-broiled food, and the mixture of the two different varieties of the same basic ingredients—the fresh and the cured pork—is typical of Italian cooking. The pork tenderloin can be served on a bed of finely shredded lettuce—previously dressed with a little oil, sugar, salt and lemon juice—and lemon quarters all round. If you want something more substantial, then have a dish of rice as well.

To serve 3 or 4

1 lb.	pork tenderloin, cut into 1-inch [2½-cm.] cubes	½ kg.
	white bread with the crusts removed, cut into an equal number of cubes, quite a bit smaller than the meat	
4 to 6 oz.	salt pork without the rind, blanched in boiling water for 5 minutes, drained and cut into twice as many thin slices as pork cubes	125 to 175 g.
	olive oil	
	freshly ground pepper and salt	
	marjoram, thyme or sage	

Sprinkle the fresh pork, bread cubes, and salt-pork slivers with a generous amount of olive oil, pepper and a little salt, and marjoram or thyme (the Italians use sage).

Thread the ingredients onto long skewers, in the following order: bread, salt pork, fresh pork, salt pork, bread and so on, until each skewer is about three quarters full. These quantities will fill five or six 9-inch [23-cm.] skewers.

Broil gently for about 15 to 20 minutes, not too close to the heat, turning the skewers from time to time.

ELIZABETH DAVID
SPICES, SALT AND AROMATICS IN THE ENGLISH KITCHEN

Deviled Pork and Bacon

Filets de Porc au Diable

To serve 4

1 lb.	pork tenderloin, cut into 1-inch [2½-cm.] cubes	½ kg.
½ lb.	bacon, thickly sliced and cut into 1-inch [2½-cm.] pieces	¼ kg.
¼ cup	prepared mustard	50 ml.
1½ cups	fresh bread crumbs	375 ml.
4 tbsp.	butter, melted	60 ml.

Thread the pork cubes onto skewers, alternating with the pieces of bacon. Paint the meat with the mustard, then roll it in the bread crumbs. Basting with the melted butter, grill over hot coals or broil, turning the skewers regularly, for about 10 to 15 minutes.

CURNONSKY
A L'INFORTUNE DU POT

Baked Spareribs with Apple-Onion Dressing

To serve 4

4 lb.	spareribs, parboiled for 2 minutes	2 kg.
2 tbsp.	flour	30 ml.
⅛ tsp.	salt	½ ml.
	pepper	
	Apple-onion dressing	
3 cups	diced tart apples	¾ liter
1 cup	chopped onions	¼ liter
1 cup	raisins, soaked in boiling water for 5 minutes and drained	¼ liter
7 cups	soft bread crumbs	1¾ liters
12 tbsp.	butter	180 ml.
1	chopped garlic clove	1
1 cup	chopped celery	¼ liter
¼ cup	finely chopped fresh parsley	50 ml.
1½ tsp.	salt	7 ml.
¼ tsp.	paprika	1 ml.

Preheat the oven to 500° F. [260° C.].

To make the dressing, add the raisins to the bread crumbs; melt the butter and sauté the chopped onions, garlic and celery. Add these ingredients to the bread crumbs and raisins with the apples, parsley, salt and paprika.

Cut the parboiled spareribs into two pieces. Spread one piece with the apple and onion dressing. Cover the dressing with the other piece of meat. Tie the two pieces together. Rub the outside of the meat with the flour, salt and pepper.

Place the spareribs on a rack in an uncovered roasting pan and reduce the heat at once to 325° F. [160° C.]. Bake for about one and a half hours. Baste the meat every 10 minutes with the fat in the pan.

IRMA S. ROMBAUER AND MARION ROMBAUER BECKER
JOY OF COOKING

Barbecued Spareribs, Chinese-Style

	To serve 6	
4 lb.	spareribs	2 kg.
½ cup	soy sauce	125 ml.
½ cup	dry sherry	125 ml.
½ cup	water	125 ml.
¼ cup	dark brown sugar	50 ml.
2	garlic cloves, crushed	2

Preheat the oven to 350° F. [180° C.]. Arrange the ribs in a large roasting pan. Combine all of the other ingredients, stir well and pour this marinade over the ribs. Cover the pan with foil. Bake for 45 minutes, turning the ribs once or twice. Take the ribs from the pan and save the marinade for basting. Set the barbecue grill as high above the bed of coals as possible. When the coals are gray, arrange the ribs on the grill. Cook them for 20 to 30 minutes until the meat is browned and tender, turning and basting frequently with the soy marinade so they won't dry.

ELEANOR GRAVES
GREAT DINNERS FROM LIFE

Stuffed Spareribs

	To serve 6	
4 lb.	lean spareribs, divided into 2 strips, each about 10 inches [25 cm.] long	2 kg.
4 or 5	cooking apples, peeled, cored and thickly sliced	4 or 5
1 lb.	dried prunes, parboiled in water for 15 minutes, drained and pitted	½ kg.
	salt	
	pepper	
	brown sugar	
	ground cinnamon	

Cook the apples in a small amount of water until almost tender. Drain. Place one strip of the spareribs on a rack in a shallow roasting pan and sprinkle it with a little salt and pepper. Spread the cooked apples evenly over the ribs. Cover with the prunes, then sprinkle with a little brown sugar, cinnamon and more salt. Place the second strip of ribs on top and link the edges together, here and there, with skewers. Bake in a preheated 325° F. [160° C.] oven for about two hours or until a fork pierces the meat easily.

THE EDITORS OF AMERICAN HERITAGE
THE AMERICAN HERITAGE COOKBOOK

Barbecued Spareribs

These spareribs can be barbecued on a charcoal grill instead of in the oven, but in that case the amounts of marinade ingredients should be doubled to allow for more frequent basting.

	To serve 6	
2½ lb.	spareribs, in one piece, excess fat removed, cut between ribs but not separated	1 kg.
	salt	
	sugar	
2 tbsp.	honey (optional)	30 ml.
1 tsp.	soy sauce (optional)	5 ml.
	Soy-sauce marinade	
1 cup	soy sauce	¼ liter
1	garlic clove, crushed	1
3	slices fresh ginger root, crushed	3
1 tbsp.	sugar	15 ml.
1 tbsp.	sherry	15 ml.

Before marinating, the ribs may be rubbed with salt and sugar and left for one hour.

To prepare the marinade, combine the crushed garlic and ginger with the soy sauce, sugar and sherry. Rub the marinade over the ribs and into the cuts as well. Put the ribs in a shallow pan and pour the rest of the marinade over them. Let stand two to four hours at room temperature, basting and turning the meat occasionally. (Do not marinate for a longer period: the meat will toughen.) Drain; reserve the marinade.

Preheat the oven to 375° F. [190° C.]. Place the marinated ribs on a metal rack over a roasting pan nearly filled with water (this will catch the drippings and keep them from burning). Roast for about 45 minutes, basting frequently with the reserved marinade. Turn the spareribs at 15- to 20-minute intervals for even browning. Halfway through the cooking, the ribs may be glazed with the combined honey and soy sauce, if desired.

The heat may be turned up to 450° F. [230° C.] during the last five minutes of roasting, to crisp the ribs, but cooking them any longer at high heat tends to dry them out.

GLORIA BLEY MILLER
THE THOUSAND RECIPE CHINESE COOKBOOK

Spareribs Orchard-Style

To serve 6

3 lb.	spareribs, in two parts	1½ kg.
2 tbsp.	chopped onion	30 ml.
6	tart apples, peeled, cored and chopped	6
¼ cup	brown sugar	50 ml.
1½ cups	toasted bread cubes	375 ml.
¼ tsp.	salt	1 ml.
⅛ tsp.	pepper	½ ml.

Combine the chopped onion, chopped apples, sugar and bread cubes. Cover half of the spareribs with this stuffing; place the other section of spareribs on top. Sprinkle with salt and pepper. Bake uncovered in a preheated 350° F. [180° C.] oven for two hours.

THE SALVATION ARMY WOMEN'S AUXILIARY, ROCHESTER, N.Y.
ROCHESTER HERITAGE COOK BOOK

Ormania Stuffed Pork Belly

To serve 6

2 lb.	fresh pork belly	1 kg.
2	bread rolls, soaked in 1 cup [¼ liter] milk, then squeezed dry	2
2	eggs	2
5 oz.	mixed pork liver and salt pork, coarsely chopped	150 g.
⅓ cup	finely chopped onion, fried in 4 tbsp. [60 ml.] lard	75 ml.
1	garlic clove, crushed	1
1½ tsp.	salt	7 ml.
	black pepper	
	marjoram	
⅓ tsp.	paprika	1½ ml.
3 tbsp.	lard	45 ml.
1 cup	stock *(recipe, page 165)*	¼ liter

With a sharp knife, cut horizontally into the middle of the pork belly to open a pocket between the layers of meat. Prepare the stuffing as follows: Place the squeezed, soaked bread rolls in a dish, beat in the eggs, add the minced liver and bacon, the fried onions, the garlic, 1 tsp. [5 ml.] of salt, a pinch each of black pepper and marjoram, and the paprika. Mix together thoroughly. Put this stuffing into the pocket cut in the meat, sew the end up with string and press on the stuffing until it is evenly distributed. Rub the remaining salt over the pork and roast it at 325° F. [170° C.], basting regularly, until it is brown and crisp, two to two and a half hours. Dish it up in its own gravy, first degreased, then thinned with the stock. Remove the string before serving. Serve with a potato and onion salad.

JÓZSEF VENESZ
HUNGARIAN CUISINE

Colne Loaf

Colne is in Lancashire, in the mountainous north of England.
This is a fine stamina food which probably owes its origin to the exacting climate and steep climbs for which Colne is noted. Some folk like the loaf made with rather more onion, but this is a matter of taste.

To serve 4

1 lb.	lean or fat slab bacon, parboiled for 10 minutes and drained	½ kg.
1	medium-sized onion	1
½ lb.	pork sausage meat	¼ kg.
2	firm tomatoes, finely chopped	2
2	ribs celery, chopped	2
	salt	
⅔ cup	water	150 ml.
½ cup	bread crumbs	125 ml.
	dried sage	
1	egg, well beaten	1
3	eggs, hard-boiled	3
	butter	

Mince the bacon and onion and mix with the sausage meat and tomatoes. Simmer the celery in seasoned water for 10 minutes. Add the celery and 3 tablespoons [45 ml.] of the celery's cooking water to the bacon mixture, also the bread crumbs, a little sage and the well-beaten egg. Put half of this mixture in a buttered loaf pan, disperse the whole hard-boiled eggs over it, then smother with the remaining bacon mixture. Place in a larger pan containing hot water and bake for about an hour at 350° F. [180° C.]. Serve hot or cold.

JOYCE DOUGLAS
OLD PENDLE RECIPES

Hot Ham Loaf

To serve 4

½ lb.	smoked ham	¼ kg.
1 lb.	boneless lean pork	½ kg.
1	egg	1
½ cup	milk	125 ml.
1 cup	dry bread crumbs	¼ liter
2 tbsp.	finely chopped onion	30 ml.
	salt and pepper	
¾ cup	brown sugar	175 ml.
1 tbsp.	prepared mustard	15 ml.
½ cup	vinegar	125 ml.
½ cup	water	125 ml.

Grind the ham and pork together, add the egg, milk, bread crumbs, onion, and salt and pepper to taste. Mold into a loaf and place in a roasting pan. Mix the brown sugar, mustard, vinegar and water, and pour this sauce over the loaf. Bake in a preheated 300° F. [150° C.] oven for one hour, basting occasionally with the sauce.

RUTH R. TYNDALL
EAT YOURSELF FULL

Ham Baked in a Crust

Prager Schinken

To serve 6 to 8

2 to 2½ lb.	boned smoked ham, soaked in cold water overnight	1 kg.
1 tsp.	marjoram	5 ml.
	pepper	
½ cup	gin	125 ml.
1 lb.	whole-wheat flour	½ kg.
about ½ cup	lukewarm water	about 125 ml.

Dry the ham well, place it in a pot and season it with the marjoram and a generous grinding of pepper. Pour on the gin, cover and let the ham stand at room temperature for 30 minutes, turning it occasionally.

Gradually stir enough lukewarm water into the flour to make a soft, pliable, but not sticky, dough. Knead the dough until smooth, and roll it out on a floured board to the thickness of a finger. Remove the meat from the marinade. Wrap the meat securely in the dough, sealing the edges by moistening them with cold water so that no juices can escape. Put the dough-wrapped ham on a floured baking sheet and bake in a preheated 350° F. [180° C.] oven for three to four hours, or until the crust is firm and dark brown.

To serve, cut the crust away and slice the meat. The flavorless crust is not eaten, but the ham cooked inside it is extremely succulent. Serve with asparagus, green peas or spinach, mashed potatoes and Madeira sauce. The ham is also good cold, on homemade bread, with scrambled eggs.

LILO AUREDEN
DAS SCHMECKT SO GUT

Roast Ham with Cider Sauce

To serve 16 to 20

12 lb.	smoked ham	6 kg.
½ cup	sliced onion	125 ml.
½ cup	sliced carrot	125 ml.
2	sprigs fresh parsley	2
½	bay leaf	½
	whole cloves	
5	peppercorns	5
1 quart	fresh apple cider	1 liter
	sugar	
	fine bread crumbs	
	paprika	
	Cider sauce	
3 tbsp.	butter	45 ml.
¼ cup	flour	50 ml.
2 cups	ham liquor	½ liter
¼ cup	fresh apple cider	50 ml.
	salt and pepper	

Soak the ham for several hours, or overnight, in cold water to cover. Wash thoroughly, scrape, and trim off the hard skin near the end of the bone. Put in a kettle with the onion, carrot, parsley, bay leaf, four cloves and peppercorns. Cover with cold water, bring slowly to the boiling point, and let simmer until tender, the time required being about four hours. After two hours of the cooking, add 1 quart [1 liter] of cider. Allow the ham to cool in the liquor. Remove the ham from the liquor, take off the skin, sprinkle the ham with sugar and fine bread crumbs. Put dashes of paprika over the ham, at about 2-inch [5-cm.] intervals, and insert a clove in the center of each dash. Bake for one hour in a preheated 350° F. [180° C.] oven.

Just before serving, prepare the sauce. Melt the butter, add flour and pour on gradually, while stirring constantly, the hot ham liquor. Add the cider and season with salt and pepper, if necessary.

Serve the ham hot, accompanied by the sauce.

FANNIE MERRITT FARMER
A BOOK OF GOOD DINNERS FOR MY FRIEND

Baked Ham Slice

To serve 4

1½ lb.	smoked ham slice, cut about 2 inches [5 cm.] thick	¾ kg.
½ cup	brown sugar	125 ml.
1 tbsp.	flour	15 ml.
½ tsp.	dry mustard	2 ml.
1 cup	boiling water	¼ liter
¼ cup	vinegar	50 ml.
¼ cup	seedless raisins	50 ml.

Place the ham slice in a baking dish. In a saucepan, combine the sugar with the flour and mustard. Stir in the boiling water and vinegar and bring to a boil. Remove this sauce from the heat and add the raisins. Pour the sauce over the ham and bake in a preheated 375° F. [180° C.] oven until the ham is tender, about one and a half hours. Serve with sauce spooned over the ham.

BEATRICE VAUGHAN
THE OLD COOK'S ALMANAC

Barbecued Ham Steak

To serve 4 to 6

2	smoked ham center-slice steaks (1 inch [2½ cm.] thick)	2
1 cup	cider	¼ liter
3 tbsp.	brown sugar	45 ml.
1 tbsp.	dry mustard	15 ml.
3	whole cloves, crushed	3

Place the ham steaks in a large frying pan and cover them with water. Parboil for five minutes, then pour off the water. Remove the pan from the heat.

Make a marinade mixture from the cider, brown sugar, dry mustard and cloves. Let the ham soak in the marinade for 15 minutes.

Remove the ham steaks, saving the marinade, and slash the fat around the edges. Grease the grill of a barbecue with a piece of ham fat and place the steaks on the grill over medium hot coals. Baste with the marinade and turn the steaks often. Allow 25 to 30 minutes total cooking time.

MONETTE R. AND ROBERT W. HARRELL JR.
THE HAM BOOK

Poaching

Fresh Ham Boiled with Hay and Beer

Nastoyashchaya Buzhenina, v Sennoy Trukhe s Pivom

The technique of cooking ham in hay is demonstrated on pages 54-55. The traditional accompaniments to this dish are chestnuts, either braised or puréed; cabbage or sauerkraut; and boiled potatoes. The chestnuts should be braised—or boiled before puréeing—in milk or in a mixture of meat stock and dry red wine.

To serve 6 to 8

3 to 4 lb.	fresh ham roast	1½ to 2 kg.
	salt	
½ lb.	fresh sweet hay	¼ kg.
8 to 10	peppercorns	8 to 10
2	bay leaves	2
1	carrot, sliced	1
1	turnip, sliced	1
1	onion, sliced	1
1	leek, sliced	1
3 cups	dark beer	¾ liter
1 tbsp.	flour	15 ml.

Salt the ham, wrap it in a cloth, put it in a pan with the hay, and cover the ham and hay generously with cold water. Cover the pan—leaving the lid slightly ajar—and bring the water to a boil; remove the pan from the heat and let stand for 30 minutes. Then bring the water back to a boil once more; remove the pan from the heat and let the ham cool.

Take the ham out of the cloth and put it in another pan. Add the peppercorns, bay leaves and vegetables. Pour in the beer, cover the pan and cook over low heat until the meat is done, about one hour, turning the meat several times.

Remove the meat to a serving platter. Strain and degrease the cooking liquid, and blend in the flour. Bring this sauce to a boil, reduce its volume slightly if necessary and pour the sauce over the ham.

ELENA MOLOKHOVETS
PODAROK MOLODÝM KHOZYAÏKAM

Loin of Pork Stuffed with Truffles

Enchaud de Porc à la Perigourdine

For those who like pork, this is one of the loveliest dishes in the whole repertoire of cookery from southwestern France.

To serve 10

4 lb.	pork loin roast, boned and the bones reserved	2 kg.
	salt and pepper	
2 or 3	truffles, fresh or canned, cut into thick little pieces	2 or 3
¼ lb.	fresh pork rind, cut into thin strips	125 g.
1	garlic clove, slivered	1
2½ cups	heated stock *(recipe, page 165)* or ⅔ cup [150 ml.] dry white wine heated with 2 cups [½ liter] water	625 ml.

Lay the meat on a board, salt and pepper it, and lay the truffle pieces at intervals along the meat. Add a few little slivers of garlic. Roll up the meat and tie it round with string so that it is the shape of a long, narrow bolster.

Put the meat in a baking dish with the bones and the strips of rind. Let it cook for about 30 minutes in a preheated 325° F. [170° C.] oven. When the meat has turned golden, pour in the hot stock or the wine and water, plus the liquid from the truffles if they were canned. Now cover the dish and let the meat cook for another two to two and a half hours.

Pour off the liquid from the dish into a bowl, refrigerate and, when it has set, remove the fat from this jelly. Chop the jelly and arrange it around the cold pork in a serving dish.

ELIZABETH DAVID
FRENCH PROVINCIAL COOKING

Poached Pork with White Cabbage

Gedämpftes Schweinefleisch mit Weisskraut

To serve 4 to 6

1½ to 2 lb.	lean blade-end pork roast	¾ to 1 kg.
	salt and pepper	
1	sprig marjoram, tarragon or thyme	1
1 tsp.	caraway seeds	5 ml.
½ tsp.	anise seeds	2 ml.
1	large cabbage (about 3 lb. [1½ kg.]), quartered, cored and blanched	1
4 to 6	small tomatoes, skinned, seeded and coarsely chopped	4 to 6
	paprika	

Put the meat, seasoned with salt and pepper, into a saucepan. Add the marjoram, tarragon or thyme, and the caraway seeds and anise seeds tied in a cheesecloth bag. Pour on boiling water to cover. When the water returns to a boil, skim, cover the pan, reduce the heat and simmer slowly for two hours, turning the meat occasionally.

After the first hour of cooking, put the blanched cabbage quarters into a second saucepan that will just hold them; add a pinch of caraway seeds, and scoop onto the cabbage one or two ladles of the pork broth taken from the top fatty layer. Simmer, covered, for 30 minutes. Then add the tomatoes and a pinch of paprika and cook for 15 minutes more.

When serving, place the cabbage on a round warmed platter and surround it with the sliced meat sprinkled with a little of the cooking broth. Serve with potatoes of any kind.

GRETE WILLINSKY
KOCHBUCH DER BÜCHERGILDE

Pork Loin Boiled in Sauerkraut Brine

Svinsko File, Vareno v Zelev Sok

Although this recipe calls for pork loin, any of the less tender and less expensive pork cuts can be substituted. The natural acetic acid in sauerkraut brine, combined with very slow cooking, tenderizes the meat and makes it highly aromatic. With its red coating, the pork looks very attractive as a dish for a cold buffet. It can be kept refrigerated for three or four days.

To serve 4 to 6

2 lb.	boneless pork loin roast	1 kg.
2 quarts	sauerkraut brine, strained	2 liters
Red glaze		
1 to 2 tbsp.	paprika	15 to 30 ml.
10	garlic cloves	10
	salt	
1 tsp.	freshly ground pepper	5 ml.
½ tsp.	freshly ground cumin	2 ml.

Place the meat in a pan that will just contain it easily. Cover the meat with the strained sauerkraut brine, put on the lid, and bring the brine very slowly to the simmering point. Let it cook over very low heat, with the liquid just trembling, for about two hours or until the meat is tender.

Transfer the cooked meat to a platter. To make the glaze, crush the garlic cloves in a mortar with a pinch or two of salt until they form a paste. Brush this paste over the meat while it is still warm. Then combine the paprika, pepper and cumin, and use this mixture to coat the warm meat. Serve the meat cold, cut into thin slices.

L. PETROV, N. DJELEPOV, E. IORDANOV AND S. UZUNOVA
BULGARSKA NAZIONALNA KUCHNIYA

Cold Pork Loin in Jelly

Porc Piqué

For instructions on larding a pork loin and coating it with aspic, see pages 56-57. If the stock you use for the pork does not set into a jelly when both are cooled, use ¼ cup [50 ml.] of the stock to soften 2 tablespoons [30 ml.] of powdered gelatin; then warm the remaining stock and dissolve the gelatin in it before starting to glaze the pork.

	To serve 6	
2 to 2½ lb.	boned pork loin roast, trimmed of all but a thin layer of fat	1 kg.
¼ lb.	fresh pork fat, cut into larding strips ¼ inch [6 mm.] thick and as long as the piece of pork	125 g.
	salt	
	sugar	
about 1½ quarts	rich gelatinous stock *(recipe, page 165)*, heated	about 1½ liters

Roll the strips of pork fat in a little salt, and use them to lard the piece of pork lengthwise, following the grain of the meat. Roll up the loin and tie it with string at 1-inch [2½-cm.] intervals, starting at the middle and working outward to form a regular cylindrical shape. Sprinkle the pork lightly all over with sugar. Color it on all surfaces, either in a skillet over high heat, or in an oven preheated to 425° F. [220° C.]. Place the pork in an oval casserole just large enough to hold it and cover it generously with the hot stock. Bring to a simmer, cover the casserole and place in a preheated 325° F. [170° C.] oven for 35 minutes, or poach the pork over low heat on top of the stove.

Strain and degrease the cooking stock, and return it to the casserole. Allow the pork to cool in the stock. Transfer the pork to a rack and remove the strings. Gently warm about 1 cup [¼ liter] of the cooking stock, pour it into a bowl and set in cracked ice. When the stock begins to thicken, but is not yet jellied, spoon several layers of it over the pork to glaze the surface. Serve the pork cold, in slices.

P. E. LALOUE
LE GUIDE DE LA CHARCUTERIE

Pork Stew

To make caramel syrup for this recipe boil ¼ cup [50 ml.] of sugar with 1 teaspoon [5 ml.] of water until caramelized.

This stew can be made in advance and reheated repeatedly. It keeps well in the refrigerator for about one week, and can be frozen very successfully.

	To serve 6	
2 to 2½ lb.	boneless lean fresh ham, cut into 3-inch [8-cm.] cubes	1 kg.
2	shallots, finely chopped	2
1 tsp.	salt	5 ml.
1 tbsp.	sugar	15 ml.
1 tsp.	caramel syrup	5 ml.
¼ tsp.	pepper	1 ml.
¼ cup	*nuoc mam* fish sauce	50 ml.
1½ quarts	water	1½ liters

Combine the shallots with the salt, sugar, caramel syrup, pepper and fish sauce, and pour the mixture over the pork cubes. Marinate at room temperature for about one hour.

Bring the water to a boil in a heavy pot. Put the pork and its marinade into the boiling water and bring to a boil again. Skim off the scum, reduce the heat to medium low, cover, and simmer until the pork is tender (about three hours).

Serve the pork stew hot with rice and salad.

JILL NHU HUONG MILLER
VIETNAMESE COOKERY

Boiled Pork

Rafutei

	To serve 4	
1 lb.	boneless lean pork	½ kg.
1 cup	*sake* wine	¼ liter
½ cup	*mirin* wine	125 ml.
2 tbsp.	sugar	30 ml.
½ cup	dried bonito shavings (about 1 oz. [50 g.])	125 ml.
½ cup	soy sauce	125 ml.
	snow peas, parboiled for a few seconds and drained	

Place the pork in a bowl, pour on the *sake*, work it into the meat with your fingers and let stand for 30 minutes. Place the pork in a pot with water to cover, and simmer for one hour over a low heat, skimming. Remove the pork and cut it into four pieces.

Place the pork in another pot with 2 cups [½ liter] of its cooking broth, the *mirin* and the sugar. Cook for 30 minutes, then add the dried bonito shavings and half of the soy sauce. Cook for one more hour, then add half of the remaining soy sauce and cook for an additional hour, adding the remaining soy sauce halfway through.

Place the pork in a warmed serving dish and garnish with the cooked snow peas.

MICHIKO SHO
JOY COOKING—PORK SIDE DISHES

Brianza Casserole

Cazzoeula

A *cazzoeula* typical of the Brianza region of Italy should be quite thick and almost glutinous; it must be stirred frequently to prevent sticking. In Inverigo, a little tomato sauce is added with the carrots and celery.

To serve 6 to 8

1½ lb.	spareribs, cut into 6 to 8 pieces	¾ kg.
¼ lb.	fresh pork rind, cut into strips	125 g.
1	pig's foot, cut into 4 pieces	1
½ lb.	fresh Italian-style sausages, pricked with a fork	¼ kg.
4	small onions, sliced	4
2 tbsp.	butter	30 ml.
4	carrots, sliced	4
1	rib celery, sliced	1
1	large cabbage, coarsely shredded	1
	salt and pepper	

In a large pot, soften the onions in the butter over medium heat. Add the rind and pig's foot and brown them lightly. Pour on enough water to cover them, and simmer, partly covered, for one hour, turning them occasionally to prevent sticking. When the water has nearly all evaporated, add the ribs. Cook for about 15 minutes, then add the carrots and celery. After another 15 minutes, add the cabbage. Cook for 30 minutes, add the sausages and cook the *cazzoeula* for 30 minutes longer. Correct the seasoning before serving.

OTTORINA PERNA BOZZI
VECCHIA BRIANZA IN CUCINA

Cold Stuffed Pork Belly

Gefüllte Schweinsbrust (Kalt)

To serve 8

3 lb.	fresh pork belly	1½ kg.
1 lb.	fresh pork bones and rind	½ kg.
2 quarts	water	2 liters
1	carrot	1
1	Hamburg parsley root	1
1	small celeriac	1
	thyme	
	salt	
10	peppercorns	10
5	allspice berries	5
1	bay leaf	1
Liver stuffing		
1 lb.	pork liver, very finely chopped	½ kg.
½ lb.	boneless pork Boston shoulder, very finely chopped	¼ kg.
2	bread rolls with the crusts removed, soaked in water and squeezed dry	2
3 oz.	fresh pork fat, very finely chopped	100 g.
1 tbsp.	finely chopped shallot	15 ml.
	salt and pepper	
	grated nutmeg	
1 tsp.	marjoram	5 ml.

Put the pork bones and rind in a large saucepan with the water, carrot, parsley root, celeriac, a pinch of thyme, salt, peppercorns, allspice and bay leaf. Simmer, with the lid ajar, for 30 minutes.

To prepare the stuffing, mix all of the ingredients well together. With a sharp knife, cut a pocket in the pork belly between the layers of meat. Score the rind. Fill the pocket with the stuffing, sew up the opening and roll up the stuffed meat in a cloth. Tie the roll tightly with string. Place the meat in the broth and simmer for two hours.

Allow the meat to cool slightly in the broth. Lift it out onto a dish, unwrap the cloth, and tie the meat up tightly in another cloth. Place on a board with another board on top. Weight the top board to press the meat; let the meat cool completely, before serving it.

OLGA HESS AND ADOLF FR. HESS
WIENER KÜCHE

Pickled Pork Hocks

Paksiw Na Pata

To serve 4

4	fresh pork hocks (1 lb. [½ kg.] each)	4
2 cups	water	½ liter
½ cup	distilled white vinegar	125 ml.
1	small bay leaf	1
6	medium-sized garlic cloves, peeled and crushed slightly	6
2 tbsp.	dark brown sugar	30 ml.
1 tbsp.	salt	15 ml.
½ tsp.	whole black peppercorns	2 ml.
2 tbsp.	soy sauce, preferably Japanese	30 ml.

Combine the water, vinegar, bay leaf, garlic, brown sugar, salt and peppercorns in a heavy 4- to 5-quart [4- to 5-liter] casserole and stir until the sugar and salt dissolve. Add the pork hocks, turning them about with a spoon until they are evenly coated with the vinegar mixture. Bring to a boil over high heat, reduce the heat to low, cover tightly and simmer for one and a half hours. (Check the pork from time to time; if the liquid seems to be cooking away, replenish it with boiling water.) Stir in the soy sauce, cover again and simmer for 30 minutes longer, or until the pork is tender and shows no resistance when pierced with a small, sharp knife.

To serve, arrange the pork hocks attractively on a heated platter. Discard the bay leaf, garlic and peppercorns and pour the cooking sauce over the meat. *Paksiw na pata* is traditionally accompanied by plain rice, boiled without salt.

FOODS OF THE WORLD
PACIFIC AND SOUTHEAST ASIAN COOKING

Pork Hocks with Vegetables

To serve 4

2	pork hocks	2
1 tsp.	salt	5 ml.
¼ tsp.	pepper	1 ml.
4	carrots	4
4	medium-sized onions	4
4	medium-sized potatoes	4
1	small cabbage, cut into thick wedges	1

In a large pot, cover the hocks with water, put the lid on the pot and simmer for about one and a half hours, or until the hocks are almost cooked.

Add the salt and pepper, carrots, onions and potatoes, peeled but whole, and cook for another 15 minutes. Add the wedges of cabbage, and continue to cook everything until all the vegetables are tender. Serve on a platter with the vegetables piled around the hocks.

ROBIN HOWE
COOKING FROM THE COMMONWEALTH

Vietnamese Meat Loaf

This meat loaf is made with pork and is steamed; it has a quite different flavor and texture from a baked loaf and is very quick to make.

To serve 4

1 lb.	pork, finely chopped or ground	½ kg.
about ½ cup	dried bean thread, soaked in hot water for at least 10 minutes, drained and coarsely chopped	about 125 ml.
6	dried mushrooms, soaked in hot water for 20 minutes, drained, stems removed and coarsely chopped	6
3	shallots, sliced thin	3
1	small onion, coarsely chopped	1
1 tbsp.	*nuoc mam* fish sauce	15 ml.
½ tsp.	salt	2 ml.
	pepper	
4	eggs	4

Measure out 8 tablespoons [120 ml.] of the soaked and chopped bean thread for use in this recipe. Add the mushrooms, shallots, onion, fish sauce, salt and pepper, and mix thoroughly with your hands into the chopped pork. Break the eggs into the meat mixture and mix in well.

Place the meat loaf in a heatproof dish and put the dish in the top section of a steamer. Put water into the bottom section of the steamer, set the top section containing the meat loaf in place, cover and steam over high heat until the loaf is firm (about 20 minutes). Alternatively, place the dish on a trivet in a covered saucepan with water in the bottom of the pan. To test, remove the lid and test the firmness of the loaf with a fork. It is done when the loaf feels quite firm and the fork's tines emerge clean.

This meat loaf is especially good served with leaf lettuce. Wrap a bite-sized portion of the meat loaf in a leaf of lettuce, dip it into fish sauce and eat it, while making appropriate noises of appreciation.

JILL NHU HUONG MILLER
VIETNAMESE COOKERY

Hot Poached Sausage

Saucisson Chaud Lyonnais

To serve 3 or 4

1 lb.	large pork poaching sausage	½ kg.
3 or 4	medium-sized potatoes	3 or 4
7 tbsp.	butter, melted	105 ml.
2 tbsp.	chopped fresh parsley	30 ml.

Put the sausage into a large pan of cold water and bring it slowly to just below the simmering point, about 160° F. [70° C.], being careful not to let the water come to a boil. This way the sausage will stay moist. With the lid slightly ajar, poach the sausage for 40 to 45 minutes.

In another pan, boil the potatoes in their skins for 30 minutes or until just done. While they are still hot, peel them, slice them thickly, put them on a warmed plate, sprinkle with parsley and pour over the melted butter. Drain the sausage, slice thickly and serve with the hot potatoes.

FERNAND POINT
MA GASTRONOMIE

Steamed Pork with Szechwan Preserved Vegetables

Cha-Ts'ai Cheng Chu-Jou Ping

Szechwan preserved vegetables, or cha-ts'ai, are a kind of spicy vegetable pickle made from Chinese mustard greens; the pickle can be obtained from Oriental food shops.

To serve 2

4 oz.	boneless pork, with some marbling of fat, chopped not too finely	125 g.
1 tbsp.	chopped water chestnuts	15 ml.
	salt	
2 to 3	slices fresh ginger root, crushed and chopped	2 to 3
½ tbsp.	Chinese rice wine	7 ml.
1 tbsp.	water	15 ml.
5	slices Szechwan preserved vegetables, cut ⅛ inch [3 mm.] thick	5

Mix the pork with the water chestnuts, salt, ginger, wine and water. Put the vegetable slices on top of the meat mixture. Put the bowl in a bamboo steamer set in a wok or pan over boiling water, cover the steamer and cook for 30 minutes. Alternatively, place the bowl on a trivet in a large saucepan with boiling water under the trivet and steam, covered, for 30 minutes.

CECILIA SUN YUN CHIANG
THE MANDARIN WAY

Pork Pot with Cabbage

Potée aux Choux

To serve 8

6 to 7 lb.	salt-cured ham shank, soaked in water overnight and drained	3 kg.
1	*cervelas* or other large poaching sausage, pricked with a fork	1
½ lb.	salt pork, soaked overnight in water and drained, the rind removed, cut into small pieces and reserved	¼ kg.
4 tbsp.	lard	60 ml.
2	small turnips, cut into chunks	2
2	medium-sized carrots, cut into chunks	2
4 or 5	leeks	4 or 5
1	large onion, stuck with a whole clove	1
1	bouquet garni with garlic and celery	1
1	large cabbage, halved, cored, blanched for 10 to 12 minutes in boiling salted water and drained	1
4	medium-sized, firm-fleshed potatoes, quartered	4
	salt and pepper	
	thinly sliced bread, toasted in the oven (optional)	

In an earthenware pot if possible, or in an enameled-iron pan, melt the lard over low heat. Place the salt-pork rind in the bottom of the pot. Put in the ham shank, then the salt pork, turnips, carrots and leeks. Add the onion and the bouquet garni. Pour in enough water just to cover the contents of the pot, cover and simmer over low heat for one and a half hours. Add the cabbage, the sausage and the potatoes; sprinkle with salt. Cook for another one and a half hours, then correct the seasoning with salt and pepper.

To serve, arrange the vegetables and meats on a heated serving platter. Discard the bouquet garni and onion. Pour the cooking broth into a soup tureen and serve it separately, with slices of toasted bread if you wish.

IRÈNE LABARRE AND JEAN MERCIER
LA CUISINE DU POITOU ET DE LA VENDÉE

Ham with Dried Apples and Dumplings

Schnitz-un-Gnepp

Schnitz means "cut" and, in Pennsylvania Dutch usage, it has come to mean cut dried apples. There are both sweet and sour *schnitz*; the sour *schnitz* are used for pies; the sweet apples go into sweet *schnitz*, served with dumplings *(gnepp)* as in this recipe.

	To serve 6 to 8	
2½ to 3 lb.	smoked ham with bone	1 to 1½ kg.
2 cups	dried apples	½ liter
2 tbsp.	brown sugar	30 ml.
	Baking-powder dumplings	
3 tsp.	baking powder	15 ml.
1½ cups	sifted all-purpose flour	375 ml.
½ tsp.	salt	2 ml.
1 tbsp.	butter	15 ml.
about ¼ cup	milk	about 50 ml.
1	egg, well beaten	1

In a large pot, cover the ham almost completely with cold water. Bring to a boil, reduce the heat, cover and simmer gently for two hours. Meanwhile, put the dried apples in a bowl and cover with cold water to soak. When the ham has been cooked for two hours, add the drained apples and the brown sugar. Simmer for one hour, then lift the ham onto a large warmed platter and spoon the apples around it. Reserve the ham broth.

To make the dumplings, sift together the flour, baking powder and salt into a bowl. Pinch in the butter with your finger tips until it is well distributed, then stir in enough milk to make a soft dough. Add the egg and beat the dough briefly. Then drop the dumpling dough from a soup spoon into the boiling ham broth, cover tightly, and simmer the dumplings for 10 to 12 minutes. Arrange the dumplings on the platter around the meat and spoon a little broth over them. The broth may be thickened by stirring in a little flour, mixed to a smooth paste with water.

THE EDITORS OF AMERICAN HERITAGE
THE AMERICAN HERITAGE COOKBOOK

Poached Ham

Jambon Genre "York ou d'Arleuf"

For a demonstration on the poaching of a whole ham with hay, see pages 54-55. Lime flowers are sold dried at pharmacies, health-food stores or herbal specialists, for use in preparing tisane or herb tea.

	To serve 30 to 40	
1	lightly smoked ham (about 16 to 18 lb. [8 kg.]), soaked in cold water overnight	1
½ lb.	hay or ¼ lb. [125 g.] dried lime flowers, tied in a cheesecloth (optional)	¼ kg.

According to the size of the ham, it will need seven to eight hours of slow cooking in unsalted water to cover, without letting the water boil. Keep the temperature about 180° F. [85° C.]. In general, the cooking time is 20 to 25 minutes to the pound [½ kg.]. The ham is cooked when the small shank bone can be removed easily. These hams may be cooked with hay or with lime flowers, by adding a handful of one or the other to the poaching liquid.

To serve the ham cold, let it cool in its cooking liquid.

ALEXANDRE DUMAINE
MA CUISINE

Ham Poached in Red Wine

Jambon Chaud

In wine-growing regions of France, hams are sometimes cooked in the lees of wine—the sediment found at the bottom of the barrel after the clear red wine has been drawn off.

	To serve 20 to 30	
1	smoked or salt-cured ham (13 lb. [6 kg.]), soaked in cold water overnight	1
4 to 5 quarts	dry red wine	4 to 5 liters
1	onion	1
1	bouquet garni	1
1	bunch fines herbes (including tarragon or hyssop)	1
⅓ cup	chopped fresh parsley	75 ml.
	freshly ground pepper	
½ cup	dry bread crumbs	125 ml.

Tie up the ham in a cheesecloth or a large, clean dish towel and put it into a pan just large enough to hold it. Add the wine, onion, bouquet garni and fines herbes. Bring to a boil, cover and then cook very slowly for five to six hours. The ham is done when it is easily pierced by a skewer.

Unwrap the ham, remove the rind and press the parsley, pepper and bread crumbs onto the ham. Place it in a very hot oven, preheated to 475° F. [250° C.], for five to 10 minutes to brown it slightly before serving.

MAURICE BÉGUIN
LA CUISINE EN POITOU

Pork Pot from Champagne

Potée Champenoise

For the technique of making a large poaching sausage, see the demonstration on pages 20-21.

To serve 10 to 12

1½ lb.	lean salt pork, rind removed, blanched for 10 minutes and drained	¾ kg.
1½ lb.	salt-cured ham, blanched for 3 minutes and drained	¾ kg.
1	pork poaching sausage, pierced on all sides with a fork	1
2 cups	dried white beans (about ¾ lb. [⅓ kg.]), soaked in cold water overnight and drained	½ liter
	salt and freshly ground pepper	
3	medium-sized carrots	3
1	small rutabaga	1
3	medium-sized turnips	3
2	small green cabbages, cored and blanched	2
1	stewing chicken, trussed	1
6 to 8	large potatoes	6 to 8
	slices of old bread	

Put the soaked beans into a large saucepan and cover them generously with cold water. Bring to a boil over medium heat and boil for 10 minutes. Then skim and put in the salt pork, the ham and the root vegetables. Reduce the heat, cover and cook for 30 minutes. Add the cabbage and the chicken and cook for about one hour and 10 minutes. Add the potatoes and the sausage, and cook for 30 minutes longer or until everything is done. To serve, taste the broth for seasoning and ladle it over slices of stale bread in a warmed soup tureen. Slice the meats and serve them in a heated dish, with the vegetables arranged around them.

ROGER LALLEMAND
LA VRAIE CUISINE DE LA CHAMPAGNE

Ham Poached with Hay

Jambon au Foin

For a demonstration of preparing a ham for poaching with hay, see pages 54-55. If desired, you can ask your butcher to cut the shank bone and remove the pelvic bone from the ham.

To serve 8 to 10

1	smoked ham (6 to 7 lb. [3 kg.])	1
½ lb.	good hay	¼ kg.
1	sprig thyme	1
2	bay leaves	2
6	whole cloves	6
10	juniper berries	10

The day before serving, prepare the ham by sawing off the knuckle end of the shank bone and removing the pelvic bone. Soak the ham overnight in cold water to cover. The following day, put the ham in a large pot, cover it completely with fresh cold water, and add the hay and the flavorings.

Place the pot on low heat and bring it to simmering; do not let it boil. Maintain a constant temperature of 180° F. [85° C.]. Poach the ham for 15 minutes to the pound [30 minutes per kg.]. When the ham is cooked, remove the rind. The ham may be served hot or cold.

PAUL BOCUSE
PAUL BOCUSE'S FRENCH COOKING

Salt Pork

Comment Faire le Petit Salé de Cochon

While it is being salted, the pork must be kept in the refrigerator for six or seven days, or in a comparably cool —40° F. [5° C.]—pantry or basement.

All cuts of pork are good for preparing *petit salé*, but the tenderloin is considered to be the best. After salting, you may poach the pork and serve it with pea or lentil purée, or use it in a stew made with cabbage, turnips or mixed vegetables. Be careful not to salt the stew; and if the salt pork is too salty, soak it in warm water before cooking it.

To salt 15 pounds [7 kg.] of pork

15 lb.	pork, of any cut you wish	7 kg.
1 lb.	salt	½ kg.

Rub the pieces of meat all over with the salt, and put them into a large crock. When it is full, cover the crock tightly to keep out the air. The pork may be used after five or six days; if you wish to keep it a long time, add more salt, but the fresher salt pork is the better it is.

MENON
LA CUISINIÈRE BOURGEOISE

Pease Pudding

If this pudding is to be served with salted pork, it can be cooked with the pork as in the demonstration on pages 52-53. The pudding cloth called for in the recipe is a large square of doubled cheesecloth.

	To serve 4	
1 cup	dried split peas (about ½ lb. [¼ kg.]), soaked in water for one hour	¼ liter
2 tbsp.	butter	30 ml.
1	egg, beaten	1
	flour	

Cover the split peas with water, bring to a boil and simmer until tender, about one hour. Pass them through a sieve into a bowl. Stir in the butter and egg, beating well. Flour a pudding cloth, put the pea purée in it, and tie up loosely. Put the wrapped purée into a pot of simmering water and cook for one hour over low heat. Untie the cloth and put the pudding on a warmed dish. Serve sliced, with salted pork.

TERENCE CONRAN AND MARIA KROLL
THE VEGETABLE BOOK

Braising and Stewing

Pork Pot Roast

Arrosto di Maiale in Casseruola

	To serve 6	
3 lb.	pork loin roast	1½ kg.
⅔ cup	stock *(recipe, page 165)*	150 ml.
2 tbsp.	butter	30 ml.
	salt and pepper	
1	garlic clove	1
1	sprig rosemary	1
½ cup	dry white wine	125 ml.

Place the pork in a heavy casserole and add all of the other ingredients. Cover and cook gently over low heat for at least one hour. When the pork has absorbed almost all of the liquid, remove the casserole from the heat, take out the meat, bone it and cut it into thin slices. Arrange the slices, overlapping them, on a warmed serving dish and strain over them the juices remaining in the casserole. The pork may be served hot or cold with equal success, with green vegetables and mashed potatoes.

GUGLIELMA CORSI
UN SECOLO DI CUCINA UMBRA

Braised Pork with Onion Sauce

Palette de Porc "Pauvre Femme"

The cabbage with salt pork that is suggested as an accompaniment to this dish consists of a parboiled cabbage, roughly cut up, then mixed with a few lardons of sliced, sautéed salt pork, and finally baked or braised until tender. A few spoonfuls of boiling vinegar should be poured on the cabbage just before serving.

	To serve 4	
2 lb.	pork Boston shoulder roast or 1½ lb. [¾ kg.] pork tenderloin with ½ lb. [¼ kg.] additional bones	900 g.
3	garlic cloves, halved lengthwise	3
	salt and pepper	
7 tbsp.	butter	105 ml.
5	medium-sized onions (about 1¾ lb. [875 g.]), thinly sliced	5
1	large potato (about 1¾ lb. [875 g.]), sliced	1
1	bouquet garni	1
1 cup	milk	¼ liter
2 tbsp.	coarsely chopped fresh parsley	30 ml.

Make six small cuts in the meat and insert the halved garlic cloves. Season with salt and pepper. Melt 1½ tablespoons [22 ml.] of the butter in a heavy iron casserole. Brown the pork on both sides over medium heat for 20 minutes. At the same time, cook the onions in another pan with the remaining butter until lightly colored. Add them to the pork with the potato and the bouquet garni.

Bring the milk to a boil and pour it over the pork. Cover the casserole and bake in a preheated 325° F. [160° C.] oven for one and a quarter hours, turning the meat occasionally.

Remove the meat and keep it warm in an ovenproof dish. Remove the bouquet garni and put the onions, potatoes and cooking liquid through a food mill to obtain a light, puréed sauce. Skim the excess fat from the surface and adjust the seasoning, which should include quite a lot of pepper. Pour the sauce over the meat and allow it to simmer for a few moments. Sprinkle the meat with the parsley and serve it in the cooking dish, accompanied by cabbage with salt pork.

JEAN & PIERRE TROISGROS
THE NOUVELLE CUISINE OF JEAN & PIERRE TROISGROS

Pork Roast with Beer

Arrosto di Maiale alla Birra

To serve 6 to 8

3 lb.	pork center-loin roast	1½ kg.
3 tbsp.	butter	45 ml.
4	medium-sized onions, thinly sliced	4
1 tsp.	salt	5 ml.
½ tsp.	white pepper	2 ml.
1	garlic clove, crushed	1
3	bay leaves	3
2 cups	beer	½ liter
1 tbsp.	flour	15 ml.

Melt the butter in a Dutch oven or heavy casserole; add the onions and cook over low heat until the onions are soft and yellow. Add the pork and brown it on all sides. Sprinkle with salt and pepper; add the garlic, bay leaves and beer. Cover and simmer for two and a half hours. Slice the pork, transfer to a warmed platter and keep it warm.

Remove the bay leaves from the pan juices and skim off the fat. Add the flour to the onions and pan juices; stir and cook until thickened. Pour over the pork and serve.

TERESA GILARDI CANDLER
THE NORTHERN ITALIAN COOKBOOK

Braised Loin of Pork

Carré et Filet de Porc Frais

To serve 6 to 8

3 lb.	pork loin roast	1½ kg.
2	carrots	2
1	onion, stuck with 2 whole cloves	1
1	garlic bulb	1
2	leeks, white parts only	2
1	celery rib	1
	salt	
2 to 3 tbsp.	lard	30 to 45 ml.
	sauce Robert or piquant sauce (recipes, page 166)	

Do not bone the loin, but have the chine bone sawn through at 1½-inch [3-cm.] intervals to make the loin easier to carve. Place the loin in a stockpot or heavy casserole with the car-

rots, onion, leeks and celery. Cover with water to about 1½ inches [3 cm.] above the level of the meat.

Add about 1 teaspoon [5 ml.] of salt to every 1 quart [1 liter] of water. Bring to a boil and skim. Reduce the heat, using a heat-diffusing pad if necessary, to poach the pork very slowly at about 160° F. [80° C.]—a gentle simmer—without further boiling. Cook for 13 to 15 minutes per pound [25 to 30 minutes per kg.].

When the pork is cooked, drain it. Heat the lard in a roasting pan. Place the loin in the pan, baste it with the hot lard and put the loin in a preheated 450° to 475° F. [230° to 240° C.] oven to brown it quickly. Serve with a *sauce Robert* or a piquant sauce.

PAUL BOCUSE
PAUL BOCUSE'S FRENCH COOKING

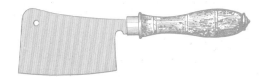

Pork Loin with Sherry

Solomillo de Cerdo al Jerez

For instructions on larding pork roast, see the demonstration on pages 58-59. The technique of boning a pork loin is demonstrated on pages 12-13.

To serve 6

3 to 4 lb.	pork loin roast, boned, with the bones reserved and chopped with a cleaver into 3 or 4 pieces	1½ to 2 kg.
⅔ cup	dry sherry	150 ml.
2 oz.	raw cured ham such as prosciutto, cut into thin larding strips	75 g.
4 to 5 oz.	fresh pork rind in 1 piece	125 to 150 g.
3 tbsp.	stock (recipe, page 165)	45 ml.
	salt and pepper	
12	boiling onions, peeled	12

Using a larding needle, lard the interior of the pork with the strips of ham. Roll and tie the roast with string, so that it is enclosed in its own layer of fat. Put any trimmings from the pork in the bottom of a roasting pan, and place the pork on top. Surround with the bones. Pour the sherry and stock over the pork, season and roast in a preheated 375° F. [190° C.] oven, basting occasionally, for one hour. Put the onions around the pork halfway through the cooking time. Toward the end of the cooking time, increase the oven heat to 400° F. [200° C.] if necessary to brown the onions.

To serve, cut off the string, carve the pork and arrange it on a serving dish surrounded by the onions. Serve pan-fried potatoes separately.

MANUAL DE COCINA

Braised Pork with Chestnuts

Porc Braisé aux Marrons

When buying chestnuts, avoid those with the little holes that indicate worms. With the point of a sharp paring knife, slit each chestnut on both sides. The incisions help the skin release during cooking. Put the chestnuts on a baking sheet (they should not overlap) and place in a preheated 400° F. [200° C.] oven for 30 minutes. Remove from the oven and, using a towel to avoid burning your hands, peel the chestnuts. Both inner skins and outer shells should come off. Discard any bad chestnuts; you may lose up to a third.

To serve 8

6 lb.	pork picnic or Boston shoulder roast, boned and tied	3 kg.
5½ to 6½ cups	water	1375 to 1625 ml.
1½ lb.	fresh chestnuts, peeled	¾ kg.
1 tsp.	salt	5 ml.
½ tsp.	freshly ground pepper	2 ml.
2	onions, coarsely sliced	2
3	rutabagas (about 3½ lb. [1¾ kg.]), cut into 2-inch [5-cm.] chunks	3

Sprinkle the meat with the salt and pepper. Place it in a large heavy kettle, fat side down. Add ½ cup [125 ml.] of water and place over medium heat. Cover and cook for 15 minutes. Uncover the meat and continue cooking until all of the liquid has evaporated and the meat starts to brown. Turn the meat to brown it on all sides. (This takes about 12 minutes.) Add the onions, 5 cups [1¼ liters] of water, cover and cook over medium heat for one hour. Add the chestnuts and cook covered for another hour.

Meanwhile, shape the pieces of rutabaga with a small knife so that they are equal in size and will cook uniformly. You will have about 2½ pounds [1 kg.] left. Add to the pork another cup [¼ liter] of water and cook for another 45 minutes, covered. Taste the cooking liquid for seasoning. It probably will need salt and pepper. By this time there should not be much liquid left.

Remove the roast to a warmed serving platter. Using a slotted spoon, scoop out the chestnuts and rutabagas and place them around the meat. Tip the kettle to one side so that all of the liquid accumulates in one corner, then skim off as much fat as you can. If you have less than 1 cup [¼ liter] of liquid left, add 1 cup [¼ liter] of water to the kettle and boil over high heat for one or two minutes to melt the solidified juices and to blend the sauce. Pour the sauce over the meat or into a sauceboat and serve immediately.

JACQUES PÉPIN
A FRENCH CHEF COOKS AT HOME

Stuffed, Braised Pork Shoulder

For instructions on braising a Boston shoulder roast, see the demonstration on pages 62-63. The technique of boning a Boston shoulder roast is demonstrated on pages 12-13. If you have meat trimmings left over from boning the roast, they may be chopped and added to the stuffing.

To serve 8

4 lb.	pork Boston shoulder roast, boned	2 kg.
2 tbsp.	olive oil	30 ml.
about 2 cups	boiling stock (recipe, page 165)	about ½ liter
White wine marinade		
1 cup	dry white wine	¼ liter
2 tbsp.	olive oil	30 ml.
1	sprig rosemary	1
2	bay leaves	2
1 tsp.	mixed dried herbs	5 ml.
2	garlic cloves, lightly crushed	2
6	juniper berries, lightly bruised	6
Herb-flavored stuffing		
2 tbsp.	chopped parsley	30 ml.
1 tsp.	mixed dried herbs	5 ml.
2	garlic cloves	2
	salt and pepper	
1	egg	1
¼ cup	bread crumbs	50 ml.
	meat trimmings (optional)	

Combine all of the marinade ingredients and put in the meat. Let it marinate at room temperature for several hours, turning it occasionally. Remove the meat from the marinade and pat it dry with paper towels. Reserve the marinade.

For the stuffing, pound the garlic to a purée with some salt and pepper. Combine with the remaining stuffing ingredients until the mixture has the consistency of a paste. Smear the stuffing onto the top surface of the meat with your hands. Tie up the meat to enclose the stuffing, sewing all of the ends together with kitchen string and tying the resulting package into a roughly spherical shape. Rub the meat with olive oil.

Place the meat in a roasting pan and sear it in a preheated 425° F. [220° C.] oven for 30 to 45 minutes or until the surface is golden brown. Remove the meat to a pot just large enough to contain it. Drain off the fat from the roasting pan, then strain the marinade into the pan and heat, stirring, to deglaze the pan juices.

Pour the marinade over the meat and add enough boiling stock to come one half or two thirds of the way up the meat. Cover the pot and place it in a 325° F. [170° C.] oven for about one and a half hours, basting the meat occasionally. During the last half hour remove the lid, increase the heat to 375° F. [190° C.] and baste often to form a glaze.

Transfer the meat to a warmed platter. Strain the liquid from the pot into a small saucepan and simmer, skimming, until the sauce is reduced and free of fat. Remove the strings from the meat, slice it or cut it into wedges, and serve with the sauce and, if desired, with a white vegetable purée combining potatoes, celeriac, turnips, onions and garlic.

PETITS PROPOS CULINAIRES

Pork Stew with Eggplant

Daube de Porc aux Bélangères

To serve 6

3 lb.	boneless lean pork roast, in 1 piece	1½ kg.
4	medium-sized eggplants (about 3 lb. [1½ kg.]), peeled and cut into 1-inch [2½-cm.] cubes	4
3 tbsp.	flour	45 ml.
2 tbsp.	peanut oil	30 ml.
2 tbsp.	lard	30 ml.
½ tsp.	thyme	2 ml.
¼ tsp.	sage	1 ml.
6	*melegueta* peppercorns or allspice berries, wrapped in a cheesecloth bag	6
	salt and pepper	
1 cup	water	¼ liter

Dredge the pork with the flour. Heat the oil and lard in a heavy, covered casserole and sauté the pork until it is golden all over. Add the thyme, sage, wrapped *melegueta* peppercorns or allspice, a little salt and freshly ground pepper, and the water. Cover and cook over low heat until the pork is almost tender, about two hours. Degrease the cooking liquid and discard the cheesecloth bag. Add the eggplants, cover and cook for 15 minutes, or until the eggplants are done.

ELISABETH LAMBERT ORTIZ
THE COMPLETE BOOK OF CARIBBEAN COOKERY

Fillet of Pork with Almonds

Lomo de Cerdo Almendrado

To roast the almonds called for in this recipe, place blanched almonds on a baking sheet in a 400° F. [200° C.] oven for 10 minutes or until lightly browned.

Almonds are one of Majorca's major products and they are probably the finest grown anywhere. They are carefully harvested and stripped of their green covering by hand and so are expensive even on their native island. They are used in many dishes and this one is especially nice. There is a similar recipe from Aragon, using red wine and water and no cream—this is equally good, and is usually served with potatoes and a salad of lettuce and raw onions.

To serve 4 to 6

2 to 2½ lb.	pork tenderloin roast, cut into two long pieces	1 kg.
	salt and pepper	
1 cup	crushed roasted almonds	¼ liter
½ cup	flour	125 ml.
4 tbsp.	lard	60 ml.
½ cup	dry sherry	125 ml.
2 tbsp.	chopped scallions or shallots	30 ml.
1 cup	stock *(recipe, page 165)*	¼ liter
3 tbsp.	heavy cream	45 ml.

Make two longitudinal incisions in each half of the tenderloin without cutting right through the meat. Sprinkle with salt and press a layer of crushed almonds into each incision. Tie the halves together again neatly and roll them in seasoned flour. Heat the lard in a large heavy pan and carefully brown the meat all over. Reduce the heat, add the sherry and allow to bubble, then add the onions or shallots and cook gently for a few minutes. Pour in the stock and cover the pan. Cook gently for an hour, turning the meat once and making sure it does not stick. Degrease, and stir in the cream. Serve the tenderloin in slices with the juices poured over it. Garnish with triangles of fried bread. Creamed potatoes are a good foil for the crunchy texture of the almonds.

ANNA MACMIADHACHÁIN
SPANISH REGIONAL COOKERY

Stuffed Pork Tenderloin

To serve 4 to 6

2	pork tenderloins, each slit twice lengthwise so that it opens out like a book	2
2	large slices cooked ham, cut into strips ½ inch [1 cm.] wide	2
3 oz.	Lancashire or white Cheddar cheese, cut into strips ½ inch [1 cm.] wide	100 g.
8	sage leaves, halved and blanched in boiling water for 1 minute, or 1 tsp. [5 ml.] chopped thyme	8
2	large onions, chopped	2
½ to ¾ cup	brown sherry, Madeira or port	125 to 175 ml.
4	thick slices bacon	4

Put a line of both ham and cheese strips into each slit in the pork tenderloins (some cheese will be left over). Put the sage leaves (or sprinkle the thyme) along the slits with the ham and the cheese. Tie each tenderloin at 1½-inch [4-cm.] intervals. Put the onion all over the base of a long narrow dish. Pour in the wine. Lay the tenderloins on top with the slices of bacon over them to keep the tenderloins basted with fat. Put into an oven preheated to 375° F. [190° C.] and leave for 40 minutes. Chop and sprinkle the remaining cheese over them and put them back for five minutes. Untie before serving. At table, carve the tenderloins across diagonally to produce the broadest possible slices.

JANE GRIGSON
ENGLISH FOOD

Piquant Pork Chops

To serve 4

4	pork loin chops, cut 1 inch [2½ cm.] thick	4
3 tbsp.	butter	45 ml.
1 tbsp.	finely chopped fresh parsley	15 ml.
2 tsp.	finely chopped capers	10 ml.
1	anchovy fillet	1
½ cup	dry white wine	125 ml.
½ cup	crushed, drained canned tomatoes	125 ml.
½ tsp.	basil	2 ml.

Melt 1 tablespoon [15 ml.] of butter in a skillet that will snugly hold the four chops. When the butter is hot, quickly brown the chops on both sides and sprinkle them with pepper. Remove the chops from the skillet, pour out the fat, rinse the skillet and wipe it clean.

Add the remaining 2 tablespoons [30 ml.] of butter to the skillet and melt it. Add the anchovy fillet and stir for a minute or so, until it has melted. Stir in the wine, tomatoes, parsley, capers and basil.

Return the chops to the skillet, cover, and reduce the heat. Simmer the meat and sauce for 30 minutes, turning the chops two or three times. Place the chops on a serving dish and spoon the sauce liberally over each chop.

CAROL CUTLER
THE SIX-MINUTE SOUFFLÉ AND OTHER CULINARY DELIGHTS

Stuffed Pork Chops

For the technique of preparing pork chops for stuffing, see the demonstration on pages 66-67.

A double pork loin chop is two rib bones thick, about 1 to 1½ inches [2½ to 4 cm.].

To serve 4

4	double pork loin chops with a pocket cut in each one	4
Mushroom stuffing		
1 cup	finely chopped fresh mushrooms	¼ liter
1	onion, finely chopped	1
3 tbsp.	butter	45 ml.
½ tsp.	thyme	2 ml.
2 tbsp.	chopped fresh parsley	30 ml.
½ cup	fine bread crumbs, toasted	125 ml.
	salt and pepper	
1	egg, lightly beaten	1

To make the stuffing, sauté the onion in the butter until transparent, about 10 minutes. Add the mushrooms, thyme, parsley and bread crumbs. Mix thoroughly and remove from the heat. Season to taste with salt and pepper, and stir in the egg. Stuff the pockets in the chops, and secure with small skewers or toothpicks.

Sear the chops very quickly in a lightly oiled skillet, over high heat. Turn the chops carefully so that you do not disturb the stuffing and the skewers. When the chops are nicely browned, cover the pan and cook over very low heat for an hour or until the chops are tender. Or you may place the chops in a baking dish and roast them in a preheated 325° F. [160° C.] oven for one hour or until tender and nicely browned. Serve with a green vegetable or a salad.

JAMES A. BEARD
THE FIRESIDE COOK BOOK

Pork Chops with Sausages

Cotolette di Maiale alla Monzese

To serve 4

4	pork chops	4
4	small fresh pork sausages, pierced on all sides with a fork	4
1 tbsp.	flour	15 ml.
2 tbsp.	butter	30 ml.
1	sprig fresh sage	1
1	large ripe tomato, peeled, seeded and chopped	1
	salt	

Coat the pork chops lightly with the flour and fry them in the butter until browned on both sides, adding the sage to the frying pan. Scatter the tomato on top of the chops, season with a little salt, cover the pan and reduce the heat. Cook slowly for about 45 minutes. After 30 minutes, add the sausages. When the sausages and chops are done, serve each chop with a sausage and some of the cooking juices.

OTTORINA PERNA BOZZI
VECCHIA BRIANZA IN CUCINA

Pork Chops with Hominy

To serve 4

4	lean pork chops, cut about ¾ inch [2 cm.] thick	4
	flour	
1 tsp.	salt	5 ml.
1	medium-sized onion, sliced	1
1	garlic clove, crushed	1
2 cups	drained, canned hominy	½ liter
⅛ tsp.	pepper	½ ml.

Trim the fat off the edges of the chops and render the fat in a large heavy skillet. Coat the chops with the flour and brown them slowly in the hot fat. Turn the chops, sprinkle them with ½ teaspoon [2 ml.] of the salt, and brown them on the other side slowly. Pour off the excess drippings and remove bits of fat. Push the chops to the edge of the skillet and add the onion and garlic. Cook until the onion is tender but not browned. Add the hominy, mix it well with the pan drippings, and arrange the chops over the hominy. Heat for three or four minutes. Sprinkle the chops with the pepper and the remaining salt.

JEANNE A. VOLTZ
THE FLAVOR OF THE SOUTH

Pork Chops with Ham and Pickles

Sertésborda Hentes Módra

To serve 6

6	pork loin chops, cut about ¾ inch [2 cm.] thick	6
	salt and freshly ground black pepper	
¾ cup	flour	175 ml.
3 tbsp.	lard	45 ml.
1 cup	finely chopped onions	¼ liter
1	small garlic clove, finely chopped	1
1 tbsp.	sweet Hungarian paprika	15 ml.
1 cup	chicken stock (recipe, page 165)	¼ liter
¼ cup	puréed tomato	50 ml.
1 cup	sour cream	¼ liter
6 oz.	thinly sliced boiled ham, cut into fine julienne	200 g.
6 oz.	sour gherkins, cut into fine julienne	200 g.

Sprinkle the pork chops generously with salt and a few grindings of pepper, then dip them in flour and shake off the excess. Heat the lard over high heat in a heavy skillet, then add the chops two or three at a time. Cook them for about four minutes on each side, or until they are lightly browned.

Remove the chops to a dish and pour off from the skillet all but a thin film of the fat. Reduce the heat; add the onions and the garlic to the fat and, stirring occasionally, cook them for eight to 10 minutes, or until the onions are lightly colored. Off the heat, stir in the paprika, continuing to stir until the onions are well coated.

Return the pan to high heat and pour in the stock and tomato purée. Stir, bring the liquid to a boil, add the chops, and reduce the heat to its lowest point. Cover the pan tightly and simmer for about 40 minutes, or until the chops show no resistance when pierced with the tip of a small, sharp knife. Turn the chops once while they are simmering.

Arrange the chops on a warmed platter and keep them warm while you make the sauce. With a wire whisk, beat 1 teaspoon [5 ml.] of flour into the sour cream in a mixing bowl, then whisk the mixture into the skillet. Stirring constantly, cook over low heat for two or three minutes, or until the sauce is thick and smooth. Add the ham and gherkin julienne and simmer for one to two minutes, until they are heated. Taste for seasoning. Pour some of the sauce over the chops and serve the rest separately.

FOODS OF THE WORLD
THE COOKING OF VIENNA'S EMPIRE

Pork-Chop Sweet-Potato Casserole

To serve 2

2	thick pork loin chops, trimmed of excess fat	2
4	small sweet potatoes, cut into ¼-inch [6-mm.] slices	4
1 tbsp.	butter	15 ml.
¾ tbsp.	salt	10 ml.
	coarsely ground black pepper	
1	large cooking apple, peeled, quartered, cored and sliced	1
2	medium-sized onions, sliced	2
1 tbsp.	light brown sugar	15 ml.
1	lemon, the peel grated and the juice strained	1
1 tbsp.	hot water	15 ml.

Preheat the oven to 350° F. [180° C.]. Butter a 1-quart [1-liter] baking dish and put in the sweet potatoes. Dot with butter and sprinkle with the salt and a dash of pepper. Make a layer of the apple and onion slices on top. Combine the brown sugar with the lemon juice and peel, and spread the mixture over the apples and onions. Add the hot water and then the pork chops. Cover the dish and bake until the chops are very tender, or for about one and a half hours. Remove the cover for the last 30 minutes to brown the chops.

JUNE PLATT
JUNE PLATT'S NEW ENGLAND COOK BOOK

Pork and Apple Stew

To serve 6

6	pork blade steaks or blade chops, trimmed of excess fat, the fat cut into thin strips	6
4	medium-sized cooking apples, peeled, cored and sliced	4
3	onions, thinly sliced	3
1½ tbsp.	brown sugar	22 ml.
	salt and freshly ground pepper	
1 tbsp.	water	15 ml.

In a wide casserole put a layer of half of the onions, then half of the apples, then half of the brown sugar. Put the chops on

top and season with a little salt and a generous grinding of black pepper. Add the water and cover with the remaining onions, then the rest of the apples. Toss the strips of pork fat in the remaining brown sugar. Lay them, crisscross, on top of the apples and throw the remaining sugar over all. Season again with salt and black pepper.

Cover the casserole and cook in a preheated 350° F. [180° C.] oven for one hour. Reduce the heat to 250° F. [120° C.] and cook for one hour more. This stew is just as good if you cook it at 250° F. for three hours.

MONICA SHERIDAN
MY IRISH COOK BOOK

Pork Chops with Creamed Cabbage

Côtes de Porc Pilleverjus

To serve 4

4	pork loin chops, trimmed and pounded lightly to flatten	4
1	small, young cabbage (about 2 lb. [1 kg.]), outer leaves removed, halved, cored and cut into julienne	1
	salt and pepper	
2 tbsp.	lard	30 ml.
⅓ cup	finely sliced onion, parboiled and drained	75 ml.
1	bouquet garni	1
2 tbsp.	butter or lard	30 ml.
½ cup	heavy cream	125 ml.
	small potatoes, boiled	
1 tbsp.	vinegar	15 ml.
⅓ cup	stock *(recipe, page 165)*	75 ml.

Season the chops with salt and pepper. Fry in the lard until both sides are well browned, about five minutes on each side. Add the onion to the pan, add a bouquet garni, cover the pan and cook over low heat for 35 minutes.

Meanwhile, in a covered saucepan, cook the shredded cabbage, lightly salted, in the butter or lard as slowly as possible. As soon as the cabbage is done, after about 30 minutes, moisten it with the cream and simmer for a few moments, stirring all the time.

Arrange the chops on a foundation of the cabbage. Garnish with the boiled potatoes. Dilute the frying-pan juices with the vinegar and stock, bring to a boil, and pour this sauce over the chops.

PROSPER MONTAGNÉ
THE NEW LAROUSSE GASTRONOMIQUE

Pork Cutlets in White Wine

Bracioline di Maiale al Vino Bianco

Allow one or two cutlets per person. If you are using pork loin chops, which also can be prepared in this manner, allow one chop per person.

	To serve 3 to 6	
6	pork cutlets, flattened lightly with a wooden mallet	6
1	garlic clove, finely chopped	1
1	sprig rosemary, finely chopped	1
	salt	
	cayenne pepper	
3 tbsp.	olive oil	45 ml.
½ cup	dry white wine	125 ml.
⅔ cup	hot beef stock *(recipe, page 165)* or water	150 ml.

Trim off all of the fat from the cutlets, cut the fat into small pieces and pound these to a paste with the garlic, the rosemary, a little salt and a pinch of cayenne pepper. Spread this paste on both sides of each cutlet. Heat the oil in a skillet large enough to hold all of the cutlets, and fry them first on one side until brown, then turn and brown them on the other side. Pour the wine into the pan and cook, uncovered, until it is reduced by about half to a syrupy glaze. Add the stock or water to the pan, cover and cook gently until the liquid is completely absorbed. Serve immediately.

ADA BONI
ITALIAN REGIONAL COOKING

Pork Scallops Cooked in the Oven

Schweineschnitzel aus dem Backofen

	To serve 4	
4	pork scallops (about 6 oz. [200 g.] each), pounded flat	4
2 tbsp.	lard	30 ml.
2	medium-sized potatoes, thinly sliced	2
1	large onion, thinly sliced	1
	salt and pepper	
½ tsp.	caraway seeds	2 ml.
1 cup	sour cream	¼ liter

Fry the scallops briefly in the lard, over high heat, until lightly browned on both sides. Mix the potato and onion slices together and put a layer of them in a buttered baking dish. Season with salt, pepper and caraway seeds. Put the scallops on top of the potato and onion layer. Cover with the remaining potatoes and onions, season again, and pour on the sour cream.

Cover the dish tightly with its lid or foil and put into a preheated 350° F. [180° C.] oven. Bake for 40 minutes, without uncovering the dish. Serve with a lettuce salad.

HANS KARL ADAM
DAS KOCHBUCH AUS SCHWABEN

Pork Cutlets à la Mirepoix

The French half of this fractured-English recipe title describes the finely chopped herbs and shallots that are used to flavor the cutlets.

Be sure you send a little newly made mustard to the table with this dish. Applesauce or tomato sauce add considerably to the zest.

	To serve 6	
12	pork cutlets, fat removed and reserved	12
	salt	
	cayenne pepper	
5	slices bacon	5
¼ cup	finely chopped fresh parsley	50 ml.
2	shallots, finely chopped	2
12	fresh sage leaves, finely chopped	12
1 tbsp.	veal stock *(recipe, page 165)* or water	15 ml.
3 tbsp.	strained fresh lemon juice	45 ml.
1 tbsp.	chili-flavored vinegar (or substitute a few drops Tabasco sauce)	15 ml.

Strew a few grains of salt and cayenne pepper over the pork cutlets. Mince the reserved fat with the bacon and put this in a stewpan, with the parsley, shallots and sage leaves; on these lay the cutlets, place them over a slow heat, well covered, for 15 minutes; then turn them and cook, covered, for another 15 minutes. Take the cutlets out and keep them warm whilst you mix the stock with the pan seasonings. Strain the juices, pressing the vegetables firmly, and skim the strained sauce quite free from fat; when this is done add the lemon juice and chili vinegar; warm up the sauce, and pour it quite hot over the cutlets.

MRS. RUNDELL
MODERN DOMESTIC COOKERY

Pork Scallops, Polish-Style

Suropieki

	To serve 4	
8	pork scallops (about 1¼ lb. [⅔ kg.]), pounded flat	8
	salt	
½ cup	flour	125 ml.
4 tbsp.	lard	60 ml.
1 tbsp.	chopped fresh parsley	15 ml.
Beer sauce		
2 cups	beer	½ liter
4 tbsp.	lard	60 ml.
1	Hamburg parsley root, julienned or coarsely grated	1
1	onion, thinly sliced	1
1	beet, julienned or coarsely grated	1
1	carrot, julienned or coarsely grated	1
1	rib celery, thinly sliced	1
¾ cup	sliced fresh mushrooms	175 ml.
¼ cup	puréed tomato	50 ml.
½ cup	sour cream	125 ml.
2 tbsp.	raisins, soaked in warm water for 10 minutes and drained	30 ml.
½ cup	pitted prunes, soaked in warm water for 10 minutes and drained	125 ml.
1	bouquet of thyme, lovage, dried chili and juniper berries (optional), tied in cheesecloth	1
3 tbsp.	strained fresh lemon juice	45 ml.
	salt and pepper	
1	apple, peeled, cored and chopped	1
Fried bread		
4	large slices homemade-style white bread	4
½ cup	milk	125 ml.
1	egg, lightly beaten	1
3 tbsp.	butter	45 ml.

Dust the pork scallops with salt and flour, heat the lard in a skillet over high heat and fry the scallops until they are brown on both sides. Drain the slices on paper towels.

To make the sauce, heat the lard and add the vegetables. Cook over medium heat until the vegetables are soft, then add the beer, the puréed tomato mixed with the sour cream, and the raisins. Reserve some of the prunes for garnish, and add the rest to the sauce with the herb bouquet, lemon juice, and a little salt and pepper. Stir in the fried pork scallops, and stew over low heat until the meat is very tender, about 30 minutes. About 10 minutes before the end of the cooking time, add the apple pieces.

To make the fried-bread garnish, dip the bread slices in the milk and then in the egg. Heat the butter and fry the slices until they are golden.

To serve, arrange the pork on the fried-bread slices. Discard the bouquet of seasonings and pour the sauce over the scallops. Sprinkle the scallops with chopped parsley and garnish them with the reserved prunes.

B. SNAGLEWSKA AND I. ZAHORSKA
POTRAWY STAROPOLSKIE I REGIONALNE

Stuffed Pork Slices

Polpette

The mortadella called for is a mild-flavored Italian bologna studded with pieces of fat.

	To serve 6	
1 lb.	boneless lean pork, cut into 6 thin slices and pounded flat	½ kg.
1 tbsp.	lard or oil	15 ml.
Sausage forcemeat		
½ lb.	pork sausage meat	¼ kg.
¼ cup	chopped mortadella	50 ml.
2	slices prosciutto, chopped	2
1	egg, beaten	1
2 tbsp.	freshly grated Parmesan cheese	30 ml.
2 tbsp.	chopped fresh parsley	30 ml.
½ tsp.	finely chopped garlic	2 ml.
	salt and pepper	

Mix the forcemeat ingredients thoroughly, seasoning them lightly with salt and pepper, and spread the mixture on the pork slices. Roll up the slices and place them close together in a pan greased with the lard or oil, placing the rolls flap sides down so that they do not unroll.

Cook over high heat for 10 minutes, turning the rolls to brown them on all sides after they have sealed. Season the rolls with salt and pepper, cover the pan, reduce the heat, and cook the rolls gently for one hour.

OTTORINA PERNA BOZZI
VECCHIA BRIANZA IN CUCINA

Pork and Potato Casserole

Hökarepanna

To serve 4 to 6

¾ lb.	boneless pork loin, cut into slices ¼ inch [½ cm.] thick	⅓ kg.
2 tbsp.	butter	30 ml.
2 tbsp.	vegetable oil	30 ml.
3	medium-sized onions, thinly sliced	3
4	lamb kidneys, or 1 veal or 2 pork kidneys	4
1½ cups	beer	375 ml.
1½ cups	stock *(recipe, page 165)*	375 ml.
½ tsp.	sugar	2 ml.
6	medium-sized potatoes (about 2 lb. [1 kg.]), thinly sliced and set aside in a bowl of cold water to prevent discoloration	6
	salt and freshly ground pepper	
1	bay leaf	1

Preheat the oven to 350° F. [180° C.]. Heat the butter and the oil in a heavy 10- to 12-inch [25- to 30-cm.] skillet over medium heat, add the onions and cook them until they are soft and lightly browned. Remove them to a dish. Add more butter and oil to the skillet if necessary, and in it brown the kidneys and the pork slices quickly, turning them several times to brown them evenly.

Remove the meats from the skillet and slice the kidneys ¼ inch [½ cm.] thick. Deglaze the pan by adding the beer, stock and sugar and boiling them over high heat for two to three minutes, meanwhile scraping into the liquid any browned bits clinging to the bottom and the sides of the pan. Remove the pan from the heat and set aside.

Drain the potatoes. Arrange two or three layers of potatoes, meat and onions alternately in a heavy 3-quart [3-liter] casserole, finishing with a layer of potatoes. Season each layer with a little salt and pepper as you proceed, and place the bay leaf in the center of the top layer. Pour in the deglazing liquid; it should just cover the top layer in the casserole. Add more stock if it does not.

Bring the casserole to a boil over high heat and then bake, uncovered, in the center of the oven for about one hour and 40 minutes, or until the top layer of potatoes is brown and tender when pierced with a sharp knife. Serve directly from the casserole.

FOODS OF THE WORLD
THE COOKING OF SCANDINAVIA

Skewers of Meat, Calabrian-Style

Spiedini di Carne alla Calabrese

To serve 6

1 lb.	boneless fresh ham or pork loin	½ kg.
1 lb.	boneless veal rump	½ kg.
¼ cup	olive oil	50 ml.
	salt and pepper	
1 tbsp.	finely chopped fresh basil	15 ml.
1 tsp.	crushed fresh oregano	5 ml.
½ tsp.	crushed dried hot chilies	2 ml.
½ cup	water	125 ml.

Cut the meat into small thin slices. Thread the slices onto six skewers, alternating pork and veal. Pour the oil into a small roasting pan, and brown the skewered meat in the oil over high heat. Sprinkle all of the seasonings over the skewers, add the water to the pan, cover and cook for 45 minutes in a preheated 325° F. [170° C.] oven.

WILMA REIVA LASASSO
REGIONAL ITALIAN COOKING

Black Loin of Pork

Lomo Negro

To serve 8

2 lb.	boned pork loin, cut into 12 to 16 thin steaks	1 kg.
¼ cup	strained fresh lemon juice	50 ml.
¼ cup	water	50 ml.
2 tbsp.	lard	30 ml.
½ cup	vinegar	125 ml.
	salt and pepper	

Sprinkle the pork steaks with the lemon juice and water and let stand for 30 minutes. Pat them dry with paper towels.

Melt the lard in a skillet over medium heat and fry the steaks in it to a golden brown on each side. Sprinkle with salt and pepper. Add the vinegar. Cover the skillet and simmer over low heat for about 30 minutes or until the steaks are tender and a deep rich brown.

CORA, ROSE AND BOB BROWN
THE SOUTH AMERICAN COOK BOOK

Pork with Rice, Onions, and Tomatoes

This recipe may be prepared hours in advance, or the day before, stopping at the point before you add the cheese. It can be taken from its retirement and steam-heated for at least half an hour so the heat fully penetrates and then the cheese is folded in. Crisp French bread is all you need on the side.

	To serve 6 to 8	
3 lb.	boneless lean pork, cut into cubes	1½ kg.
4 oz.	lean salt pork with the rind removed, cut into lardons 1½ inches [4 cm.] long	125 g.
2 tbsp.	olive oil	30 ml.
2	small onions, sliced	2
1 cup	raw unprocessed rice	¼ liter
1 cup	beer	¼ liter
about 2 cups	chicken stock (recipe, page 165)	about ½ liter
	salt and pepper	
4	garlic cloves, mashed	4
½ tsp.	thyme	2 ml.
¼ tsp.	ground saffron or turmeric	1 ml.
1	bay leaf, crumbled	1
4	small tomatoes (about 1 lb. [½ kg.]), peeled and chopped	4
1 cup	freshly grated Parmesan cheese	¼ liter

Blanch the salt-pork lardons in boiling water for 10 minutes. Drain, dry and brown them lightly with the olive oil in a skillet over medium heat. Drain the lardons and place them in a 3-quart [3-liter] enameled iron casserole.

Make sure that the cubes of pork are as dry as possible. Increase the heat and brown the pork cubes, a few pieces at a time, in the fat remaining in the skillet. Place the cubes in the casserole as they brown, taking them from the skillet with a slotted spoon so that you do not transfer too much oil to the casserole. Reduce the heat under the skillet and brown the onions lightly. Then put these in the casserole.

Keeping the skillet over medium heat, use a wooden spoon to stir your rice into the oil until the rice turns a milky color. Remove the rice and place this in a separate bowl. Remove as much fat as possible from the skillet, then add the beer and stir with the wooden spoon over high heat, scraping and scouring coagulated fragments from the bottom and sides of the pan. When all has been cleaned and the frothing has subsided, pour this into the casserole.

Add the stock to the casserole so that the meat is covered; salt and pepper to taste. Add the garlic and the herbs. Bring to the simmering point, cover tightly and place the casserole in the lower part of a preheated 325° F. [170° C.] oven. Simmer slowly for one hour.

Remove the casserole from the oven and stir in the toma-toes. Again on top of the stove, bring to the simmering point. Then place it in the oven for one and a half to two hours, after reducing the oven temperature to 250° F. [130° C.]. At the end of this time the meat should be completely tender. Take the casserole from the oven and place it to one side.

Increase the oven temperature to 375° F. [190° C.]. What little fat there is should have risen to the top, so tilt the casserole and skim off this fat. You should have about 2 to 2½ cups [½ liter to 625 ml.] of liquid. Stir in the rice (adding more stock if the pork mixture looks a bit dry). Bring the casserole to the simmering point on top of the stove, cover and pop it back into the oven. The casserole needs to be kept at full simmer for 20 minutes so that the rice cooks. At no time during this period must you stir or disturb it.

Remove the casserole from the oven and check your seasoning, adjusting to taste. Just before serving, delicately fold in the cheese so that it permeates the dish.

BILL RICE
FAR FLUNG FOOD

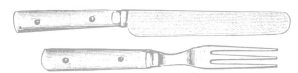

Italian Pork Stew
Spezzatino di Maiale

	To serve 6	
2 to 2½ lb.	lean pork, cubed	1 kg.
¼ cup	olive oil	50 ml.
2	garlic cloves	2
1 tbsp.	fresh sage leaves	15 ml.
	salt and pepper	
	grated nutmeg	
1 cup	dry red wine	¼ liter
1 cup	puréed tomato or tomato sauce, diluted with a little stock	¼ liter
1 lb.	dried red kidney or white beans, soaked in water overnight, parboiled for 10 minutes and simmered until tender (1½ to 2 hours)	½ kg.

Heat the oil in a heavy pan and brown the garlic and sage leaves. Add the pork and season it with salt, pepper and nutmeg. When the meat is well browned, add the wine, and cook over low heat until the wine has almost completely evaporated. Add the tomato, and let most of this liquid, too, evaporate gently—remembering, however, that at the end of cooking the meat must have plenty of sauce. Fifteen minutes before removing the meat from the heat, add the separately cooked beans.

MARIÙ SALVATORI DE ZULIANI
LA CUCINA DI VERSILIA E GARFAGNANA

Pork and Sauerkraut Layer

Rakottkáposzta d'Ormánság

To serve 6

2 lb.	boneless lean pork, cut into cubes	1 kg.
1	large onion, finely chopped	1
7 tbsp.	lard	105 ml.
2 tbsp.	Hungarian paprika	30 ml.
1¼ cups	water	300 ml.
2	green peppers, halved, seeded, deribbed and coarsely chopped	2
1	tomato, coarsely chopped	1
½ cup	flour	125 ml.
1¼ cups	heavy cream	300 ml.
2 lb.	sauerkraut (about 2 quarts [2 liters]), rinsed in cold water and drained	1 kg.
1 cup	rice, boiled and drained	¼ liter

Lightly brown the onion in the lard, then stir in the paprika and dilute the mixture with the water. Add the pork and scatter the pieces of green pepper and tomato over the top. Cover and simmer for about 45 minutes. Mix the flour with the cream and stir this mixture into the meat. Bring to a boil.

Spread half of the sauerkraut in a 4-quart [4-liter] casserole, cover it with half of the rice and top with the pork. Cover with the remaining rice and sauerkraut. Pour in the paprika-and-vegetable sauce, cover and cook in a preheated 350° F. [180° C.] oven for 35 to 45 minutes.

ROSE KORANYI
LIVRE DE LA BONNE CHÈRE

Pork Stew, Philippine-Style

Adobo

To serve 6

2 to 2½ lb.	boneless lean pork, cut into 1½- to 2-inch [4- to 5-cm.] cubes	1 kg.
½ cup	vinegar	125 ml.
1	bulb garlic, unpeeled but pounded to separate and lightly bruise the cloves	1
1 tsp.	pepper	5 ml.
	salt	
2 cups	water	½ liter
1 tbsp.	lard	15 ml.

Place the pork in a saucepan. Add the vinegar, garlic, pepper, salt to taste, and the water. Cover the saucepan, bring to a boil, and cook slowly for about two hours, or until the meat is tender. Strain the cooking broth into another saucepan and reduce it to about 4 or 5 tablespoons [60 to 75 ml.].

Separate the garlic from the pork, peel the cloves, and fry them gently in the lard until brown. Add the pork and fry the cubes until brown. Add the reduced broth and let the *adobo* simmer over low heat for about five minutes. Serve hot.

ENRIQUETA DAVID-PEREZ
RECIPES OF THE PHILIPPINES

Pork and Small-Turnip Pot

Sianlihaa Ja Pieniä Nauriita

To serve 4 to 6

2 to 2½ lb.	lean pork Boston shoulder, cut into 1-inch [2½-cm.] cubes	1 kg.
2 tbsp.	butter	30 ml.
10	tiny white turnips or 5 medium-sized turnips, peeled and quartered	10
2 tbsp.	unbleached white flour	30 ml.
1½ cups	stock *(recipe, page 165)*	375 ml.
½ tsp.	raw sugar or honey	2 ml.
½ tsp.	sea salt	2 ml.
¼ tsp.	white pepper	1 ml.
½ tsp.	thyme	2 ml.
1	sprig parsley	1

Preheat the oven to 350° F. [180° C.]. In a skillet, brown the pork cubes in half of the butter. Remove and place the cubes in a heavy, deep casserole or a pot with a lid. In the same skillet, brown the turnips in the rest of the butter. Sprinkle with flour, turn them, and allow the turnips to brown but not burn. Pour the stock over the turnips, a small amount at a time, stirring and letting the broth come to a simmer after each addition. Simmer until this sauce thickens. Add the sugar or honey, salt, pepper and a pinch of thyme. Stir.

Pour the turnip mixture over the pork in the pot. Mix and add the sprig of parsley. Cover, and put the pot in the oven for 20 minutes. Reduce the heat to 250° F. [120° C.] and cook until the turnips are soft, about one and a half to two hours. Do not let the turnips become overdone.

Serve with potatoes and/or bread to dip into the sauce, and some tart pickle or salad.

ULLA KÄKÖNEN
NATURAL COOKING THE FINNISH WAY

Pork and Chestnut Stew

Porc Limousine

To serve 6

2 to 2½ lb.	boneless lean pork, cubed	1 kg.
2 tbsp.	lard	30 ml.
1	garlic clove, crushed	1
1	onion, thinly sliced	1
2 tbsp.	flour	30 ml.
1 cup	dry white wine	¼ liter
	stock *(recipe, page 165)* or water	
	salt and pepper	
1 lb.	chestnuts, the flat ends slit crosswise, parboiled for 15 minutes, peeled and skinned	½ kg.

In a heavy pan, brown the pork in the lard. Add the garlic and onion, let them color lightly, sprinkle with the flour, stir until the flour is lightly browned and pour in the wine. Add enough stock or water to cover the meat, and season with salt and pepper. Cover and simmer for 45 minutes. Add the chestnuts and simmer for 45 minutes more, without stirring. Degrease before serving.

HUGUETTE COUFFIGNAL
LA CUISINE PAYSANNE

Skewered Pork and Vegetables

Kushisashi-Nabé

To serve 4

1 lb.	boneless lean pork, cut into 1½-inch [4-cm.] squares, ½ inch [1 cm.] thick	½ kg.
3	leeks, trimmed and cut into 1½-inch [4-cm.] lengths	3
4	green peppers, halved, seeded, deribbed and cut into 1½-inch [4-cm.] squares	4
¾ cup	flour	175 ml.
2 tbsp.	oil	30 ml.
2 cups	stock *(recipe, page 165)*	½ liter
1 tbsp.	red bean paste	15 ml.
¼ cup	*mirin* (rice wine)	50 ml.
¼ cup	soy sauce	50 ml.
2 tbsp.	sugar	30 ml.
	seven-flavors pepper	

Spear onto small metal skewers the leek, pork and pepper pieces in that order. Roll in the flour and sauté in the oil, over high heat, until brown on both sides, about seven to 10 minutes. Meanwhile, bring the stock to a boil in a wide, shallow pan. Stir in the red bean paste (diluted first with a little stock), *mirin*, soy sauce and sugar. Reduce the heat and add the skewers of sautéed pork and vegetables.

Cook for two to three minutes over medium heat, turn the skewers and cook their contents on the other side for one to two minutes. Remove the skewers, push off the pork and vegetables into bowls, and pour on the stock. Sprinkle with seven-flavors pepper.

MASARU DOI
JAPANESE ONE-POT COOKERY

Rice with Pork

Arroz con Carne de Cerdo

To serve 4 to 6

1 lb.	boneless lean pork, cut into 1-inch [2½-cm.] cubes	½ kg.
2 cups	raw unprocessed long-grain rice	½ liter
3	garlic cloves, crushed	3
1	medium-sized onion, finely chopped	1
1	fresh red or green hot chili, stemmed, seeded and chopped	1
1	bay leaf, crumbled	1
1 tbsp.	chopped fresh parsley, preferably flat-leafed parsley	15 ml.
2 tbsp.	distilled white vinegar	30 ml.
	salt	
1 oz.	boiled ham, coarsely chopped (about ¼ cup [60 ml.])	50 g.
2	slices bacon, coarsely chopped	2
4 tbsp.	lard	60 ml.
¼ cup	puréed tomato	50 ml.
1 tbsp.	capers, preferably Spanish type, rinsed and drained well	15 ml.
12	small pimiento-stuffed green olives, halved	12
1 quart	boiling water	1 liter

Mix together the pork, garlic, onion, chili, bay leaf, parsley, vinegar, salt, ham and bacon, and marinate at room temperature for about an hour.

In a heavy saucepan, heat the lard and fry the marinated mixture for two or three minutes. Add the puréed tomato, the rice, capers, olives and boiling water. Stir to mix, bring to a boil, cover and cook over very low heat until the rice is tender and has absorbed all of the liquid, about 20 minutes.

ELISABETH LAMBERT ORTIZ
THE COMPLETE BOOK OF CARIBBEAN COOKERY

Eggplant Stew with Pork

To serve 8

1 lb.	boneless pork, cut into ¾-inch [2-cm.] cubes	½ kg.
¼ lb.	smoked ham, cut into small pieces	125 g.
3	small eggplants (about 2 lb. [1 kg.]), cut into 1-inch [2½-cm.] cubes	3
2 tbsp.	lard	30 ml.
2	green peppers, halved, seeded, deribbed and cut into small pieces	2
2	onions, cut into small pieces	2
2	tomatoes, peeled, seeded and cut into small pieces	2
¼ cup	water	50 ml.
1 tbsp.	salt	15 ml.

Fry the pork cubes and ham lightly in the lard, add the peppers and onions and, a few minutes later, the tomatoes. Cook for about five minutes and stir in the water, eggplants and salt to taste. Cover and cook over low heat for about 45 minutes or until the pork is tender.

BERTA CABANILLAS AND CARMEN GINORIO
PUERTO RICAN DISHES

Pork with Winter Radish

Svinsko s Ryapa

The winter radish, with either a black or white skin, has white flesh and loses most of its sharpness in cooking. If these radishes are unavailable, turnips may be substituted.

To serve 5

1½ lb.	boneless pork, cubed	¾ kg.
1 lb.	winter radish, peeled and cut into chunks	½ kg.
	salt	
4 tbsp.	oil	60 ml.
1 tsp.	Hungarian paprika	5 ml.
10	small fresh sweet red peppers, cut into rings	10

Place the meat and radish chunks in a braising pan and season with salt. Add half of the oil and about ½ cup [125 ml.] of warm water. Simmer, covered, for about one hour or until the meat is tender, adding more water if necessary.

Heat the paprika in the remaining oil, without allowing it to fry. Add this mixture to the stew with the peppers, and simmer a little longer, until the peppers are soft. Let the stew rest for five minutes, then serve with hot garlic bread.

L. PETROV, N. DJELEPOV, N. IORDANOV AND S. UZUNOVA
BULGARSKA NAZIONALNA KUCHNIYA

Pork and Vegetable Stew

Ghiveciu

To serve 6 to 8

2 to 2½ lb.	boned pork Boston shoulder, cut into large cubes	1 kg.
2	onions, thinly sliced	2
4 tbsp.	lard	60 ml.
1	small cabbage, halved, cored and cut into pieces	1
1	large carrot, diced	1
1	Hamburg parsley root, diced	1
½	celeriac, diced	½
¼ lb.	okra, sliced	125 g.
1 cup	fresh white beans or ½ cup [125 ml.] dried navy or pea beans, soaked in water overnight, drained and parboiled for 10 minutes	¼ liter
1 cup	shelled fresh peas	¼ liter
1	small zucchini, diced	1
1	small eggplant, diced	1
2 or 3	potatoes, diced	2 or 3
1	small cauliflower, cut into small florets	1
2 or 3	large tomatoes, sliced	2 or 3
	salt and pepper	

Fry the onions in the lard for three to four minutes. Then add the pork cubes and brown them. Combine all of the remaining vegetables in a large bowl.

In a large earthenware dish, alternate layers of browned pork and onions with layers of the mixed vegetables. Season each layer with a little salt and pepper. Add a little water to the juices in the skillet. Heat, stirring, and pour these deglazed pan juices into the dish. Cover and bake for two hours in a preheated 350° F. [180° C.] oven, shaking the dish from time to time. Uncover for the last 20 minutes, so that the surface browns and the excess juices evaporate. Serve the stew from the cooking dish.

SANDA MARIN
CARTE DE BUCATE

Baked Shish Kebab

Kebap po Shopski

The volatile oils in hot chilies may irritate your skin. Wear rubber gloves when handling them.

To serve 5 or 6

2 to 2½ lb.	boneless pork, cut into 1-inch [2½-cm.] cubes	1 kg.
	salt and freshly ground pepper	
5	fresh red hot chilies (or fewer, according to taste), sliced into rings and seeded	5
½ cup	olive oil	125 ml.
1 cup	chopped onions	¼ liter
2 tbsp.	flour	30 ml.
1 tsp.	Hungarian paprika	5 ml.
½ cup	puréed tomato	125 ml.
½ cup	heated stock *(recipe, page 165)* or warm water	125 ml.

Yogurt topping

1 cup	plain yogurt	¼ liter
2	eggs, lightly beaten	2
	salt and pepper	
1 tsp.	crumbled dried summer savory	5 ml.
1 tbsp.	chopped fresh parsley	15 ml.

Season the pork cubes with a little salt and pepper, and thread them onto wooden or metal skewers alternately with the rings of chili pepper, allowing five or six pork cubes for each skewer. Heat the oil in a large skillet and fry the kebabs on the skewers, turning them until lightly browned on all sides. Then arrange them side by side in a lightly greased shallow baking dish.

In the oil left in the skillet, fry the onions for 10 minutes or until softened. Add the flour and paprika, stir to blend, then add the puréed tomato and pour in the hot stock or water. Season to taste, bring this sauce to a boil, and pour it over the skewered meat. Bake, uncovered, in a preheated 350° F. [180° C.] oven for about 30 minutes or until tender.

For the topping, whisk the eggs and yogurt together. Season with some salt and pepper, and pour the mixture over the meat. Sprinkle with the savory, return to the oven, and bake for about 30 minutes more or until the topping is set and golden brown on top. Serve in the baking dish, sprinkled with parsley. Deep-fried, julienned potatoes and buttered peas go well with this dish.

L. PETROV, N. DJELEPOV, E. IORDANOV AND S. UZUNOVA
BULGARSKA NAZIONALNA KUCHNIYA

Pork Braised in Beer

Schweinskeule in Bier Geschmort

To serve 4

1 lb.	boneless fresh ham, cubed	½ kg.
	salt	
6 tbsp.	lard or dripping	90 ml.
1	onion, finely chopped	1
1 cup	beer	¼ liter
	water	
2 tbsp.	flour	30 ml.
1	slice black bread, crumbled	1
1	lemon peel, grated	1
1	garlic clove, chopped	1
½ tsp.	caraway seeds	2 ml.

Season the meat with salt and fry it in the lard until browned on all sides. Add the onion, the beer, and enough water to almost cover the meat. Cover and simmer over low heat for one and a half hours or until the meat is tender. Remove the meat and keep it warm.

Blend the flour with a little more beer or with some of the sauce, and stir it into the sauce. Add the crumbled bread, lemon peel, garlic and caraway seeds, and cook, stirring, until the sauce is thickened and reduced to the desired consistency. Strain the sauce, return the meat to it to reheat, and serve the dish with dumplings or potatoes.

JOZA BŘÍZOVÁ AND MARYNA KLIMENTOVÁ
TSCHECHISCHE KÜCHE

Pork and Prune Hotpot

To serve 4

1 lb.	boneless lean pork, cut into 1-inch [2½-cm.] cubes	½ kg.
½ cup	dried prunes, soaked in warm water for 15 minutes and drained	125 ml.
1	lemon, peel removed and cut into strips, juice strained	1
¼ cup	flour	50 ml.
1 tsp.	salt	5 ml.
	pepper	
1 tbsp.	lard	15 ml.

Cover the prunes with cold water and stew them with the lemon peel for about 20 minutes, until quite tender. Strain off the juice and keep it. Discard the lemon peel. Remove the pits from the prunes if necessary.

Mix the flour with the salt and pepper and roll the pork pieces in the seasoned flour to coat them. Melt the lard in a skillet and fry the pork until brown. Place the pork and prunes in alternate layers in a casserole or pie dish. Add to the skillet whatever seasoned flour is left from coating the pork pieces. Stir in about 1¼ cups [300 ml.] of the prune cooking juice, bring to a boil and pour this thickened gravy over the pork and prunes. Add the lemon juice. Cover and stew in a preheated 350° F. [180° C.] oven for at least one hour. Serve in the casserole.

D. D. COTTINGTON TAYLOR
GOOD HOUSEKEEPING MENU AND RECIPE BOOK

Braised Pork with Cumin

Rojoes Cominho

To serve 4

2 lb.	boneless lean pork, cut into 1-inch [2½-cm.] cubes, dried thoroughly with paper towels	1 kg.
1½ tsp.	ground cumin	7 ml.
1 tbsp.	lard	15 ml.
¾ cup	dry white wine	175 ml.
½ tsp.	finely chopped garlic	2 ml.
1 tsp.	salt	5 ml.
	freshly ground pepper	
5	thin lemon slices, quartered	5
2 tbsp.	finely chopped fresh coriander (cilantro)	30 ml.

In a heavy 10- to 12-inch [25- to 30-cm.] skillet, melt the lard over high heat until it sputters. Add the pork cubes and brown them, turning the cubes frequently with a large spoon and regulating the heat so that they color quickly and evenly without burning. Stir in ½ cup [125 ml.] of the wine, the cumin, garlic, salt and a liberal grinding of pepper. Bring to a boil over high heat, then cover the skillet, reduce the heat to low and simmer for 25 minutes, or until the pork is tender and shows no resistance when pierced with the tip of a small, sharp knife. Add the remaining wine and the lemon slices and cook over high heat, turning the meat and lemon pieces constantly, until the sauce thickens slightly. Stir in the coriander and taste for seasoning. Serve on a heated platter.

FOODS OF THE WORLD
THE COOKING OF SPAIN AND PORTUGAL

Pork Braised with Honey

Shikar Korma

Boning a pork loin is demonstrated on pages 12-13.

To serve 6

2 lb.	pork loin, boned and cut into small pieces	1 kg.
4 tsp.	honey	20 ml.
4 tbsp.	clarified butter	60 ml.
1 cup	water	¼ liter
½ tsp.	salt	2 ml.
4	medium-sized shallots, finely chopped	4
½ tsp.	ground turmeric	2 ml.
½ tsp.	freshly ground pepper	2 ml.
1	strip fresh orange peel	1
1	strip fresh lemon peel	1
⅔ cup	plain yogurt, whisked until smooth	150 ml.
1	garlic clove, crushed	1
4	cardamom pods, seeds removed and ground	4
½-inch	cinnamon stick, splintered and pounded	1-cm.
¼ tsp.	ground mace	1 ml.

Heat a heavy saucepan over medium heat, and put in the honey. Stir until the honey sticks to the bottom of the pan but is not caramelized. Add the butter and, when hot, add the pork. Stir and brown the pork over medium heat for about 10 minutes. Add the water, season with the salt, bring to a boil and turn down the heat to low. Simmer gently, uncovered, until cooked, about 40 minutes.

Evaporate all of the liquid in the pan, turning up the heat if necessary. Add the shallots, turmeric, pepper and orange and lemon peel. Cook and stir over medium heat until the butter separates. Now add the yogurt, a little at a time, stirring well until it is all absorbed, and the butter again separates from the sauce. Add the garlic, cardamom and cinnamon. Cook over medium heat for another minute. Dust with the mace and cover tightly. Cook gently in a preheated 300° F. [150° C.] oven for 15 minutes before serving.

DHARAMJIT SINGH
INDIAN COOKERY

Pork with Icicle Radish

This dish can only be prepared when icicle radishes are in season, and the season is brief. Out of season, they have a woody texture and lack taste. Icicle radishes are found in the spring and summer months in Japanese and Chinese supermarkets. They are much bigger than American white radishes and seem like a cross between a turnip and a radish. This dish can be made ahead of time and reheated before serving. The flavor improves with reheating, so don't hesitate to make this the day before a party and keep in the refrigerator overnight.

	To serve 4	
¼ lb.	boneless pork loin, trimmed and half frozen	125 g.
2	medium-sized icicle radishes, peeled and sliced (about 3 cups [¾ liter])	2
2 tbsp.	vegetable oil	30 ml.
1 tbsp.	dry sherry	15 ml.
1 tbsp.	dark soy sauce	15 ml.
½ tsp.	salt	2 ml.
½ tsp.	sugar	2 ml.

Cut the pork into slices ¼ inch [5 mm.] thick and 1 inch [2½ cm.] square. The radishes should be sliced to approximately the same size as the pork slices. Parboil the radish slices in boiling water for three minutes. Drain.

Heat the oil in a wok or a frying pan. Add the pork and stir fry over high heat for three minutes. Add the sherry. Mix. Then add the soy sauce, salt and sugar. Mix well. Add the icicle radish slices and mix some more. Cover and cook for four to five minutes over medium heat. (If the mixture seems dry, add 2 tbsp. [30 ml.] of cold water before covering it.) Remove the pork and icicle radish to a platter and serve.

GRACE ZIA CHU
MADAME CHU'S CHINESE COOKING SCHOOL

Pork Sausages in White Wine Sauce

Salsiccia in Salsa Bianca

	To serve 2	
1 lb.	fresh pork sausages, pricked with a fork	½ kg.
½ cup	stock (recipe, page 165)	125 ml.
½ cup	dry white wine	125 ml.
½ tsp.	fennel seeds	2 ml.
1 tbsp.	freshly grated Parmesan cheese	15 ml.

Put the sausages in a saucepan with the stock, wine, fennel seeds and cheese. Cook uncovered over medium heat for about 20 minutes, turning the sausages occasionally, until they are done and the sauce has thickened. Serve hot.

EMMANUELE ROSSI (EDITOR)
LA VERA CUCINIERA GENOVESE

Pork in Red Sauce

Babi Mérak

Traditionally pork in red sauce is served as part of a rijsttafel (or "rice table")—an elaborate rice meal accompanied by a variety of side dishes. The fresh chilies called for should be prepared carefully, preferably using rubber gloves, so that their volatile oils do not make your skin tingle.

To make thick santen, or coconut milk, grate about 3½ ounces [100 g.] of fresh coconut into a bowl. Pour in 1¼ cups [300 ml.] of boiling water, leave for five minutes and strain the liquid through a cloth. Squeeze the cloth hard to extract all of the coconut milk.

	To serve 4	
1 lb.	boneless lean pork loin or shoulder, diced	½ kg.
8	fresh red hot chilies, halved lengthwise and seeded, parboiled for 8 minutes and drained	8
4	garlic cloves, chopped	4
2	onions, chopped	2
5	slices laos (galanga root)	5
1 tbsp.	chopped seréh (lemon grass)	15 ml.
½ tsp.	trassi (Indonesian dry shrimp paste), crumbled	2 ml.
1 tsp.	asem (tamarind pulp or jelly)	5 ml.
	salt	
4 tbsp.	lard or vegetable oil	60 ml.
1 cup	thick santen (coconut milk)	¼ liter

In a mortar, pound the drained peppers together with the garlic, onions, laos, seréh, trassi and asem until a smooth paste is formed. Season with salt to taste.

Heat the lard or oil in a saucepan and sauté the pungent paste for five minutes over medium heat, stirring occasionally. Add the meat and brown it on all sides. Add the santen and simmer, stirring all the time, for 15 to 20 minutes or until the sauce thickens and the meat is tender. Serve with plain boiled rice.

J. M. J. CATENIUS-VAN DER MEIJDEN
GROOT NIEUW VOLLEDIG INDISCH KOOKBOEK

Pork and Brown Cabbage

Flaesk i Brunkaal

To serve 4 to 6

2 to 2½ lb.	spareribs, fresh or salt-cured	1 kg.
1	white cabbage	1
2 tbsp.	sugar	30 ml.
2 tbsp.	butter	30 ml.
	soy sauce (optional)	
1 cup	water	¼ liter

Divide the head of cabbage into eight parts and shred them coarsely. Cook the sugar in a pot over low heat until caramel colored. Add the butter and brown the cabbage in it. If a deeper color is desired, add a little soy sauce. Add the water, cover and steam the cabbage until very tender. This will take about two hours. Add the pork in one piece one hour before the cabbage is done.

SUSANNE
DANISH COOKERY

Pork in Horseradish Cream

Krenfleisch

The technique of boning a Boston shoulder roast is demonstrated on pages 12-13.

To serve 4

2 lb.	pork Boston shoulder roast, boned and cut into 4 pieces	1 kg.
2 tbsp.	wine vinegar	30 ml.
1	onion, chopped	1
4	peppercorns	4
2	bay leaves	2
4 oz.	fresh pork rind	125 g.
	salt	
2 tbsp.	grated horseradish	30 ml.
1 cup	heavy cream	¼ liter

Bring 2 cups [½ liter] of water to a boil with the vinegar, onion, peppercorns, bay leaves, pork rind and a pinch of salt. After cooking for five minutes, put in the pieces of pork. Cover and simmer gently for two hours. Take out the meat, sprinkle it with the horseradish and keep it warm in a serving dish. Remove all fat from the cooking liquid and boil it over high heat until reduced by half, then strain it into a saucepan. Stir in the cream, reheat, and pour the sauce over the meat. Serve with sauerkraut and mashed potatoes.

LILO AUREDEN
DAS SCHMECKT SO GUT

Pork with Celery and Egg-and-Lemon Sauce

Hirino Me Selinorizes

To serve 6 to 8

3 lb.	boneless lean pork, cut into serving pieces	1½ kg.
4 tbsp.	butter	60 ml.
2	medium-sized onions, chopped	2
2 tbsp.	flour	30 ml.
½ cup	dry red or white wine	125 ml.
2 tbsp.	chopped fresh parsley	30 ml.
	salt and pepper	
1 lb.	celeriac, peeled and cubed, or 1 large bunch celery, thickly sliced crosswise, including the leaves	½ kg.
Egg-and-lemon sauce		
4	egg yolks	4
¼ cup	strained fresh lemon juice	50 ml.

Heat the butter in a large pan over medium heat and quickly brown the meat. Add the onions and, as they begin to brown, stir in the flour, blend, then add the wine and parsley. Pour in enough hot water to cover, add some salt and pepper, and simmer over low heat for at least two hours. If you are using celeriac, it must be put with the meat after the meat has been simmering for about 30 minutes. Celery can be added to the meat about 45 minutes before the meat is ready.

To make the egg-and-lemon sauce, beat the egg yolks and slowly add the lemon juice, beating all the while. Gradually add 2 or 3 tablespoons [30 or 45 ml.] of the liquid from the meat. Stir the sauce back into the pan with the meat, and continue stirring over low heat for a few minutes without permitting the sauce to approach a boil. Let the pan stand on the side of the stove, covered, for five minutes before serving.

ROBIN HOWE
GREEK COOKING

Stuffed Pork Belly

Gefüllte Schweinsbrust

To prepare a pork belly for stuffing, open up the natural pocket between the layers of lean belly flesh with the tip of a knife.

To serve 6

2 to 2½ lb.	fresh pork belly, prepared for stuffing, rind scored	1 kg.
2	crusty rolls, soaked in milk, squeezed dry and crumbled	2
2 tbsp.	butter	30 ml.
1 tbsp.	chopped fresh parsley	15 ml.
1 tbsp.	marjoram	15 ml.
1	cardamom pod, seeds removed and ground	1
	salt and pepper	
1	egg	1
⅔ cup	dried raisins, soaked in warm water for 15 minutes and drained	150 ml.
⅔ cup	hot water	150 ml.
1 cup	stock *(recipe, page 165)*	¼ liter
½ cup	sour cream	125 ml.

Fry the crumbled rolls briefly in the butter. Season with the parsley, marjoram, ground cardamom and a little salt and pepper, and remove from the heat. Add the egg and raisins, and mix well. Fill the pocket in the meat with this stuffing and sew up the opening.

Place the meat in a large pan, pour in the water and roast the meat in a preheated 425° F. [220° C.] oven for about 15 minutes, or until the meat is brown. Pour in some of the stock, reduce the oven temperature to 325° F. [160° C.], cover the pan and braise the meat for about one and a half hours, basting and occasionally adding more stock.

Transfer the meat to a warmed platter. Degrease the cooking liquid and thicken it with the sour cream. Serve the meat with this sour-cream gravy and a dish of red cabbage.

DOROTHEE V. HELLERMANN
DAS KOCHBUCH AUS HAMBURG

Chaurice with Creole Sauce

Chaurice, Sauce à la Créole

Chaurice is a spicy pork sausage highly seasoned with red pepper. A recipe for this Louisiana specialty is on page 87. Hot Italian sausages or Spanish chorizos may be substituted.

To serve 6

12	*chaurice* (about 2 lb. [1 kg.])	12
½ tsp.	lard	2 ml.
1	large onion, chopped	1
1	garlic clove, finely chopped	1
4	tomatoes, peeled and roughly chopped	4
1 tsp.	salt	5 ml.
1 tsp.	black pepper	5 ml.
½ cup	boiling water	125 ml.

Place the lard in a frying pan or stewpan over medium heat. When it heats, add the onion. Let this brown slightly and then add the garlic. Add the tomatoes. As this mixture browns, put in the sausages, which you have pricked gently. Cover and let the sausages simmer for about five minutes, then add the salt. Add the boiling water. Cover well and let all simmer for 20 minutes. This is very nice for breakfast.

THE PICAYUNE CREOLE COOK BOOK

Sausage Roasted in the Coals

Cervelas Truffé sous la Cendre

A cervelas is a large French poaching sausage, to which diced, fresh truffles are sometimes added. The technique for making such a sausage is demonstrated on pages 20-21; the recipe is on page 88. Heavy-duty aluminum foil will produce the strongest wrapping for the sausage.

To serve 4

1	*cervelas* (1 lb. [½ kg.]), preferably made with truffles	1
2 cups	Beaujolais or other light, dry red wine	½ liter
4	medium-sized potatoes, scrubbed but not peeled	4

Enclose the sausage loosely in a large double sheet of heavy-duty aluminum foil. Roll one end of the foil tightly to make a cone, and pinch the edges firmly. Fill the cone with the wine and close the wide end tightly. Fold this closed roll inside a dampened newspaper.

Scrape the coals away from the hearth, which should be well heated by the fire. Place the roll and the potatoes on the hot hearth, cover them with hot ashes, and pile glowing embers on top. Cook for 45 minutes. Take off the paper and carefully unwrap the foil. The sausage will be lightly roasted and will have a delicious taste of caramelized wine. Serve accompanied by the roasted potatoes.

FELIX BENOIT AND HENRY CLOS JOUVE
LA CUISINE LYONNAISE

Stewed Pork Rolls

The original version of this recipe calls for tying the pork rolls with strings made by blanching the leaves of a fresh (not dried) garlic bulb and then separating the leaves lengthwise into narrow strips.

	To serve 4	
1 lb.	pork tenderloin, cut into 14 slices and pounded flat	½ kg.
2	dried black mushrooms, soaked in warm water for 15 minutes, stems discarded, cut into 14 pieces	2
1 cup	bamboo shoots, cut into 1½-inch [4-cm.] strips	¼ liter
3	scallions, split lengthwise and cut into 1½-inch [4-cm.] strips	3
⅓ cup	soy sauce	75 ml.
1 tbsp.	*shaoh sing* wine or dry sherry	15 ml.
5 cups	peanut oil	1¼ liter
3 tbsp.	sugar	45 ml.
3 tbsp.	brown Chinese vinegar or red wine vinegar	45 ml.
3 cups	boiling water	¾ liter
1½ tsp.	dark sesame oil	7 ml.

On each pork slice, place a mushroom piece, bamboo-shoot strip and scallion strip. Then roll up the pork well and secure it with a toothpick. Marinate the pork rolls in the soy sauce and wine or sherry at room temperature for about 20 minutes. Drain the rolls and pat dry; reserve the marinade.

Heat the peanut oil in a wok or deep frying pan and deep fry the pork rolls for about one minute, until brown. Remove the rolls and pour off the oil from the pan. Put the pork rolls back into the pan with the marinade, sugar, vinegar and boiling water, and stew, uncovered, for about 30 minutes or until tender. When the sauce is reduced to ½ cup [125 ml.], add the sesame oil and serve.

FU PEI MEI
PEI MEI'S CHINESE COOKBOOK

Wrapped Boiling Sausage

Coteghino Fasciato

Part of the cooking liquid from this dish may be strained off, thickened and used as a sauce with macaroni for a first course. Melt a small piece of butter in a saucepan, add a tablespoon of flour and, when this roux begins to brown, strain into it at least half of the sausage cooking liquid. Boil the sauce briefly to thicken it, add the mushrooms that have been cooked with the sausage and pour this sauce over buttered macaroni. Pass grated cheese on the side.

	To serve 4	
½ lb.	fresh pork sausage, peeled	300 g.
1	large, thin, boneless veal or beef round steak (about ½ lb. [¼ kg.]), pounded flat	1
3 tbsp.	butter	45 ml.
1	rib celery, coarsely chopped	1
1	carrot, coarsely chopped	1
¼	onion, coarsely chopped	¼
¼ to ½ cup	slivered bacon or ham (optional)	50 to 125 ml.
3 tbsp.	dried mushroom caps, soaked in water for 30 minutes	45 ml.

Wrap the sausage in the veal or beef. Tie up with string and place the roll in a casserole with the butter, celery, carrot and onion, and the ham or bacon if used. Salt and pepper are not needed because the sausage contains enough. Fry over medium heat, turning the sausage roll until it is browned on all sides, then pour on enough water to come halfway up the roll. Add the dried mushrooms with their soaking liquid and simmer, covered, for about one hour or until tender.

Serve the sausage with some of the cooking liquid poured around it; use the rest to make a sauce for the macaroni.

PELLEGRINO ARTUSI
LA SCIENZA IN CUCINA E L'ARTE DI MANGIAR BENE

Sausage Braised in Wine

Cervelas Chaud à la Beaujolaise

The authors of this recipe demand a large truffled poaching sausage no more than one day old, which has not begun to dry. You can produce a delicious—if less perfect—dish with a freshly made, but untruffled sausage produced as demonstrated on pages 20-21.

	To serve 4	
1 lb.	truffled poaching sausage	½ kg.
1 tbsp.	butter	15 ml.
3 or 4	shallots, finely chopped	3 or 4
3 to 4 tbsp.	finely chopped fresh parsley	45 to 60 ml.
2 tbsp.	finely chopped fresh chervil	30 ml.
	salt and pepper	
1 cup	young Beaujolais or other dry, light red wine	250 ml.

Thickly butter a gratin dish, and sprinkle with the chopped shallots, chervil and 2 tablespoons [30 ml.] of parsley. After pricking it several times with a needle, put the sausage onto this bed. Season the sausage lightly with salt and pepper, and pour in the wine. Cover the dish and put it into a preheated 325° F. [170° C.] oven for 20 minutes.

Sprinkle the sausage with the remaining chopped parsley. Serve the sausage hot, accompanied with potatoes in vinaigrette sauce or with a salad of warm lentils.

FELIX BENOIT AND HENRY CLOS JOUVE
LA CUISINE LYONNAISE

Sausages and Chestnuts

	To serve 6	
1 lb.	finely ground pork, formed into 6 flat oval cakes	½ kg.
40	chestnuts, with the flat ends slit crosswise, roasted in a 425° F. [220° C.] oven for 10 minutes, shelled and skinned	40
2 tbsp.	butter	30 ml.
1 tbsp.	flour	15 ml.
1½ cups	strong beef or veal stock (recipe, page 165)	375 ml.
1 cup	dry sherry or Madeira	¼ liter
1	bouquet garni	1
	salt and black or cayenne pepper	

Fry the sausages gently in the butter until they are well browned. Lift them out, and pour the greater part of the fat in which they have been fried into a clean saucepan. Mix the flour into the fat, and stir over medium heat until well browned; then pour in by degrees the stock and wine. Add the bouquet garni and season the whole properly; give it a boil, lay in the sausages round the pan, and the chestnuts in the center; stew them, covered, very gently for nearly an hour. Take out the bouquet, arrange the sausages neatly on a dish, and heap the chestnuts in the center. Strain the sauce over them and serve them very hot.

ELIZA ACTON
MODERN COOKERY

Pork and Rice Patties

Zrazy Wieprzowe z Ryzem

	To serve 6 to 8	
2 lb.	boneless pork Boston shoulder, ground or finely chopped	1 kg.
1	onion, finely chopped and lightly browned in butter	1
	salt and pepper	
1 cup	raw unprocessed rice, boiled in 2 cups [½ liter] stock for 10 minutes	¼ liter
1	egg	1
½ cup	flour	125 ml.
4 tbsp.	butter	60 ml.
1 cup	stock (recipe, page 165)	¼ liter
2 cups	sour cream	½ liter

Combine the pork, onion, salt and pepper, rice and egg. Shape the mixture into 12 to 16 patties, dust them with the flour, and brown them quickly on both sides in the butter. Put the patties close together in a large heavy casserole, and pour over them the butter in which they were browned. Add the stock, bring to a boil, cover and simmer for 30 minutes. Stir in the sour cream blended with 1 teaspoon [5 ml.] of the flour left from dusting the patties, and heat until the sauce bubbles up once. Serve with pan-fried potatoes.

MARIA OCHOROWICZ-MONATOWA
POLISH COOKERY

Cabbage Leaves Stuffed with Pork

Sarmale cu Varză Dulce

Sarmale are made with either fresh or pickled cabbage leaves. The pickled variety uses whole cabbage leaves, preserved in the same brine used for shredded sauerkraut. If pickled leaves are not available, core a whole head of firm white cabbage. Place it in a bowl, pour on salted boiling water and let it stand for about 25 minutes or until the leaves can be easily detached.

To serve 6

1½ lb.	boneless lean pork, finely chopped or ground	¾ kg.
2	onions, finely chopped	2
2 tbsp.	lard	30 ml.
2 tbsp.	raw unprocessed rice	30 ml.
2 tbsp.	chopped mixed fresh parsley, dill and thyme	30 ml.
	salt and pepper	
1	large slice firm, homemade-type white bread, soaked in water and squeezed dry	1
24	cabbage leaves, fresh or pickled	24
1 lb.	sauerkraut, drained and the juice reserved	½ kg.
1 tbsp.	puréed tomato	15 ml.

In a heavy skillet over low heat, cook the onions in the lard until they are soft but not colored. Add the rice and stir until it is transparent. Season this mixture with the chopped herbs and a little salt and pepper. In a bowl, combine the onion mixture and the pork with the soaked bread, and work by hand until this stuffing is smooth, adding water if necessary to give it a creamy consistency.

Cut the hard center ribs out of the cabbage leaves. To make each roll, spread a leaf out flat and place a little stuffing in the center. Fold the edges over, then roll up the leaf tightly. The real Moldavian *sarmale* are no thicker than 1 inch [2½ cm.].

Line the bottom of a large glazed earthenware pot with a layer of sauerkraut. Arrange a layer of the cabbage rolls close together on top. Repeat these layers until all of the rolls are used up, ending with a sauerkraut layer.

Almost cover the rolls with the sauerkraut juice mixed with the puréed tomato. If the sauerkraut juice is very salty, dilute it with water. Over low heat, using a heat-diffusing pad if necessary, bring the mixture slowly to a simmer. Cook for two hours, shaking the pot occasionally to prevent sticking. Then cover the pot and place it in a 300° F. [150° C.] oven for one to two more hours or until not more than 1 cup [¼ liter] of liquid is left.

Serve accompanied by a bowl of sour cream and by po-lenta or cornbread. This dish is even better cooked the day before and then reheated slowly in the oven.

SANDA MARIN
CARTE DE BUCATE

Oven-baked Spiced Meat Loaf

Gekruid Gehakt uit de Oven

The *ketjap benteng manis* called for here is a sweet Indonesian soy sauce. It is obtainable where Oriental foods are sold.

To serve 4

1 lb.	ground pork	½ kg.
2 to 3	slices stale, homemade-type bread with the crusts removed, soaked in a little milk	2 to 3
1	egg, lightly beaten	1
	salt and pepper	
	grated nutmeg	
1½ tsp.	ground cumin	7 ml.
¾ tsp.	ground ginger	4 ml.
1	onion, finely chopped	1
1 tbsp.	finely chopped leek green	15 ml.
2 to 3 tsp.	*ketjap benteng manis*	10 to 15 ml.
	butter	
2 to 3 tbsp.	grated Gouda or Cheddar cheese	30 to 45 ml.
3 tbsp.	dry bread crumbs	45 ml.
2 tbsp.	chopped fresh parsley	30 ml.

Combine the pork in a bowl with the bread, egg, salt, pepper, nutmeg, cumin, ginger, onion, leek and *ketjap benteng manis*, and mix it thoroughly with two forks.

Butter a 1-quart [1-liter] enameled cast-iron casserole. Fill it with the spiced ground meat and press the meat down lightly with a fork. Sprinkle the surface with the mixed cheese, bread crumbs and parsley. Spread slivers of butter on the surface and bake, uncovered, in a preheated 375° F. [190° C.] oven for the first 10 minutes. Lower the temperature to 325° F. [160° C.] and bake for 30 minutes longer, or until the meat loaf is done and nicely browned on top.

HUGH JANS
BISTRO KOKEN

Fried Tasty Meat Mince

Chow Yook Soong

To serve 2

½ lb.	lean pork, finely chopped or ground	¼ kg.
4 tbsp.	vegetable oil	60 ml.
½ cup	peanuts or blanched almonds	125 ml.
2 tbsp.	soy sauce	30 ml.
1 tbsp.	cornstarch	15 ml.
	sugar	
	salt and pepper	
2 tbsp.	water	30 ml.
1 tbsp.	dry sherry	15 ml.
4	dried Chinese mushrooms, soaked in warm water for 30 minutes, drained, water reserved, mushrooms finely diced	4
8	water chestnuts, finely diced	8
¼ cup	snow peas	50 ml.
2	celery ribs, finely diced	2
1	garlic clove, chopped	1
2	slices fresh ginger root	2
1	small lettuce, cored and coarsely chopped	1

Heat 1 tablespoon [15 ml.] of the oil and fry the nuts until they are golden. Drain, cool and crush them.

Mix the pork with half of the soy sauce, 1 teaspoon [5 ml.] of the cornstarch, the salt, pepper, almost all of the sugar, and the water. Make a mixture of the sherry and the remaining soy sauce and cornstarch, a pinch of sugar, and the reserved mushroom liquid.

Heat 2 tablespoons [30 ml.] of the oil in a wok or skillet and fry all of the diced ingredients. Sprinkle with salt, cover and braise for three minutes. Remove to a dish. Fry the garlic and ginger, add the pork mixture, stir one minute over high heat, then braise, covered, for two minutes over low heat. Add the braised vegetables; stir until well mixed.

Arrange a hollow in the center of the ingredients and pour in the sherry sauce. Heat until the sauce is slightly thickened, then stir it into the other ingredients. Cover the wok or pan and braise the mixture for about three minutes longer or until the pork is well cooked.

Meanwhile, braise the lettuce in the remaining 1 tablespoon of oil, sprinkling it with salt. When tender, add the lettuce to the meat mixture. Arrange in a warmed serving dish, sprinkle with the nuts and serve.

DOREEN YEN HUNG FENG
THE JOY OF CHINESE COOKING

Braised Ham in Cream Sauce

Le Jambon Braisé Sauce à la Crème

Instructions for preparing a ham for cooking appear on pages 10-11. To cook the ham until three quarters done, as required here, poach an uncooked ham for 15 minutes a pound [½ kg.], but poach a ready-to-eat ham for a total of only 30 minutes.

To serve 10 to 20

1	whole smoked ham (about 15 lb. [7½ kg.])	1
4 tbsp.	butter	60 ml.
4 to 5	medium-sized carrots, finely diced	4 to 5
1	celery rib, finely diced	1
2	medium-sized onions, finely diced	2
1 lb.	veal bones, cut into small pieces	½ kg.
4	chicken necks, cut up	4
2 cups	dry white wine	½ liter
1 cup	Madeira	¼ liter
1 quart	veal stock (recipe, page 165)	1 liter
4	tomatoes, halved and seeded	4
1	bouquet garni	1
	confectioners' sugar	
3 cups	heavy cream	¾ liter
	salt and pepper	

Poach the ham until it is three quarters cooked. Trim off the excess fat. Melt half the butter in a saucepan and add the carrots, celery, onions, veal bones and chicken necks. Stew for about 10 minutes, then put the mixture in a large braising pan. Add the ham, and pour the white wine over it.

Put the pan into a preheated 375° F. [190° C.] oven. Bake for 30 minutes or until the wine has a syrupy consistency.

Pour in the Madeira, add the stock, the tomatoes and the bouquet garni. Bring to a boil over high heat, cover the pan and return it to the oven. Turn the heat down to 350° F. [180° C.] and cook the ham for about one hour or until done, basting regularly and turning it occasionally.

Transfer the ham to an ovenproof dish. Sprinkle the surface with confectioners' sugar, and return the ham to the oven to caramelize the surface. Meanwhile, strain the cooking liquid into a saucepan and reduce it by half. Add 2 cups [½ liter] of the cream and correct the seasoning. Lightly whip the remaining cream and, off the heat, beat it into the sauce with the remaining butter and Madeira.

Slice the ham and reassemble it in its original shape on the ovenproof dish. Coat the surface with the sauce and return the ham to the oven—at 475° F. [240° C.]—for a few minutes to glaze. Serve the remaining sauce in a sauceboat.

ALEXANDRE DUMAINE
MA CUISINE

Ham Braised in Madeira

Jambon Braisé

A ham of the size specified can provide more than one meal. The leftover ham may be eaten cold, or it may be sliced and warmed in a sauce.

	To serve 10 to 20	
1	smoked ham (14 to 16 lb. [6 to 8 kg.]), soaked in cold water for 24 hours	1
1 cup	Madeira (or substitute white wine or Champagne)	¼ liter
	sugar	
3 cups	velouté sauce *(recipe, page 166)*	¾ liter

Place the ham in a large pan of fresh cold water and bring it gently to a boil. At the first sign of boiling, reduce the heat, using a heat-diffusing pad if necessary, and poach at just below the simmer for 20 minutes to the pound [½ kg.]. Allow the ham to cool partially in its poaching liquid, and then drain it and take off the skin and part of the layer of fat.

Place the ham in a roasting pan, pour the wine over it, and sprinkle the surface lightly with sugar. Roast in a preheated 350° F. [180° C.] oven for 45 minutes, basting frequently. When cooked, the ham should be well glazed, like a true roast. Remove all traces of fat from the basting liquid and add the liquid to the hot velouté sauce.

Prepared in this way, the ham may be accompanied by a variety of vegetables: spinach, peas, mixed vegetables, mushrooms, truffles, and so on. Present the velouté sauce separately in a bowl.

HENRI-PAUL PELLAPRAT
LE NOUVEAU GUIDE CULINAIRE

Smoked Pork Chops and Lentils

	To serve 6	
6	smoked pork loin chops (6 oz. [200 g.]), cut about 1 inch [2½ cm.] thick	6
2½ cups	dried lentils	625 ml.
¼ cup	vegetable oil	50 ml.
1 tsp.	finely chopped garlic	5 ml.
2½ cups	chicken stock *(recipe, page 165)*	625 ml.
1 cup	finely chopped scallions, including 2 inches [5 cm.] of the green tops	¼ liter
¼ cup	finely chopped fresh parsley	50 ml.

In a heavy 4- to 5-quart [4- to 5-liter] casserole, heat the vegetable oil over medium heat. Add the garlic and stir for a

minute or so, then pour in the chicken stock and bring to a boil over high heat. Stir in the lentils, scallions and parsley and, when the mixture returns to a boil, add the pork chops and turn them about with tongs to moisten them evenly.

Cover the casserole tightly, reduce the heat to low and simmer for about 45 minutes, or until the lentils are tender but not falling apart. Taste for seasoning and serve at once, directly from the casserole or, if you prefer, mound the lentils on a heated platter and arrange the pork chops attractively around them.

FOODS OF THE WORLD
AMERICAN COOKING: THE EASTERN HEARTLAND

Salt Pork Hocks with Sauerkraut

Berliner Eisbein

In Bavaria, this dish is usually made with smoked or fresh pork hocks instead of the salt-cured hocks called for in the Berlin version.

	To serve 6	
3 or 4	salt-cured pork hocks	3 or 4
1½ lb.	sauerkraut, rinsed in cold water and drained	¾ kg.
1	onion, finely chopped	1
2 tbsp.	lard	30 ml.
1	bay leaf	1
5	juniper berries	5

Soak the hocks in cold water for a few hours. Then sweat the onion in the lard in a large casserole, and add the sauerkraut, bay leaf, juniper berries and just enough water to prevent the sauerkraut from burning. Put the pork hocks on top, cover the casserole and stew for two to two and a half hours over low heat or in an oven preheated to 325° F. [160° C.]. Turn the hocks from time to time during cooking.

It is traditional to serve *Berliner Eisbein* with peas, and the hocks may be garnished with fried onion rings.

GRETE WILLINSKY
KOCHBUCH DER BÜCHERGILDE

Cured Pork and Salt-Turnip Pot

Potée Colmarienne ou Süri Rüewe

Salt turnips are coarsely grated turnips, salted in layers in a crock or small barrel and fermented under a weight exactly as sauerkraut is. They are rinsed before using to rid them of excess salt. Sauerkraut may be substituted for the turnips.

	To serve 4	
1 lb.	boneless smoked Boston shoulder	½ kg.
2	salted pork hocks	2
3 lb.	salt turnips, rinsed and squeezed dry	1½ kg.
1	large onion, finely sliced	1
10 tbsp.	lard	150 ml.
2	garlic cloves, crushed	2
1¼ cups	dry white Alsatian wine	300 ml.
1¼ cups	water	300 ml.

In a heavy, covered casserole, sweat the onions in the lard without letting them color. Distribute half of the turnips in a layer on the onions, then add the meats and the garlic and cover with the remaining turnips. Pour in the wine and water. Cover tightly and bring to a boil on top of the stove, then put in a preheated 325° F. [170° C.] oven for about one and a half hours. Take out the meat and slice it. Transfer the turnips to a serving dish and arrange the meat on top. Serve steaming hot, with potatoes baked or boiled in their skins.

JOSEPH KOSCHER AND ASSOCIATES
LES RECETTES DE LA TABLE ALSACIENNE

Ham Slice with Cranberries

	To serve 4	
1 lb.	center-slice smoked ham	½ kg.
1 cup	cranberries	¼ liter
½ cup	water	125 ml.
3 tbsp.	honey or ¼ cup [50 ml.] brown sugar, packed	45 ml.
½ tsp.	ground cloves	2 ml.

Trim a few bits of fat off the ham and heat the fat in a skillet until crisp. Remove the fat bits, add the ham and cook slowly until browned, about 10 minutes. Turn the ham and brown the other side. Add the cranberries, water, honey and cloves. Bring to a boil and cook until the berries pop open. Remove the ham to a warmed platter. If a thicker sauce is wanted, boil the cranberry mixture, uncovered, for three or four minutes. Pour the sauce over the ham.

JEANNE A. VOLTZ
THE FLAVOR OF THE SOUTH

Pork and Bean Stew

Plockfinken

If your butcher does not sell salt pork, you can prepare it yourself with any cut of pork you wish. Several days in brine or dry salt (pages 14-15) will be sufficient for this recipe.

	To serve 6	
1½ lb.	salt pork	¾ kg.
1½ cups	dried white beans (about ½ lb. [¼ kg.]), soaked in water overnight and parboiled for 1 hour	375 ml.
½ lb.	pork heart, washed, trimmed, dried well and diced	¼ kg.
½ lb.	pork kidney, split in half, trimmed of fat, soaked in salted water for 2 hours, drained, membranes removed, and diced	¼ kg.
2	leeks, chopped	2
3	carrots, chopped	3
3	medium-sized potatoes, diced	3
1 lb.	green beans, cut small	½ kg.
	salt and pepper	
	vinegar	
	chopped fresh parsley	
2 tbsp.	flour	30 ml.

Put the pork in a large saucepan, cover generously with water, and bring to a boil. Simmer uncovered for 30 minutes. Add the parboiled dried beans, the heart, kidney, leeks and carrots, and cook for 20 minutes. Add the diced potatoes, and cook for 15 minutes, or until the potatoes are almost done. Add the green beans and cook for 15 minutes, or until done.

Remove the salt pork, cut it into small pieces and set it aside. Season the cooking liquid with salt, pepper and vinegar, and stir in chopped parsley to taste. Mix the flour with a little of the cooking liquid and return the mixture to the pan. Cook until the liquid thickens into a sauce, about 10 minutes. Return the pork to the pan, reheat, and serve.

JUTTA KÜRTZ
DAS KOCHBUCH AUS SCHLESWIG-HOLSTEIN

Bacon with Dried Apples and Potatoes

Schnitz und Kartoffeln

In this winter stew from the Swiss canton of Aargau, dried apples take the place of fresh vegetables. In the canton of Lucerne, a similar dish is made with fresh pears in place of dried apples. To make the dish with fresh pears, first parboil the bacon. Lightly brown the sugar with a little butter, pour in the water in which the bacon was cooked, add quartered pears and finally the potatoes and cook until both are tender.

To serve 4		
10 oz.	bacon or smoked meat, in one piece	300 g.
10 oz.	dried apples, soaked in cold water for a few hours, and drained	300 g.
3	medium-sized potatoes (about 1 lb. [½ kg.]), quartered	3
1 to 2 tbsp.	sugar	15 to 30 ml.
	salt	
	butter (optional)	

Let the sugar brown lightly in a dry saucepan, add the apples and the bacon, cover with cold water and cook gently, covered, for 50 minutes. Then add the potatoes, salt to taste and continue cooking until the potatoes are soft (about 30 minutes). Shake the pan to mix all of the ingredients well. If lean meat is used, a little butter can be added with the meat.

EVA MARIA BORER
TANTE HEIDI'S SWISS KITCHEN

Ammerschwihr Sauerkraut

Choucroute d'Ammerschwihr

This recipe is the creation of Pierre Gaertner, a pupil of Fernand Point at the Pyramide restaurant in Vienne, France. Gaertner established his own reputation at Les Armes de France, at Ammerschwihr in Alsace.

To serve 4 to 6		
1 lb.	bacon or salt pork	½ kg.
1	onion, finely chopped	1
2 tbsp.	rendered goose fat or lard	30 ml.
1 lb.	sauerkraut, rinsed and drained	½ kg.
1 cup	dry white Alsatian wine	¼ liter
1	apple, diced	1
10	juniper berries, tied in cheesecloth	10
about 1 cup	stock *(recipe, page 165)*	about ¼ liter
¼ cup	kirsch	50 ml.

In an earthenware or tin-lined copper pot, cook the onion in the goose fat or lard until it is golden. Add the sauerkraut. Cook for five minutes, stirring with a fork, and add the wine,

apple and juniper berries. Pour in enough stock almost to cover the sauerkraut. Cover and simmer for two to three hours. An hour before serving, add the bacon or salt pork and, half an hour later, add the kirsch. Serve with potatoes boiled in their jackets.

FERNAND POINT
MA GASTRONOMIE

The Fat Pig Casserole

To clean pig's ears and feet, singe off any hairs over an open flame. Scrub well, then sprinkle with salt, rubbing it into the skin. Rinse well with cool water; pat dry.

To serve 8		
1 lb.	boneless lean pork, cut into 1-inch [2½-cm.] cubes	½ kg.
2	pig's ears, halved	2
2	pig's feet, coarsely chopped	2
¼ lb.	lean salt pork without the rind, blanched in boiling water for 10 minutes, drained and sliced	125 g.
¾ lb.	*cotechino* or other spicy pork sausages, sliced	⅓ kg.
3 tbsp.	vegetable oil	45 ml.
2 tbsp.	butter	30 ml.
1	onion, thinly sliced	1
⅔ cup	dry white wine	150 ml.
2	ribs celery, finely chopped	2
2	carrots, finely chopped	2
1	cabbage, quartered	1

Put the pig's ears, pig's feet and salt pork into a pot with water to cover, and simmer for one hour. Remove the meat with a slotted spoon, reserving the stock; cut the ears into thin strips; remove any loose bones from the feet.

Heat the oil and butter in a large skillet. Sauté the onion until lightly browned. Add the pork cubes and brown them on all sides. Add the wine, celery, carrots, ears and feet, salt pork and 2 cups [½ liter] of the cooking stock. Simmer, uncovered, for 30 minutes. Place the cabbage quarters on top of the meat and continue cooking for 30 minutes longer. Finally add the sausages, cover and cook for 20 minutes. Skim off any excessive fat before serving.

JANA ALLEN AND MARGARET GIN
OFFAL

Hunter's Stew, Polish-Style
Bigos Polski

The kielbasa called for in this recipe is a garlic-flavored Polish pork sausage found in most American supermarkets and delicatessens.

Any type of meat, game or smoked meat may be used for *bigos*—the more types, the better. The addition of red wine enhances the taste greatly. *Bigos* can be made by substituting additional sauerkraut for the fresh cabbage.

To serve 6		
½ lb.	boneless lean pork in 1 piece	¼ kg.
½ lb.	boneless lean veal in 1 piece	¼ kg.
¼ lb.	smoked bacon in 1 piece	100 g.
½ lb.	kielbasa, peeled and sliced	¼ kg.
1 lb.	sauerkraut, finely chopped	½ kg.
1	small cabbage (about 1 lb. [½ kg.]), halved, cored and finely chopped	1
2 or 3	dried mushrooms, soaked in warm water for 20 minutes, drained and chopped	2 or 3
	salt	
2 tbsp.	lard	30 ml.
¼ cup	chopped onion	50 ml.
2 oz.	fresh pork rind, diced and browned to render its fat, fat reserved	75 g.
3 tbsp.	flour	45 ml.
½ cup	puréed tomato	125 ml.
	pepper	
	sugar (optional)	

Cover the sauerkraut with a small amount of boiling water and cook covered for one hour. In a separate covered pan, cook the fresh cabbage and the mushrooms in a small amount of boiling water for 30 to 40 minutes.

Salt the pork and veal and fry them with the bacon in the hot lard until the meats are brown on all sides. Add the pork, veal and bacon to the the sauerkraut and cook until the meats are tender, about 40 minutes. When done, remove the meats, cut into cubes and reserve.

Meanwhile, sauté the onion in the fat rendered from the pork rind, add the flour and stir until blended. Add this roux to the sauerkraut with the drained, cooked fresh cabbage and mushrooms, the sliced kielbasa, cubed meats, puréed tomato, salt and pepper, and sugar if desired. Heat thoroughly and serve.

HELENA HAWLICZKOWA
KUCHNIA POLSKA

Alsatian Sauerkraut
Choucroute Hansi

This recipe was given to Curnonsky by the Alsatian artist-cartoonist Hansi. Paul Haeberlin of the Auberge de l'Ill in Illhaeusern, Alsace, informs us that colmarettes are small sausages made with equal parts of lean veal, lean pork, and pork fat, pounded to a paste; frankfurters may be substituted. The salted pork loin is a single section of meat, put in brine without being cut into individual chops.

To serve 3		
1 lb.	slab bacon, unsliced	½ kg.
about 1 lb.	salted pork center loin, 3 ribs thick	about ½ kg.
6	*colmarettes*, frankfurters or smoked sausages, pierced with a fork	6
1 lb.	sauerkraut	½ kg.
1	onion, finely chopped	1
2 to 3 tbsp.	rendered goose fat or lard	30 to 45 ml.
1 cup	dry white wine	¼ liter
1	apple, peeled, halved, cored and diced	1
12	juniper berries, tied in cheesecloth	12
½ to 1 cup	stock *(recipe, page 165)*	125 to 250 ml.
2 tbsp.	kirsch	30 ml.
6	small potatoes, boiled in their jackets	6

In a heavy pot, sauté the onion in the fat until it is golden, 10 to 15 minutes. Add the sauerkraut, unwashed or very briefly rinsed, and cook for five minutes, stirring with a fork. Add the wine, apple, then the juniper berries. Pour on enough stock almost to cover the sauerkraut. Cover the pot and cook over low heat for two to three hours. One hour before serving, add the bacon in one piece. Thirty minutes before serving, add the kirsch.

Meanwhile, in a separate saucepan, poach the salted pork in water to cover, keeping it just below the simmer (160° F. [70° C.]) for one to one and a half hours. Heat the sausages for 10 minutes either in the sauerkraut pot or in a separate pan of simmering water.

Serve the sauerkraut on a heated round platter. Cut the bacon into thin slices and cut the pork loin into pieces one rib thick. Arrange the bacon slices, ribs and sausages around the sauerkraut. Serve at the same time a bowl of potatoes boiled in their jackets.

CURNONSKY
A L'INFORTUNE DU POT

Braised Mixed Grill

Meshana Skara bo Preslavski

This dish from Preslav, the ancient capital of Bulgaria, should be made with pure pork sausages containing no cereal fillers. For best results, use homemade sausages, made as demonstrated on pages 20-21. The sauce is extremely hot and is usually eaten with mashed potatoes, boiled rice or bread.

To serve 5

½ lb.	boneless lean pork, cubed	¼ kg.
5	pork chops	5
½ lb.	small fresh pork sausages, pierced on all sides with a fork	¼ kg.
2 tbsp.	lard (optional)	30 ml.
5	fresh or dried hot chilies, stemmed and seeded	5
⅓ cup	chopped onion	75 ml.
1¾ cups	sliced fresh mushrooms	375 ml.
1	sprig dried summer savory, crumbled	1
	salt	
1 tsp.	peppercorns, coarsely crushed	5 ml.
2 tbsp.	strained fresh lemon juice	30 ml.

Thread the cubed pork onto five skewers. Broil the chops, the sausages and the skewered pork for about 15 minutes, turning them once or twice. Or fry them—in batches—in the lard in a large skillet.

Remove the skewers and place all of the meats in a wide earthenware dish. Bury the hot chilies in among the pieces of meat, and sprinkle the onion, mushrooms and savory over the top. Season well with salt and pepper. Pour in 2 cups [½ liter] of hot water, and cover the dish with a well-fitting lid or with a double thickness of foil. Braise in a 350° F. [180° C.] oven for about one hour, by which time the meat should be tender. There will be a fair amount of sauce in the casserole, which should not be reduced. Sprinkle the meat with lemon juice, and bring the casserole to the table.

L. PETROV, N. DJELEPOV, E. IORDANOV AND S. UZUNOVA
BULGARSKA NAZIONALNA KUCHNIYA

Transylvanian Sauerkraut

To serve 6

1 lb.	boneless pork, finely chopped	½ kg.
8	thick slices bacon, coarsely diced	8
5 oz.	smoked pork sausage, thinly sliced	150 g.
2 lb.	sauerkraut	1 kg.
½ cup	finely chopped onions	125 ml.
7 tbsp.	lard	105 ml.
2	garlic cloves, crushed	2
1 tsp.	salt	5 ml.
	pepper	
½ tsp.	Hungarian paprika	2 ml.
⅔ cup	raw unprocessed rice, parboiled for 10 minutes and drained	150 ml.
1¼ cups	sour cream	300 ml.
1	green pepper, halved, seeded, deribbed and sliced (optional)	1
2	tomatoes, sliced (optional)	2

Boil the sauerkraut for 20 minutes in salted water; drain off the water. Fry the onion in 4 tablespoons [60 ml.] of the lard until it turns pale yellow; add the garlic, pork, salt and a little pepper, and dust with paprika. Then fry the whole slowly for 10 to 12 minutes.

Heat the bacon slightly in another skillet, then add the sliced sausage and fry for two to three minutes. Drain the bacon and sausage on paper towels.

Grease the inside of a 3- to 4-quart [3- to 4-liter] casserole with 2 tablespoons [30 ml.] of lard, place a third of the sauerkraut on the bottom, cover it with a layer of bacon and sausage, lay another third of the sauerkraut over it, sprinkle with a little sour cream, then put on the half-cooked rice, adding the fried pork in a layer, and cover with the remaining sauerkraut. A few sliced green peppers and tomatoes can be added with the pork layer.

Sprinkle the top of the sauerkraut with the remaining sour cream, dust a little paprika over it, then sprinkle with the remaining melted lard. Let it stew for one and a quarter hours in a preheated 325° F. [170° C.] oven.

JÓZSEF VENESZ
HUNGARIAN CUISINE

Dublin Coddle

This dish probably derives its name from the 16th Century, when coddle meant parboil or stew.

This is a dish that is eaten by families who have lived for generations in Dublin and who look upon the city as their local village. Sean O'Casey ate Dublin coddle. Dean Swift ate it in the Deanery of St. Patrick's Cathedral in the 18th Century. Dublin coddle is eaten especially on Saturday night when the men come home from the pubs, and is always washed down by draughts of stout. Sometimes a few sliced potatoes are added but this is not orthodox.

	To serve 6	
6	thick slices bacon	6
1 lb.	pork sausages, pierced on all sides with a fork	½ kg.
4	medium-sized onions, sliced	4
	salt and pepper	
1 cup	water	¼ liter

Put the bacon, the sausages and the onions into a saucepan. Season and add the water. Lay wax paper on top. Cover with a lid and simmer gently for 30 minutes.

MONICA SHERIDAN
MY IRISH COOK BOOK

Pork Goulash

Sikulský Guláš

	To serve 4	
1 lb.	boneless lean pork, cut into small cubes	½ kg.
1	pig's foot, quartered lengthwise	1
½ cup	chopped onions	125 ml.
4 tbsp.	lard	60 ml.
1 tbsp.	Hungarian paprika	15 ml.
1 tbsp.	caraway seeds	15 ml.
1	garlic clove, crushed	1
	salt	
1 lb.	sauerkraut, drained	½ kg.
⅔ cup	sour cream	150 ml.
2 tbsp.	cornstarch	30 ml.
3 to 4 tbsp.	strained fresh lemon juice	45 to 60 ml.

Sauté the onions in the lard for about 10 minutes or until they are golden. Add the paprika, caraway seeds, garlic and

about ½ cup [125 ml.] of water. Add the pig's foot, season with salt, cover and simmer for about 10 minutes. Season the cubed meat with salt and add it to the pot. Cook for 30 minutes, adding a little more water if necessary. Then add the sauerkraut and simmer, covered, for about one and a half hours or until the meat and sauerkraut are very tender.

When ready to serve, add the sour cream mixed with the cornstarch, and stir over medium heat until thick. Correct the seasoning with salt and lemon juice, and serve.

VOJTECH ŠPANKO
SLOVENSKÁ KUCHÁRKA

Casserole of Pork

Cassoeula

Luganega sausages are long, thin coriander-flavored pork sausages, but if these are not available other types of sausages can be used instead, for example, *cotechino* sausages, provided they are made of pure pork and are fresh. If the sausages are very large, cut them into chunks before adding them to the dish.

	To serve 6	
2 lb.	boneless lean pork, cut into 6 slices	1 kg.
1	pig's ear, washed, singed and cut in half	1
1	pig's foot, washed and coarsely chopped with a cleaver	1
½ lb.	fresh pork fat or bacon ends, cut into large pieces	¼ kg.
6	*Luganega* sausages	6
	salt	
1 tbsp.	olive oil	15 ml.
2 tbsp.	butter	30 ml.
1	onion, thinly sliced	1
½ cup	dry white wine	125 ml.
2	celery ribs, finely chopped	2
2	carrots, finely chopped	2
2	large white cabbages (about 3 lb. [1½ kg.]), quartered and cored	2
	pepper	

Put the pig's ear, the foot and the pork fat or bacon ends into a large pan of water, add salt and cook slowly for one hour. Lift out all of the meat and bones with a perforated spoon, and cut the ear into thin strips. Reserve the cooking liquid.

In a heavy casserole, heat the oil and butter, and lightly brown the onion. Add the lean pork slices and brown them on both sides. Add the wine, celery, carrots, the ear and pig's foot, the pork fat or bacon ends, and 2 cups [½ liter] of the cooking liquid. Simmer for 30 minutes.

Cook the cabbage for 10 to 15 minutes in boiling salted water. Drain well and put it on top of the meat. Continue cooking, covered, for a further 30 minutes, add the sausages, and cook for another 20 minutes. Skim off surplus fat from time to time and check the seasoning.

This is a dish which should not have too much liquid. Serve from the casserole in which it has been cooked.

ADA BONI
ITALIAN REGIONAL COOKING

Pies and Puddings

Pork Cottage Pie

To serve 4 to 6

1½ lb.	boneless, leftover cooked pork, finely chopped (about 4 cups [1 liter] chopped)	¾ kg.
5	medium-sized potatoes (about 1½ lb. [¾ kg.])	5
2 tbsp.	butter	30 ml.
	salt and pepper	
	grated nutmeg	
2	thick slices bacon, finely chopped	2
½	onion, finely chopped	½
1 tbsp.	finely chopped fresh parsley	15 ml.
about 1 cup	stock *(recipe, page 165)*	about ¼ liter

Boil the potatoes in water to cover until cooked, about 30 minutes. Drain and mash them with a knob of butter, a little salt and pepper, and a grating of nutmeg.

Mix the pork, bacon and onion and place in a shallow baking dish. Sprinkle with parsley and mix with stock until fairly moist. Season with salt and pepper. Spread the potatoes over the meat mixture, making sure that the edges are well sealed. Bubbling gravy sometimes discolors the top if gaps are left around the edge.

Bake in a preheated 350° F. [180° C.] oven for one hour. The top of the pie should be golden brown by this time. If not, brown it under a hot broiler. Hot peeled tomatoes, tomato purée, or braised celery or onions go well with this dish.

MISS READ
MISS READ'S COUNTRY COOKING

Easter Pork Pie

Pâté de Pâques à la Berrichonne

The eggs in this pastry need not be halved; the ends may be cut off and the whole eggs placed end to end in a row the length of the meat mixture. The technique of forming the pastry is demonstrated on pages 74-75.

To serve 6 to 8

2 to 2½ lb.	boneless pork, chopped	1 kg.
1 lb.	boneless veal, chopped	½ kg.
2 tbsp.	chopped fresh parsley	30 ml.
1	large onion, chopped	1
	salt and pepper	
	short-crust pastry (recipe, page 167, but double the quantities called for)	
8	hard-boiled eggs, halved lengthwise	8
	butter	
	freshly grated nutmeg	
1	bay leaf, crumbled	1
1	egg, beaten	1

On a cutting board, mix together the pork, veal, parsley, onion and a little salt and pepper, chopping until well blended. Roll out a third of the pastry dough into a large oval and place it on a baking sheet. In the middle, put half of the chopped-meat mixture spread into a flattened oval.

On each egg half, place a small piece of butter, sprinkle the eggs with a little salt and nutmeg and arrange them side by side on the meat. Cover the eggs with the remaining meat, and sprinkle on the bay leaf.

Cover the pie with the remaining pastry, crimping and sealing the edges well; decorate the top with the scraps of pastry if you like. Brush with the beaten egg. Bake for two hours in a preheated 325° F. [170° C.] oven.

AUSTIN DE CROZE
LES PLATS RÉGIONAUX DE FRANCE

Pork and Apple Pie

To serve 6

1 lb.	boneless lean pork, cut into small pieces	½ kg.
	salt and pepper	
2	cooking apples, peeled, cored and thinly sliced	2
2	onions, sliced	2
6	medium-sized potatoes, thinly sliced	6
1 tsp.	chopped fresh sage	5 ml.
2 tbsp.	lard	30 ml.
1 cup	stock *(recipe, page 165)*	¼ liter
	short-crust pastry *(recipe, page 167)* or 1½ cups [375 ml.] mashed potatoes	

Season the pork well with salt and pepper. Layer the pork with the apples, onions and potatoes in a deep, greased pie dish, sprinkling sage and seasoning over. Dot with lard, pour in the stock, and cover with foil or wax paper. Bake for one and a half hours at 325° F. [170° C.].

Cool and cover with pastry or mashed potatoes. Bake about 30 minutes at 425° F. [220° C.]. Serve hot.

KATE EASLEA
COOKING IN HAMPSHIRE PAST AND PRESENT

French Pork and Onion Pie

Tourte des Vallées

To serve 4

1½ lb.	boneless pork loin, coarsely chopped	700 g.
1	medium-sized onion, thinly sliced	1
1	garlic clove, thinly sliced	1
4 tsp.	butter	20 ml.
1	bread roll, soaked in milk and squeezed lightly	1
2	eggs	2
	salt and pepper	
	mixed spices	
7 tbsp.	Cognac	105 ml.
	short-crust or rough puff pastry (recipe, page 167, but double the quantities called for)	
¼ cup	heavy cream (optional)	50 ml.
	grated nutmeg (optional)	

Sweat the onion and garlic in the butter until soft. Add them to the soaked bread and the pork, and chop the mixture together finely. Add to this mixture one egg, the seasonings and the Cognac, and work together thoroughly.

Line a deep 8-inch [20-cm.] pie dish or 2-quart [2-liter] casserole with pastry dough rolled out to a thickness of ⅛ inch [3 mm.]. Prick the pastry on the bottom of the pie dish with a fork. Fill with the meat stuffing. Beat the remaining egg, and moisten the edges of the pastry with this glaze. Cover with another layer of pastry. Press the edges to seal them together tightly. Cut a small hole in the center of the pastry cover. Let stand in a cool place for 10 to 20 minutes. Glaze the pastry cover twice with the beaten egg, and decorate it by cutting slits with the point of a small knife.

Begin baking in a preheated 425° F. [220° C.] oven; after 10 minutes turn the heat down to 350° F. [180° C.]. Bake for a total time of 40 to 50 minutes until the crust is brown.

Before serving, you can pour a little warm heavy cream seasoned with nutmeg into the hole in the center of the pie.

JOSEPH KOSCHER AND ASSOCIATES
LES RECETTES DE LA TABLE ALSACIENNE

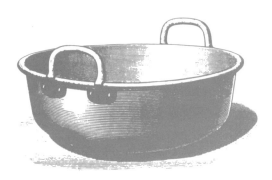

Cheshire Pork Pie

To serve 8

3 lb.	boned pork loin, sliced	1½ kg.
	salt and pepper	
	grated nutmeg	
	short-crust pastry *(recipe, page 167)*	
3	firm tart medium-sized apples (about 1 lb. [½ kg.]), peeled, cored and sliced	3
2 tbsp.	sugar	30 ml.
1¼ cups	white wine	300 ml.
2 tbsp.	butter	30 ml.

Season the pork slices with salt, pepper and nutmeg. Put a layer of pork in the bottom of a deep pie dish. Arrange the apple slices in a layer on top and sprinkle on the sugar. Cover with the remaining pork. Put in the wine, lay some butter on top, and close your pie by covering it with the pastry. Cut a slit in the top and bake in a preheated 350° F. [180° C.] oven for about one and a half hours.

THE ART OF COOKERY MADE PLAIN AND EASY

Bacon and Potato Pie

The Cornish cream suggested as a garnish is extremely thick fresh cream. You can substitute whipped cream made from the heavy—but not ultrapasteurized—cream available in many natural-food stores and specialty markets.

To serve 4

8	thick slices bacon with the rind removed, finely chopped	8
2	medium-sized potatoes, peeled, finely shredded and squeezed dry	2
2 tbsp.	finely chopped onion	30 ml.
¼ cup	flour	50 ml.
2	eggs, beaten	2
	salt and pepper	
½ cup	milk	125 ml.
1 tbsp.	rendered bacon fat	15 ml.

Mix the bacon, potatoes and onion together, and add the flour. To the beaten eggs, add a little salt and pepper, and the milk, and blend this liquid into the bacon, potato and onion mixture. Melt the bacon fat in a shallow piepan until hot, pour in the pie mixture and bake in a preheated 400° F. [200° C.] oven for about 45 minutes or until the pie is browned on top and firm to the touch.

Slice the pie and serve it hot, topped with dollops of Cornish cream and accompanied by fresh green peas.

ANN PASCOE
CORNISH RECIPES OLD AND NEW

Leek and Sausage Pie

To serve 6

12	small pork sausages, pierced with a fork	12
6	leeks, trimmed, split lengthwise and cut crosswise into 2-inch [5-cm.] lengths	6
	short-crust pastry *(recipe, page 167)*	
1 cup	stock *(recipe, page 165)*	¼ liter
2 tbsp.	butter	30 ml.
3 tbsp.	flour	45 ml.
¾ cup	heavy cream	175 ml.
2	egg yolks	2
1 tsp.	salt	5 ml.
	freshly ground black pepper	
3 to 4 tbsp.	grated horseradish, drained	45 to 60 ml.

Place a shallow, 9-inch [23-cm.] flan ring on a baking sheet, then line it with the pastry. Chill. Place the leeks in a sauce-pan and add the stock. Simmer the leeks, covered, until they are almost tender. Drain, reserving the stock. Sauté the sausages until they are browned and almost completely cooked. Drain them on paper towels.

Melt the butter in a saucepan, then remove from the heat. Stir in the flour until it is blended into a roux. Meanwhile, in another saucepan, bring the leeks' reserved cooking stock and the cream to a boil. Add this stock-and-cream mixture all at once to the roux, stirring with a whisk. When the sauce thickens, remove it from the heat and beat in the egg yolks. Return the sauce to the heat and stir it until it is a little thicker, without letting it boil. Season with the salt and pepper, and the horseradish.

Arrange the cooled leeks in the flan ring. Pour the sauce over and arrange the sausages evenly on top. Bake the flan in a preheated 450° F. [230° C.] oven for 20 minutes, or until the pastry edges are golden brown. Serve hot, in wedges.

PAULA PECK
PAULA PECK'S ART OF GOOD COOKING

Sausages Baked in Batter

Rospo nel Buco

To serve 4

8	sweet fennel-flavored Italian sausages	8
1 tbsp.	olive oil	15 ml.
6	eggs, the yolks separated from the whites	6
1 cup	milk	¼ liter
⅓ cup	flour	75 ml.
	salt and freshly ground pepper	
1 tbsp.	chopped fresh rosemary leaves	15 ml.

Preheat the oven to 400° F. [200° C.]. Prick each sausage with a fork in two or three places, then place the sausages in a 14-by-9-inch [35-by-23-cm.] baking dish with the olive oil. Bake for 20 to 25 minutes, until all of the fat has rendered out of the sausages. Meanwhile, prepare a batter by mixing the egg yolks, milk, flour, salt, pepper and rosemary leaves in a bowl with a wooden spoon. Let the batter rest for 20 minutes in a cool place; do not refrigerate.

When the sausages are ready, take the baking dish from the oven and remove all but 2 tablespoons [30 ml.] of the fat. Beat the egg whites until stiff and quickly fold them into the batter. Pour the batter over the sausages in the hot baking dish, and return it to the oven to bake for about 35 minutes. Allow to cool for five minutes before serving.

GIULIANO BUGIALLI
THE FINE ART OF ITALIAN COOKING

Pork Cake

Pounti ou Pountari

There are as many versions of *pounti* as there are farms in the Auvergne. Sometimes the ham is replaced by prunes, or prunes and raisins used in addition to the ham. The onion may be replaced by chives or shallots; the chard by spinach and sorrel. The quantity of flour may be diminished, and the number of eggs increased. Be careful about adding salt, for the ham and salt pork are already salted.

	To serve 8	
¼ lb.	lean salt pork with the rind removed, blanched in boiling water for 10 minutes, drained and finely chopped	125 g.
¼ lb.	smoked ham, finely chopped	125 g.
2 tbsp.	chopped fresh parsley	30 ml.
1	onion, chopped	1
3 cups	chopped chard (about 10 oz. [300 g.])	¾ liter
	salt and pepper	
2½ cups	flour	625 ml.
2 cups	milk	½ liter
5	eggs	5
¼ lb.	thinly sliced fresh pork fat	125 g.

Mix together all of the chopped ingredients, seasoning with salt and pepper. Mix the flour with the milk, and whisk in the eggs. This batter should be thin enough to pour. Stir the batter into the chopped mixture. Butter a baking dish and line it with the pork fat. Pour the mixture into the dish and bake it, uncovered, in a preheated 350° F. [180° C.] oven.

When the top is browned, after about 45 minutes, test for doneness with a skewer. If the skewer comes out with dough on it, cover the cake with a piece of buttered wax paper and continue baking until the skewer comes out clean.

Unmold the cake onto a warmed platter and serve it hot. It may be served with tomato sauce or gravy, but the authentic farmhouse dish is served plain.

SUZANNE ROBAGLIA
MARGARIDOU

Latvian Farmer's Breakfast

Lettisches Bauernfrühstück

	To serve 4 to 6	
5 oz.	boneless lean pork loin, cubed	150 g.
5 oz.	pork sausages, sliced	150 g.
7 oz.	boneless lean beef sirloin or tenderloin, cubed	200 g.
5 oz.	bacon, chopped	150 g.
2	medium-sized onions, chopped	2
4	medium-sized potatoes	4
2 tbsp.	lard	30 ml.
2 or 3	eggs	2 or 3
½ cup	milk or sour cream	125 ml.
	salt and pepper	
	chopped mixed herbs	

Fry all of the meats and the chopped onions together until browned, about 15 minutes. Boil the potatoes in their jackets for 15 to 20 minutes, then peel and slice them and fry them in the lard until lightly browned. Add the potato slices to the meat. Put the mixture into a deep ovenproof dish.

Beat the eggs and milk or sour cream together, and pour this mixture over the meat. Bake in a preheated 350° F. [180° C.] oven for 20 minutes or until the egg mixture is set. Season with salt and pepper and sprinkle with mixed herbs before serving. Garnish with sliced sour gherkins and tomatoes, and surround with raw chopped onion if desired.

KULINARISCHE GERICHTE

Sausages Cooked in Pudding

Toad-in-the-Hole

The batter called for in this recipe is almost identical to that used for English Yorkshire pudding or American popovers. To ensure a well-puffed pudding, the batter should be stirred gently—not beaten vigorously.

	To serve 4	
1 lb.	pork link sausages	½ kg.
3 tbsp.	lard or oil	45 ml.
1 cup	flour	¼ liter
	salt	
2	eggs	2
1¼ cups	milk	300 ml.

Make the pudding batter by sifting the flour, with a good pinch of salt, into a bowl. Form a well in the middle with the back of a wooden spoon and put in it the eggs, combined with a little milk. Amalgamate the flour and liquid slowly by stirring from the center, then stir in the rest of the milk.

Put a roasting pan in the oven, with the fat in it. The oven should be hot, about 425° F. [220° C.]. Stiffen the sausages, well pricked, in a pan of simmering water for five minutes. Watch the pan of fat in the oven to make sure it doesn't burn, take it out when the fat is sizzling hot. Pour a layer of batter over the base of the pan. It should set slightly and make a firm bed for the stiffened sausages. Arrange the sausages in the pan and pour in the rest of the batter, covering the sausages. Return the pan to the oven for 30 to 40 minutes.

The pudding should be puffed up and succulent, crisp outside and no unpleasant semiliquid dough within.

JANE GRIGSON
THE ART OF MAKING SAUSAGES, PÂTÉS, AND OTHER CHARCUTERIE

Special Presentations

Ham and Asparagus Surprise

Soufflé di Prosciutto con Punte di Asparagi

To serve 6

½ lb.	lean cooked ham, finely ground or chopped (about 1½ cups [375 ml.])	¼ kg.
18	asparagus tips, parboiled in salted water until barely tender, and drained	18
3 tbsp.	butter, softened	45 ml.
½ cup	freshly grated Parmesan cheese	125 ml.
1 cup	thick white sauce (recipe, page 166)	¼ liter
5	egg yolks	5
	freshly ground pepper	
7	egg whites	7
	salt	

Grease a 1½-quart [1½-liter] soufflé dish generously with the butter and dust the inside with 4 tablespoons [60 ml.] of the grated cheese. Mix together thoroughly the ham, the white sauce, the remaining cheese and the egg yolks. Season the mixture with a little pepper. Beat the egg whites with a pinch of salt until stiff peaks form. Fold a quarter of the whites into the ham mixture until well combined, then very gently fold in the remainder. Do not overmix.

Arrange six of the asparagus tips fanwise in the bottom of the soufflé dish, and pour in a third of the soufflé mixture.

Continue with two more layers each of the asparagus and soufflé mixture. Put the dish in a preheated 375° F. [190° C.] oven, turn the heat down to 350° F. [180° C.] and bake for about 40 minutes, or until the top is golden brown and a knife inserted in the center comes out clean. Serve at once.

LUIGI CARNACINA
GREAT ITALIAN COOKING

Molded Ham Soufflé

Sformato di Prosciutto

For a striped, layered soufflé, double all of the quantities given in this recipe, except those for the ham and the brandy. Before adding the marinated, diced ham, divide the soufflé mixture in half. Add the ham dice to one half, and add 1 cup [250 ml.] of finely chopped or puréed cooked spinach to the other half. Fold half of the beaten egg whites into each half of the soufflé, and make alternating layers of the two mixtures in a large buttered charlotte mold or deep soufflé dish. Increase the cooking time by about 15 minutes.

To serve 6

10 oz.	boiled ham	300 g.
½ cup	brandy	125 ml.
1¼ cups	thick white sauce (recipe, page 166), cooked	300 ml.
2 tbsp.	butter, melted and cooled	30 ml.
2 tbsp.	flour	30 ml.
2 tbsp.	freshly grated Parmesan cheese	30 ml.
4	eggs, the yolks separated from the whites	4
	salt and freshly ground pepper	
	freshly grated nutmeg	

Cut 6 ounces [200 g.] of the boiled ham into small dice and marinate them in the brandy for 20 to 30 minutes. Chop the remaining ham very finely and add it to the white sauce. Mix the ham and sauce together well until thoroughly combined, then add the melted butter, flour, Parmesan cheese, egg yolks, and the marinated, diced ham together with the brandy. Taste for salt and pepper; add a pinch of nutmeg. Preheat the oven to 400° F. [200° C.].

Beat the egg whites until very stiff and fold them gently into the ham mixture. Transfer to a buttered 2-quart [2-liter] soufflé dish. Place the dish in a large pan of water, so that the water comes about halfway up the sides of the soufflé dish. Put in the oven and bake for 30 to 35 minutes, then remove and allow to cool for 10 minutes.

Unmold the *sformato* onto a serving dish and serve hot.

GIULIANO BUGIALLI
THE FINE ART OF ITALIAN COOKING

Blanquette of Suckling Pig

Cochon de Lait en Blanquette

The original version of this recipe calls for verjus: the juice of unripe grapes. Lemon juice makes a satisfactory substitute.

	To serve 4	
1 lb.	leftover roast suckling pig, boned and thinly sliced	½ kg.
2 tbsp.	butter	30 ml.
2½ cups	thinly sliced mushrooms (about ½ lb. [¼ kg.])	625 ml.
2	shallots, finely chopped	2
1	garlic clove, finely chopped	1
1	bouquet garni composed of parsley, thyme and basil sprigs, a scallion, a garlic clove, 2 shallots, 2 whole cloves and a small bay leaf	1
1 tsp.	flour	5 ml.
1 cup	dry white wine	¼ liter
1 cup	stock *(recipe, page 165)*	¼ liter
	salt and freshly ground pepper	
3	egg yolks	3
2 tbsp.	strained fresh lemon juice	30 ml.

Melt the butter in a saucepan and add the mushrooms, shallots, garlic and bouquet garni. Cook over medium heat until the vegetables are softened. Add the flour, cook for two or three minutes more, then stir in the wine and ¾ cup [175 ml.] of the stock and season with some salt and pepper. Simmer, uncovered, until the sauce is reduced by half, about 30 minutes. Remove the bouquet and add the slices of meat. Heat without boiling. Beat the egg yolks with the lemon juice and the remaining stock. Beat in a little of the sauce; then, off the heat, add the yolk mixture to the pan. Return to a very low heat and stir, without letting the sauce boil, for about five minutes or until it thickens. Serve hot.

MENON
LA CUISINIÈRE BOURGEOISE

Ham in Chablis

Jambon au Chablis

	To serve 8	
8	large slices cooked smoked ham, cut ¼ inch [6 mm.] thick	8
1¼ cups	Chablis or other dry white wine	300 ml.
2 tbsp.	butter	30 ml.
3 cups	thinly sliced fresh mushrooms	¾ liter
2 tsp.	finely chopped shallot	10 ml.
1 tsp.	finely chopped garlic	5 ml.
	salt	
1 cup	heavy cream	¼ liter
1 tbsp.	white port	15 ml.
	salt and pepper	

Thickly butter a large gratin dish and arrange in it the slices of ham. Cover the slices with about ½ cup [125 ml.] of the Chablis. Cover the dish with an inverted ovenproof plate and put into a 300° F. [150° C.] oven to heat the ham through.

In a saucepan, combine the mushrooms with the shallot, garlic and the remaining Chablis. Bring to a boil rapidly, and add the cream. Boil for a few minutes, until the mixture is reduced to the consistency of a sauce. Add the wine from the ham dish and reduce the sauce, again to the desired consistency. Correct the seasoning with salt and pepper. Add the port, cover the ham with the sauce and serve very hot.

ANDRÉ GUILLOT
LA GRANDE CUISINE BOURGEOISE

Cold Ham Mousse

Mousse Froide de Jambon

The aspic jelly called for in this recipe is made from a pork stock that has been reduced enough to allow it to set firmly, and has been flavored—when almost cold—with 2 or 3 tablespoons [30 or 45 ml.] of Madeira. The technique for making the stock is on page 16; the recipe appears on page 165.

	To serve 4 to 6	
1 lb.	leftover cold cooked ham, cut into small pieces	½ kg.
1 cup	velouté sauce *(recipe, page 166)*, chilled	¼ liter
1 cup	Madeira-flavored pork aspic jelly, warmed enough to melt it partially	¼ liter
2 cups	heavy cream, lightly whipped	½ liter

Pound the ham in a mortar until it forms a perfectly smooth paste. Little by little, add the velouté sauce, which should be very cold. Pass the purée through a very fine sieve into a bowl, pressing the purée through with a pestle. Set the bowl in a bed of crushed ice and work the purée with a spatula. Incorporate—little by little—about two thirds of the half-melted aspic jelly. Correct the seasoning, then stir in the lightly whipped cream.

Line a 2-quart [2-liter] metal mold with the remaining aspic jelly by swirling the jelly around the inside of the mold while pivoting the base of the mold on a bed of crushed ice. When the jelly sets, fill the mold with the mousse mixture. Refrigerate for at least three hours or until the mousse sets.

To unmold the mousse onto a clean silver platter, dip the base of the mold for one second in hot water, dry the mold, invert the platter over it, and then invert mold and platter together. Lift off the mold. The mousse will appear pink under its coating of transparent jelly. Serve immediately.

PAUL BOCUSE
PAUL BOCUSE'S FRENCH COOKING

Ham in Cream Sauce

Jambon à la Crème de Saulieu

To serve 4

4	thick slices cooked country-style ham (about 1 lb. [½ kg.] in all)	4
1 cup	dry white wine	¼ liter
2 cups	thinly sliced fresh mushrooms	½ liter
1 tbsp.	strained fresh lemon juice	15 ml.
1 tbsp.	water	15 ml.
4 tbsp.	butter	60 ml.
1 tsp.	finely chopped shallot	5 ml.
3 or 4	tomatoes, peeled, seeded and roughly chopped	3 or 4
1 cup	heavy cream	¼ liter
	salt and pepper	

Arrange the ham slices in a gratin dish, sprinkle with a little of the wine, and put the dish, covered (with foil if it has no lid), in a 300° F. [150° C.] oven while preparing the sauce.

Place the mushrooms in a saucepan with the lemon juice, water and half of the butter. Cover and cook over high heat until they come to a foaming boil. Strain the mushroom liquid into another saucepan, reserving the mushrooms.

Add the remaining wine and the shallot to the mushroom liquid and cook the mixture, uncovered, over high heat until reduced by half. Add the tomatoes and cook for 20 minutes to reduce again. Add the cream and cook until the sauce is thick. Drain the juices from the ham dish into the sauce, and correct the seasoning of the sauce with salt and pepper. Take the sauce off the heat and whisk in the remaining butter.

Spread the mushrooms over the ham, and cover the mushrooms and ham with the sauce. Serve hot.

ROGER LALLEMAND
LA VRAIE CUISINE DE LA BOURGOGNE

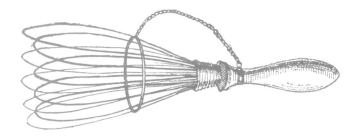

Rice Schnitzels au Gratin

Rijstschnitzels, Gegratinearde

To serve 4

4	pork scallops (about 6 oz. [200 g.] each), pounded flat	4
	salt and freshly ground white pepper	
	Hungarian paprika	
4 tbsp.	butter	60 ml.
1 cup	raw unprocessed rice, boiled in 2 cups [½ liter] water for 20 minutes and drained	¼ liter
1 cup	grated Emmenthaler cheese	¼ liter
Tomato sauce		
4	tomatoes, peeled, quartered and seeded	4
⅔ cup	oil	150 ml.
2	onions, finely chopped	2
2	garlic cloves, finely chopped	2
	salt and freshly ground white pepper	
	oregano	

To make the sauce, heat the oil and add the tomatoes, onions and garlic. Cook over high heat for five minutes, stirring constantly. Add the salt and pepper, and a pinch of oregano. Cover and simmer over low heat for 20 minutes. Purée the sauce through a strainer or food mill and return it to the pan. Stirring frequently, cook over medium heat, uncovered, until the sauce is reduced by a third.

Rub the scallops on both sides with salt, pepper and paprika. Heat 2 tablespoons [30 ml.] of the butter and fry the pork in it for five minutes on each side.

Butter a baking dish liberally, and put in one third of the rice. Cover with one third of the sauce. Now put in two scallops and sprinkle with one third of the grated cheese. Repeat these layers, finishing with a layer of rice, sauce and cheese, and dot with the remaining butter. Bake the casserole in a preheated 350° F. [180° C.] oven for 30 minutes. Serve with a cucumber salad.

LILY VAN PAREREN (EDITOR)
PRISMA VLEESBOEK 2 KALFS-EN VARKENSVLEES

Leaves of Cabbage Filled with Smoked Sausage

To serve 4

4	smoked sausages *(bratwurst, knackwurst* or *beerwurst)*, pierced with a fork	4
1	cabbage	1
1 cup	white sauce *(recipe, page 166)*	¼ liter
	salt and pepper	
¼ tsp.	savory	1 ml.
1 tbsp.	prepared mustard	15 ml.
¼ cup	grated Cheddar cheese	50 ml.

Trim the cabbage of damaged outer leaves. Carefully remove six of the outer leaves (four for wrapping and two additional ones for patching). Trim off the thick white bases and poach the leaves in boiling water for seven minutes. Remove the leaves and drain them.

Remove the hard core and coarsely chop the remaining cabbage. Place the chopped cabbage in the boiling water and cook for 20 minutes. Preheat the oven to 450° F. [230° C.]. Drain the chopped cabbage and put it through the fine disk of a food grinder. To remove excess liquid put the ground cabbage in a sieve or strainer and press out the water. Mix the ground cabbage together with the white sauce, add a little salt and pepper, and the savory.

Heat the sausages in boiling water for three minutes. Drain. Spread out the poached cabbage leaves and cover them lightly with mustard. Make a deep slit along the length of each sausage, cutting almost through. Place one sausage in the center of each cabbage leaf. Fill and cover each sausage generously with the creamed cabbage, reserving about one third for topping. Roll the filled cabbage leaves and place them side by side in a shallow ovenproof casserole. Spread the remaining cabbage mixture over the top; sprinkle with the cheese. Bake for about 30 minutes, or until the cheese is golden brown.

ALBERT STOCKLI
SPLENDID FARE: THE ALBERT STOCKLI COOKBOOK

Gratin of Leek and Ham Rolls

To serve 6

6	thin slices cooked, smoked or boiled ham	6
5 or 6	small zucchini (about 1 lb. [½ kg.]), grated through the medium blade of a food mill into a colander, salted and squeezed dry	5 or 6
7 tbsp.	butter	105 ml.
½ lb.	fresh mushrooms, grated through the medium blade of a food mill	¼ kg.
	salt	
2 tbsp.	chopped fresh parsley or fines herbes	30 ml.
1	onion, finely chopped and stewed without coloring in 2 tbsp. [30 ml.] butter for 30 minutes	1
	pepper	
1 tsp.	strained fresh lemon juice	5 ml.
12	leeks, trimmed, parboiled in salted water for 10 minutes, and drained	12
2 tbsp.	green peppercorns, parboiled if fresh, vacuum-packed or frozen; drained and rinsed if in brine	30 ml.
½ cup	freshly grated Parmesan cheese	125 ml.
½ cup	freshly grated Gruyère cheese	125 ml.
2½ cups	white sauce *(recipe, page 166)*	625 ml.

Sauté the zucchini in 2 tablespoons [30 ml.] of the butter over high heat, tossing them often, for seven or eight minutes. Set aside. Sauté the mushrooms, lightly salted, in 2 tablespoons of the remaining butter, tossing them constantly, for about three or four minutes or until all their liquid has evaporated and they begin to cling to the pan. Add the chopped herbs a few moments before removing from the heat and, at the moment of removing, grind over a bit of pepper and add a few drops of lemon juice. Mix together the zucchini, mushrooms and stewed onions.

Roll two leeks coated with 2 tablespoons of the vegetable mixture into each of the slices of ham and arrange the rolls, flap side down, in a buttered gratin dish of such a size that they barely touch. Scatter the green peppercorns over the rolls. Stir half of the grated cheese into the white sauce and spoon it evenly over the ham rolls. Sprinkle on the remaining cheese, distribute the remaining 3 tablespoons [45 ml.] of butter, chilled, in paper-thin sheets over the surface, and bake in a preheated 400° F. [200° C.] oven for 30 minutes or until the sauce is bubbling and the surface is richly golden.

RICHARD OLNEY
SIMPLE FRENCH FOOD

Holstein Ham Dumplings

Holsteiner Schinkenklösse

To make about 40 dumplings

1½ to 2 cups	diced, cooked, lean smoked ham (about ½ lb. [¼ kg.])	375 to 500 ml.
2	bread rolls, diced, or about 2 cups [½ liter] diced bread	2
4 tbsp.	butter	60 ml.
1	onion, finely chopped	1
1 cup	milk	¼ liter
1	egg	1
1	egg yolk	1
	salt	
2 cups	flour	½ liter

Fry the cubed bread in the butter until it is golden brown. Remove the bread and fry the onion in the same pan until it is soft and golden. In a bowl, mix the milk with the egg and the yolk. Season with salt and gradually add the flour, the fried bread, onion and pieces of ham. Let stand for 15 minutes or so. Form dumplings with a spoon and simmer in a large pan of salted water for 15 to 20 minutes.

JUTTA KÜRTZ
DAS KOCHBUCH AUS SCHLESWIG-HOLSTEIN

Crepe and Ham Rolls

Crepes Rondinerie

To serve 4 to 6

8 to 12	slices cooked smoked ham	8 to 12
3 or 4	shallots, thinly sliced	3 or 4
4 tbsp.	butter	60 ml.
½ cup	dry white vermouth	125 ml.
⅔ cup	heavy cream	150 ml.
¼ cup	grated Parmesan cheese	50 ml.
Crepe batter		
½ cup	flour	125 ml.
	salt	
3	eggs	3
about ¾ cup	milk or water	about ¼ liter
3 tbsp.	melted butter	45 ml.

To make the crepes, place the flour in a bowl with a pinch of salt. Add the eggs and then the liquid, whisking from the center outward until the mixture is smooth. The batter should be thin enough to lightly coat the back of a spoon. Add the butter last. Lightly grease a crepe pan or small frying pan, heat over medium heat and swirl a small ladleful of batter around to cover the bottom of the pan. When the batter is set, turn the crepe and cook the other side. Remove to a warmed plate. Make eight to 12 crepes in this way, enough for two crepes per person.

Gently sauté the shallots in half of the butter until soft. Add the vermouth, bring to a boil, reduce the heat and cook for a few minutes until the mixture is thick. Lay a ham slice on each crepe, brush the ham with the shallot mixture, add a dollop of cream and a sprinkle of cheese. Roll up the ham in the crepes and put the rolls in a buttered gratin dish.

Sprinkle the rolled crepes with the grated Parmesan and dot with the remaining butter. Put in a preheated 400° F. [200° C.] oven for 15 minutes before serving.

ARIANE CASTAING
HARPER'S AND QUEEN MAGAZINE

Individual Ham Rolls

To serve 8

16	slices boiled ham, about 6 inches [15 cm.] square and ⅛ inch [3 mm.] thick	16
1 lb.	ground cooked, smoked or boiled ham	½ kg.
6	eggs, beaten	6
½ cup	dry bread crumbs	125 ml.
2 tsp.	chopped fresh tarragon	30 ml.
3 tbsp.	capers, rinsed, drained well and chopped	45 ml.
1 tsp.	salt	5 ml.
½ tsp.	freshly ground black pepper	2 ml.
1 tbsp.	Dijon-style prepared mustard	15 ml.
2 tbsp.	finely chopped fresh parsley	30 ml.
½ cup	Madeira	125 ml.
4 tbsp.	butter, melted	60 ml.

Mix together the ground ham, eggs, bread crumbs, tarragon, capers, salt, pepper, mustard and parsley. Brush the ham squares with half of the Madeira and spoon the ground ham mixture along one edge. Roll up each slice and lay the roll, seam side down, in a buttered baking dish. (The recipe can be made in advance up to this point.) Place the dish in a preheated 350° F. [180° C.] oven and bake for 30 minutes. Baste three times during baking with the remaining Madeira mixed with the melted butter.

JULIE DANNENBAUM
MENUS FOR ALL OCCASIONS

Pig's Feet Ste-Menehould

Pieds de Cochon à la Ste-Ménéhould

To serve 8

8	pig's feet, scraped with a knife, singed and rinsed	8
	coarse salt	
1	bouquet garni	1
1	onion, stuck with 2 whole cloves	1
1	carrot	1
about 2½ cups	stock (recipe, page 165)	about 625 ml.
about 2½ cups	dry white wine	about 625 ml.
	softened butter	
	bread crumbs	

Soak the pig's feet in cold water to cover for several hours. Drain them, coat them heavily with coarse salt, and leave them in the salt for two days.

When ready to cook the feet, rinse off the salt and tie them up well, two by two, to keep them intact during cooking. Cover with cold water, bring to a boil, drain immediately and rinse in cold water. Put them in a pot with the bouquet garni, onion and carrot. Pour over enough stock and wine to cover them. Cook, covered, over very low heat, or in a 300° F. [150° C.] oven for at least four hours.

Remove the pig's feet from the pot and allow them to cool. When they are cold, take off the strings and cut each pig's foot in half lengthwise. Brush the halves with butter, roll them in dry bread crumbs, and broil them until they are golden brown on both sides.

CHARLES DURAND
LE CUISINIER DURAND

Deviled Pig's Ears

Oreilles de Porc au Diable

The flavor of pig's ears is greatly improved if they are soaked in the brine tub, or dry-salted, for two or three days. After they have been poached, they may be eaten hot with a vinaigrette sauce: 5 tablespoons [75 ml.] of oil, 1 tablespoon [15 ml.] of vinegar, salt, pepper and a little prepared mustard, mixed well and flavored with chopped onion, parsley, garlic, shallot, capers or sour gherkins to taste. Or pig's ears may be cut in strips, dipped in batter and deep fried.

To serve 6

6	pig's ears, cleaned and singed, if desired	6
1½ quarts	court bouillon (recipe, below)	1½ liters
3 tbsp.	prepared mustard	45 ml.
4 tbsp.	butter, melted	60 ml.
½ cup	bread crumbs	125 ml.

Sauce diable

2 tbsp.	finely chopped onion or shallot	30 ml.
½ cup	wine vinegar	125 ml.
1 cup	dry white wine	¼ liter
1 cup	velouté sauce (recipe, page 166)	¼ liter

In a saucepan, simmer the pig's ears in the court bouillon for about two to three hours. Watch that the delicious gelatinous covering does not fall off the cartilage—take the ears out before this happens. Put them to cool under a weight.

When the cooked ears have cooled down, cut them into halves, lengthwise. Brush them with the mustard, dip in the melted butter and then in the bread crumbs, then broil. You can equally well put them in a preheated 400° F. [200° C.] oven, if this is more convenient, but don't let them go beyond the point of crispness. Charred ears are not attractive.

To make the sauce, cook the onions, wine and vinegar until there is hardly any liquid left. Add the velouté sauce, and bring to the boil. Do not strain.

Serve the broiled ears accompanied by the sauce.

JANE GRIGSON
THE ART OF MAKING SAUSAGES, PÂTÉS, AND OTHER CHARCUTERIE

Standard Preparations

Court Bouillon

To make 1½ quarts [1½ liters] court bouillon

1½ quarts	water	1½ liters
2	onions, thinly sliced	2
2	carrots, thinly sliced	2
1	bouquet garni	1
2 tbsp.	salt	30 ml.
1 cup	dry white wine (optional)	¼ liter

In a large saucepan, boil the water with the onions, carrots, bouquet garni and salt for 10 to 15 minutes. Let the bouillon cool. When reheating for use, add the wine if desired.

Brine

This amount of brine is sufficient for about 4 pounds [2 kg.] of pork. The technique of salting pork is demonstrated on pages 14-15.

To make 2 quarts [2 liters] brine

1½ cups	sea salt	350 ml.
2 quarts	water	2 liters
¼ cup	white or brown sugar	50 ml.
2 tbsp.	juniper berries	30 ml.
8 to 10	whole cloves	8 to 10
6	bay leaves	6
2	blades mace	2
4 or 5	sprigs thyme	4 or 5

In a heavy pot, bring the water to a boil with the salt and sugar. Boil for two minutes. Remove from the heat and put in the pot a cheesecloth bag containing the remaining ingredients. Allow the brine to cool completely before removing the cheesecloth bag of aromatics.

Dry Salting Mixture

This amount of salting mixture is sufficient for about 4 pounds [2 kg.] of pork. The technique of salting pork is demonstrated on pages 14-15.

To make 1 pound [½ kg.] mixture

1 lb.	coarse salt	½ kg.
4	allspice berries	4
4	whole cloves	4
6	juniper berries	6
2	bay leaves	2
6	peppercorns	6
1 tbsp.	mixed dried herbs	15 ml.

In a mortar, crush the allspice, cloves, juniper berries, bay leaves and peppercorns together coarsely. Mix with the salt and herbs. Rub the salt mixture over the pork, making sure that all of the surfaces of the meat are evenly covered. Put a layer of the salt mixture in the bottom of the dish or bowl you are using, put in the salted pieces of pork, and sprinkle the remaining mixture over the top.

Basic Stock

This stock may be made entirely from pork bones, to use for a sauce to serve with a boned pork roast. Gelatinous elements such as ears, tails and rind will make the finished stock set to a firm jelly. Other suitable meat choices are veal knuckle, gelatinous cuts of beef—oxtail, shank or chuck—and chicken carcasses and trimmings.

To make 2 to 3 quarts [2 to 3 liters] stock

6 to 7 lb.	meaty bones and trimmings (pork, veal, beef or chicken)	3 kg.
3 to 5 quarts	water	3 to 5 liters
4	carrots, scraped and topped	4
2	large onions, 1 stuck with 2 or 3 whole cloves	2
1	whole garlic bulb, unpeeled	1
1	celery rib	1
1	leek, split and washed	1
1	large bouquet garni	1
	salt	

Put the pieces of bone on a rack in the bottom of a heavy stockpot, and place the meat and trimmings on top of them. Add cold water to cover the meats by 2 inches [5 cm.]. Bring to a boil over low heat, starting to skim before the liquid reaches a boil. Keep skimming, occasionally adding a glass of cold water, until no more scum rises. Do not stir, lest you cloud the stock.

Add the vegetables, bouquet garni and a dash of salt to the pot, pushing them down into the liquid so that everything is submerged. Continue skimming until the liquid boils again. Reduce the heat to very low, partly cover the pot and cook at a bare simmer for four hours, skimming off the surface fat three or four times.

Strain the stock by pouring the contents of the pot through a colander into a large bowl or clean pot. Discard the bones and meat trimmings, vegetables and bouquet garni. Cool the strained stock and skim the last traces of fat from the surface. If there is any residue at the bottom of the container after the stock cools, decant the clear liquid carefully and discard the sediment.

Refrigerate the stock if you do not plan to use it immediately; it will keep safely for three to four days. To preserve the stock longer, refrigerate it for only 12 hours or until the last bits of fat solidify on the top—then you can scrape off the fat and warm the stock enough so that it may be poured into four or five pint-sized freezer containers. Make sure to cover the containers tightly. The freezer stock will keep for six months, while you draw on the supply—container by container—as necessary.

Basic White Sauce

Use this recipe whenever béchamel sauce is required.

To make about 2 cups [½ liter] sauce

2 tbsp.	butter	30 ml.
2 tbsp.	flour	30 ml.
2½ cups	milk	625 ml.
	salt	
	white pepper	
	freshly grated nutmeg (optional)	
	heavy cream (optional)	

Melt the butter in a heavy saucepan. Stir in the flour and cook, stirring, over low heat for two to five minutes. Pour in all of the milk, whisking constantly to blend the mixture smoothly. Increase the heat and continue whisking while the sauce comes to a boil. Season with very little salt.

Reduce the heat to very low, and simmer for about 40 minutes, stirring every so often to prevent the sauce from sticking to the bottom of the pan. Add white pepper and a pinch of nutmeg if desired; taste for seasoning. Whisk again until the sauce is perfectly smooth, and add cream if you prefer a richer and whiter sauce.

Velouté Sauce

To make about 2 cups [½ liter] sauce

2 tbsp.	butter	30 ml.
2 tbsp.	flour	30 ml.
2½ cups	stock *(recipe, page 165)*	625 ml.
	salt and pepper	

Melt the butter in a heavy saucepan. Stir in the flour and cook, stirring, over low heat for two to five minutes. Pour in all of the stock, whisking constantly to blend the mixture smoothly. Increase the heat and continue whisking while the sauce comes to a boil.

Reduce the heat to very low, move the pan to the side of the heat and simmer for about 40 minutes, skimming occasionally. Correct the seasoning before using the sauce.

Sauce Robert

To make the variation on this sauce known as *charcutière* sauce, add about 2 tablespoons [30 ml.] of sour gherkins, cut into julienne, to the hot, finished *sauce Robert*. Do not boil or strain the sauce after this addition.

To make about 2 cups [½ liter] sauce

⅓ cup	chopped shallots or onion	75 ml.
5 tbsp.	butter	75 ml.
¼ cup	dry white wine	50 ml.
2 cups	velouté sauce *(recipe, below, left)*	½ liter
1 tsp.	prepared hot mustard	15 ml.

In a heavy saucepan over medium heat, fry the shallots or onion in 1 tablespoon [15 ml.] of the butter until they color slightly. Add the wine and boil the mixture until almost all of the liquid has evaporated. Reduce the heat to low, add the velouté sauce and simmer, uncovered, for about 30 minutes. Stir in the mustard and simmer for five minutes. Finally, blend in the remaining butter. Do not strain the sauce.

Barbecue Sauce

To make about 2 cups [½ liter] sauce

1	fresh hot chili, stemmed, seeded and chopped	1
1	garlic clove, chopped	1
1 tsp.	dry mustard	5 ml.
½ tsp.	basil	2 ml.
½ tsp.	oregano	2 ml.
1 tsp.	salt	5 ml.
2 to 3 tbsp.	fresh orange juice	30 to 45 ml.
½ cup	red wine vinegar	125 ml.
½ cup	honey	125 ml.
1	small onion, finely chopped	1
2 tbsp.	oil	30 ml.
8	medium-sized tomatoes, peeled, seeded and chopped or 3 cups [¾ liter] tomato purée made from drained, canned tomatoes	8

Using a mortar and pestle, pound the chili, garlic, mustard, basil, oregano and salt to a paste. Stir in the orange juice, vinegar and honey. Press this seasoning mixture through a strainer into a bowl and set it aside.

In a large saucepan over medium heat, cook the chopped onion in the oil until it is soft but not brown. Stir in the tomatoes and then the seasoning mixture. Increase the heat to bring the sauce to a boil, then reduce the heat enough so the sauce gently simmers. Stirring occasionally, cook the sauce, uncovered, for 30 to 40 minutes or until it thickens and is reduced to half of its original volume. Taste the sauce and correct the seasoning.

Apple Sauce

To make about 3 cups [¾ liter] sauce

7 or 8	apples, peeled, cored and sliced (about 2 lb. [1 kg.])	7 or 8
	salt	
4 tbsp.	butter (optional)	60 ml.
½ cup	sugar (optional)	125 ml.

Put the apples in a large saucepan and add a little water to keep them from sticking. Cook over medium heat, stirring frequently, until the apples are soft and almost dissolved into a lumpy purée, about 20 minutes. Stir in a pinch of salt. Add butter, if serving hot, or sugar, or both. Taste and correct the seasoning. The sauce may be sieved or left as it is, and may be served hot or cold.

Tapenade

This highly flavored mixture has many variations. If you wish, you can pound in thyme or powdered bay leaf, garlic cloves or tuna, or stir in a small amount of Cognac. If desired, the mixture may be prepared in a food processor.

To make about 1 cup [¼ liter] sauce

½ cup	pitted ripe oil-packed olives, coarsely chopped	125 ml.
2	salt anchovies, filleted, soaked in cold water for 30 minutes, patted dry and coarsely chopped	2
¼ cup	capers, rinsed and drained	50 ml.
about ¼ cup	olive oil	about 50 ml.
1 tsp.	fresh lemon juice	5 ml.
	freshly ground pepper	
1 tsp.	dry mustard (optional)	5 ml.

In a large mortar, pound together the olives, anchovies and capers until they form a paste. Little by little, stir in enough oil to make a sauce of rather firm consistency. Then season the mixture with the lemon juice, pepper to taste, and dry mustard if you are using it.

Short-Crust and Rough Puff Pastry

For a pork pie, the butter in this recipe may be wholly or partially replaced by lard. For a two-crust pie, the quantities must be doubled.

To line an 8- to 9-inch [20- to 23-cm.] flan ring or cover an 8- to 9-inch pie dish

1 cup	flour	¼ liter
¼ tsp.	salt	1 ml.
8 tbsp.	cold unsalted butter, cut into small pieces	120 ml.
3 to 4 tbsp.	cold water	45 to 60 ml.

Mix the flour and salt in a mixing bowl. Add the butter and cut it into the flour rapidly, using two table knives, until the butter is in tiny pieces. Do not work for more than a few minutes. Add half of the water and, with a fork, quickly blend it into the flour-and-butter mixture. Add just enough of the rest of the water to allow you to gather the dough together with your hands into a firm ball. Wrap the dough in plastic film or waxed paper and refrigerate it for two to three hours, or put it in the freezer for 20 minutes until the outside surface is slightly frozen.

To roll out short-crust pastry: Remove the ball of pastry dough from the refrigerator or freezer and put it on a cool, floured surface (a marble slab is ideal). Press the dough out partially with your hand, then give it a few gentle smacks with the rolling pin to flatten it and render it more supple. Roll out the dough from the center, until the pastry forms a circle about ½ inch [1 cm.] thick. Turn the pastry over so that both sides are floured and continue rolling until the circle is about ⅛ inch [3 mm.] thick. Roll the pastry onto the rolling pin, lift it up and unroll it over the flan ring or pie dish. If using the pastry for a flan, press the pastry firmly against all surfaces and trim the edges. If using the pastry to cover a pie, trim the pastry to within ½ inch [1 cm.] of the rim of the dish, turn under the pastry edges around the rim to form a double layer and press the pastry firmly to the rim with thumb and forefinger to crimp the edges.

To roll out rough puff pastry: Place the dough on a cool, floured surface and smack it flat with the rolling pin. Turn the dough over to make sure that both sides are well floured. Roll out the pastry rapidly into a rectangle about 1 foot [30 cm.] long and 5 to 6 inches [13 to 15 cm.] wide. Fold the two short ends to meet each other in the center, then fold again to align the folded edges with each other. Following the direction of the fold lines, roll the pastry into a rectangle again, fold again in the same way and refrigerate for at least 30 minutes. Repeat this process two or three more times before using the pastry. Always let the pastry dough rest in the refrigerator in between rollings.

Recipe Index

All recipes in the index that follows are listed by their English titles. Entries are organized by the cuts of pork and also by major ingredients called for in titles. Sauces, marinades and stuffings are listed separately. Foreign recipes are listed by country or region of origin. Recipe credits are on pages 174-176.

General Index/ Glossary

Included in this index to the cooking demonstrations are definitions, in italics, of special culinary terms not explained elsewhere in this volume. The Recipe Index begins on page 168.

Recipe Credits

The sources for the recipes in this volume are listed below. Page references in parentheses indicate where the recipes appear in the anthology.

Acton, Eliza, *Modern Cookery.* Published by Longman, Green, Longman, and Roberts, 1865(88, 146).
Adam, Hans Karl, *Das Kochbuch aus Schwaben.* © Copyright 1976 by Verlagsteam Wolfgang Hölker. Published by Verlag Wolfgang Hölker, Münster. Translated by permission of Verlag Wolfgang Hölker(133).
Allen, Jana and Margaret Gin, *Offal.* © Jana Allen and Margaret Gin, 1974. © Pitman Publishing 1976. First published in the United States 1974. First published in Great Britain 1976. By permission of 101 Productions, San Francisco(151).
American Heritage, the editors of, *The American Heritage Cookbook.* © 1964 American Heritage Publishing Company, Inc. Published by American Heritage Publishing Company, Inc., N.Y. Reprinted by permission of American Heritage Publishing Company, Inc.(115, 124).
Andrade, Margarette de, *Brazilian Cookery.* Copyright in Japan, 1965, by the Charles E. Tuttle Company, Inc. Published by the Charles E. Tuttle Company, Inc., Tokyo. By permission of the Charles E. Tuttle Company, Inc.(101).
Artocchini, Carmen (Editor), *400 Ricette Della Cucina Piacentina.* Published by Gino Molinari, Piacenza. Translated by permission of Carmen Artocchini and Gino Molinari(92).
Art of Cookery Made Plain and Easy, The. By a Lady. The Sixth Edition, 1758(105, 156).
Artusi, Pellagrino, *La Scienza in Cucina e l'Arte di Mangiar Bene.* Copyright © 1970 Giulio Einaudi Editore S.p.A. Published by Giulio Einaudi Editore 1970(145).
Asada, Mineko, *120 Pork Side Dishes.* © Shufunotomo Co. Ltd., 1975. Published by Shufunotomo Co. Ltd., Tokyo. By permission of Shufunotomo Co. Ltd.(93).
Aureden, Lilo, *Das Schmeckt so Gut.* © 1965 by Lichtenberg Verlag, München. Published by Lichtenberg Verlag, München, 1973. Translated by permission of Kindler Verlag GmbH, Munich(117, 143).
Bateman, Michael and Caroline Conran (Editors), *Best British Meat Dishes (The Sunday Times).* Copyright © Michael Bateman and Caroline Conran 1977. Published by Cassell & Company Limited, London. By permission of Times Newspapers Ltd., London(107).
Beard, James A., *The Fireside Cook Book.* Copyright © 1949, 1976 by Simon & Schuster, Inc. and The Artists and Writers Guild, Inc. Published by Simon & Schuster, New York. By permission of Simon & Schuster(130).
Béguin, Maurice, *La Cuisine en Poitou.* Published by La Librairie Saint-Denis, © 1933(124).
Benoit, Félix and Henry Clos Jouve, *La Cuisine Lyonnaise.* © Solar, 1975. Published by Solar, Paris. Translated by permission of Solar, Paris(144, 146).
Besson, Josephine, *La Mère Besson "Ma Cuisine Provençale."* © Éditions Albin Michel, 1977. Published by Éditions Albin Michel, Paris. Translated by permission of Éditions Albin Michel, Paris(106).
Bocuse, Paul, *Paul Bocuse's French Cooking.* Copyright © 1977 by Random House, Inc. Published by Pantheon Books, Inc., N.Y. Reprinted by permission of Pantheon Books, a division of Random House, Inc.(125, 127, 160).
Boni, Ada, *Italian Regional Cooking.* Copyright © 1969 s.c. by Arnoldo Mondadori. Published by Arnoldo Mondadori Editore SpA., Milan. Translated by permission of Arnoldo Mondadori Editore SpA.(113, 133, 154).
Borer, Eva Maria, *Tante Heidi's Swiss Kitchen.* English text copyright © 1965 by Nicholas Kaye Ltd. First published as *Die Echte Schweizer Küche* by Mary Hahns, Kochbuchverlag, Berlin W., 1963. By permission of Kaye & Ward Ltd.(150).
Bozzi, Ottorina Perna, *Vecchia Brianza in Cucina.* ©

1975 by Giunti Martello Editore, Firenze. Published by Giunti Martello Editore, Florence. Translated by permission of Giunti Martello Editore(93, 121, 131, 134).
Breteuil, Jules, *Le Cuisinier Européen.* Published by Garnier Frères Libraires-Éditeurs © 1860(94).
Břízová, Joza and Maryna Klimentová, *Tschechische Küche.* Published by Verlag Práce, Praque and Verlag für die Frau, Leipzig. Translated by permission of Práce(111, 140).
Brown, Cora, Rose and Bob, *The South American Cook Book.* First published by Doubleday, Doran & Company Inc., 1939. Republished in 1971 by Dover Publications Inc., New York(135).
Bugialli, Giuliano, *The Fine Art of Italian Cooking.* Copyright © 1977 by Giuliano Bugialli. Published by Times Books, a Division of Quadrangle/The New York Times Book Co., Inc., New York. Reprinted by permission of Times Books, a Division of Quadrangle/The New York Times Book Co., Inc.(157, 159).
Cabanillas, Berta and Carmen Ginorio, *Puerto Rican Dishes.* © University of Puerto Rico Press. Published by Editorial Universitaria, Rio Piedras. By permission of Editorial Universitaria(139).
Candler, Teresa Gilardi, *The Northern Italian Cookbook.* Copyright © 1977 by Teresa Gilardi Candler. Published by McGraw-Hill Book Company. Reprinted by permission of McGraw-Hill Book Company(127).
Carnacina, Luigi, *Great Italian Cooking.* Edited by Michael Sonino. Published in English by Abradale Press Inc., New York. By permission of Aldo Garzanti Editore and Abradale Press(159).
Castaing, Ariane, recipe taken from *Harpers and Queen* magazine, September, 1974. By permission of Ariane Castaing(163).
Chantiles, Vilma Liacouras, *The Food of Greece.* Copyright © 1975 by Vilma Liacouras Chantiles. Published by Atheneum, New York. By permission of Vilma Liacouras Chantiles(86, 110).
Chiang, Cecilia Sun Yun, *The Mandarin Way.* (As told to Allan Carr.) Copyright © 1974 by Cecilia Chiang and Allan Carr. Published by Little, Brown and Co., Boston, in association with The Atlantic Monthly Press. By permission of Cecilia Sun Yun Chiang(123).
Chu, Grace Zia, *Madame Chu's Chinese Cooking School.* Copyright © 1975 by Grace Zia Chu. Published by Simon & Schuster, a Division of Gulf & Western Corporation, New York. Reprinted by permission of Simon & Schuster, a Division of Gulf & Western Corporation(142).
Conran, Terence and Maria Kroll, *The Vegetable Book.* © Conran Ink 1976. Published by Wiliam Collins Sons & Co. Ltd., Glasgow and Crescent, New York (an imprint of Crown Publishers, Inc.). By permission of William Collins Sons & Co. Ltd.(102, 149, 100, 97, 122, 135, 141, 131).
Corsi, Guglielma, *Un Secolo di Cucina Umbra.* Published by Tipografia Porziuncola, Assisi 1968. Translated by permission of Tipografia Porziuncola(126).
Cottington, Taylor, D.D., *Good Housekeeping Menu & Recipe Book.* First published 1926. By permission of The National Magazine Co. Ltd., London(141).
Couffignal, Huguette, *La Cuisine Paysanne.* © Solar 1976. Published by Solar, Paris. Translated by permission of Solar, Paris(103, 138).
Croze, Austin de, *Les Plats Régionaux de France.* Published by Éditions Daniel Morcrette, Luzarches. Translated by permission of Éditions Daniel Morcrette(155).
Curnonsky, *A l'Infortune du Pot.* Copyright Éditions de la Couronne 1946. Published by Éditions de la Couronne, Paris(114, 152). *Recettes des Provinces de France.* Published by Les Productions de Paris, Paris(94).
Cutler, Carol, *The Six-Minute Soufflé and Other Culinary Delights.* Copyright © 1976 by Carol Cutler. Published by Clarkson N. Potter, Inc. By permission of Clarkson N. Potter, Inc.(90, 130).
Czerny, Z. Kierst, Strasburger and Kapuscinska, *Zdrowo I Smacznie.* Published by PZWL, Warsaw 1965. Translated by permission of Agencja Autorska, Warsaw, for the authors(90).
Daily Telegraph, The, *Four Hundred Prize Recipes.* © by The Daily Telegraph. Published by The Daily Telegraph,

London. By permission of The Daily Telegraph(109).
Dannenbaum, Julie, *Menus for All Occasions.* Copyright © 1974 by Julie Dannenbaum. Published by E. P. Dutton & Co., Inc., N.Y. Reprinted by permission of E. P. Dutton(163).
David, Elizabeth, *Dried Herbs, Aromatics and Condiments.* Copyright © Elizabeth David 1969. By permission of Elizabeth David(113). *French Provincial Cooking.* Copyright © Elizabeth David 1960, 1962, 1967, 1969. Published by Penguin Books Ltd. in association with Michael Joseph. By permission of Elizabeth David(110, 119). *Spices, Salt and Aromatics in the English Kitchen.* Copyright © Elizabeth David, 1970. Published by Penguin Books Ltd., London. By permission of Penguin Books Ltd.(114).
David-Perez, Enriqueta, *Recipes of the Philippines.* Copyright © by Enriqueta David-Perez. By permission of Rodrigo Perez III(137).
Doi, Masaru, *Japanese One-Pot Cookery.* Published jointly by Ward Lock & Co., Limited and Kodansha International, Ltd., Tokyo. By permission of Kodansha International, Ltd.(138).
Douglas, Joyce, *Old Pendle Recipes.* © Joyce Douglas 1976. Published by Hendon Publishing Co. Ltd., Nelson. By permission of Hendon Publishing Co. Ltd.(116).
Dumaine, Alexandre, *Ma Cuisine.* © 1972 by Pensée Moderne, Paris. Published by Éditions de la Pensée Moderne. Translated by permission of Jacques Grancher, Éditeur, Paris(89, 124, 148).
Durand, Charles, *Le Cuisinier Durand.* Privately published by the author, Nîmes, 1843(164).
Easlea, Kate, *Cooking in Hampshire Past and Present.* Published by Paul Cave Publications Ltd., Southampton. By permission of Paul Cave Publications Ltd.(156).
Famularo, Joe and Louise Imperiale, *The Festive Famularo Kitchen.* Copyright © 1977 by Joe Famularo and Louise Imperiale. Published in 1977 by Atheneum Publishers, New York. By permission of Atheneum Publishers(88).
Farmer, Fannie Merritt, *A Book of Good Dinners for My Friend.* Published by Dodge Publishing Company. Reprinted by permission of the Fannie Farmer Cookbook Corporation(117).
Feng, Doreen Yen Hung, *The Joy of Chinese Cooking.* First published by Faber and Faber Limited, London in 1952. By permission of Faber and Faber Limited(148).
Foods of the World, *American Cooking; American Cooking: Eastern Heartland; American Cooking: Southern Style; The Cooking of China; Pacific and Southeast Asian Cooking; The Cooking of Scandinavia; The Cooking of Spain and Portugal; The Cooking of Vienna's Empire.* Copyright © 1968 Time-Life Books Inc.; Copyright © 1971 Time-Life Books Inc.; Copyright © 1971 Time Inc.; Copyright © 1968 Time Inc.; Copyright © 1970 Time Inc.; Copyright © 1968 Time-Life Books Inc.; Copyright © 1969 Time-Life Books Inc.; Copyright © 1968, 1974 Time-Life Books Inc.(102, 149, 100, 97, 122, 135, 141, 131).
Fortin, Stanley, *The World Book of Pork Dishes.* © 1967 by Stanley Fortin. First published in Great Britain by Pelham Books Ltd., London, 1967. By permission of Pelham Books Ltd.(112).
Graves, Eleanor, *Great Dinners from Life.* Copyright © 1969 Time Inc. Published by Time-Life Books Inc., Alexandria(115).
Grigson, Jane, *The Art of Making Sausages, Pâtés, and Other Charcuterie.* Copyright © 1967, 1968 by Jane Grigson. Originally published in Great Britain as *The Art of Charcuterie,* 1967. Published in the United States by Alfred A. Knopf, Inc., New York. Reprinted by Alfred A. Knopf, Inc., New York(158, 164). *English Food.* Copyright © Jane Grigson 1974. First published by Macmillan 1974. Published by Penguin Books 1977. By permission of David Higham Associates Ltd.(130).
Guillot, Andre, *La Grande Cuisine Bourgeoise.* © 1976 Flammarion, Paris. Published by Flammarion et Cie. Translated by permission of Flammarion et Cie(160).
Harrell, Monette R. and Robert W. Harrell Jr., *The Ham Book.* Copyright © 1977 by Monette R. Harrell and Robert W. Harrell Jr. Published by the Donning Company/Publishers. Reprinted by permission of the Donning Company/Publishers(118).

Hawliczkowa, Helena, *Kuchnia Polska.* (Editor: Maria Librowska). Published by Panstowe Wydawnictwo Ekonomiczne, Warsaw, 1976. Translated by permission of Agencja Autorska, Warsaw, for the author(152).
Hellermann, Dorothee V., *Das Kochbuch aus Hamburg.* © Copyright 1975 by Verlagsteam Wolfgang Hölker. Published by Verlagsteam Wolfgang Hölker, Münster. Translated by permission of Verlagsteam Wolfgang Hölker(144).
Hess, Olga and Adolf Fr. Hess, *Wiener Küche,* 37th Edition 1977. Copyright © by Franz Deuticke, Vienna, 1963. Published by Franz Deuticke, Vienna. Translated by permission of Verlag Franz Deuticke(121).
Hewitt, Jean, *The New York Times Southern Heritage Cookbook.* Copyright © 1972 and 1976 by the New York Times. Published by G. P. Putnam's Sons, N.Y. Reprinted by permission of G. P. Putman's Sons(99).
Hippisley Coxe, Antony and Araminta, *The Book of the Sausage.* © Araminta & Antony Hippisley Coxe, 1978. Published by Pan Books Ltd., London. By permission of Pan Books Ltd.(86).
House and Garden, Editors of, *House & Garden's New Cook Book.* Copyright © 1967 by House & Garden's New Cook Book. Published by Simon and Schuster, New York. By permission of Condé Nast Publications Inc.(98).
Howe, Robin, *Cooking from the Commonwealth.* © Robin Howe 1958. First published 1958 by André Deutsch Limited, London. By permission of Curtis Brown Ltd., London, as Agent for the Author(122). *Greek Cooking.* © Robin Howe 1960. First published 1960 by André Deutsch Limited, London. By permission of Curtis Brown Ltd., London, as Agent for the Author(143).
Jans, Hugh, *Bistro Koken.* © Unieboek BV/C.A.J. van Dishoeck, Bussum, Holland. Translated by permission of Unieboek BV/C.A.J. van Dishoeck(147). *Vrij Nederland, March 1973.* Published by Vrij Nederland, Amsterdam. Translated by permission of Hugh Jans(106).
Käkönen, Ulla, *Natural Cooking the Finnish Way.* Copyright © 1974 by Ulla Käkönen. Published by Quadrangle/The New York Times Book Co., New York. By permission of Times Books, a Division of Quadrangle/The New York Times Book Co.(137).
Kennedy, Diana, *The Cuisines of Mexico.* Copyright © 1972 by Diana Kennedy. Published by Harper & Row, Publishers, Inc., New York. By permission of Harper & Row, Publishers, Inc.(91).
Kiehnle, Hermine and Maria Hädecke, *Das Neue Kiehnle-Kochbuch.* © Walter Hädecke Verlag. Published by Walter Hädecke Verlag, Lukas-Mosen-Weg. Translated by permission of Walter Hädecke Verlag(93, 111).
Koon, Mrs. Lee Chin, *Mrs. Lee's Cookbook.* (Editor: Mrs. Pamelia Lee Suan Yew). Published by Mrs. Lee's Cookbook, Singapore. By permission of Mrs. Pamelia Lee Suan Yew(97).
Koranyi, Rose, *Livre de la Bonne Chère.* Published by Edition Hungaria, Budapest(137).
Koscher, Joseph and Associates, *Les Recettes de la Table Alsacienne.* © Les Recettes de la Table Alsacienne, Librairie Istra, 15 rue des Juifs, Strasbourg (France). Published by Société Alsacienne d'Édition et de Diffusion, Strasbourg. Translated by permission of Librairie Istra(150, 156).
Kulinairische Gerichte: zu Gast bei Freunden. Copyright to this translation by Verlag für die Frau DDR Leipzig. Published by Verlag für die Frau, Leipzig and Verlag MIR, Moscow 1977. Translated by permission of VAAP, The Copyright Agency of the USSR, Moscow(96, 158).
Kürtz, Jutta, *Das Kochbuch aus Schleswig-Holstein.* © Copyright 1976 by Verlagsteam Wolfgang Hölker. Published by Verlagsteam Wolfgang Hölker, Münster. Translated by permission of Verlagsteam Wolfgang Hölker(150, 163).
Labarre, Irène and Jean Mercier, *La Cuisine du Poitou de la Vendée.* Copyright © Solar 1977. Published by Solar, Paris. Translated by permission of Solar(123).
Lallemand, Roger, *La Vraie Cuisine de la Bourgogne.* Published by Librairie Quartier Latin, La Rochelle. Translated by permission of Librairie Quartier Latin(161). *La Vraie Cuisine de la Champagne.* Published by Librairie Quartier Latin, La Rochelle. Translated by permission of Librairie Quartier Latin(125).
Laloue, P. E., *Le Guide de la Charcuterie.* Copyright 1950 by P. E. Laloue. Published by Le Guide de la Charcuterie(100, 120).
Lasasso, Wilma Reiva, *Regional Italian Cooking.* © By Wilma Reiva Lasasso 1958. Published by Collier Books/a Division of Macmillan Publishing Co., Inc., New York. By permission of Macmillan Publishing Co., Inc.(99, 135).
Lo, Lucy, *Chinese Cooking With Lucy Lo.* Copyright © 1979 by Lucy Lo. Published by Horwitz Publications, Hong Kong. By permission of Horwitz Group Books Pty., Ltd., Australia(95).
MacMiadhacháin, Anna, *Spanish Regional Cookery.* © Anna MacMiadacháin, 1976. Published by Penguin Books Ltd., London. By permission of Penguin Books Ltd.(129).
Manual de Cocina. Published by Editorial Almena, Instituto del Bienestar, Ministerio de Cultura, Madrid, 1965. Translated by permission of Editorial de Almena(91, 127).
Markuza-Bieniecka, B. and J. P. Dekowski, *Kuchnia Regionalna Wczoraj i dzis.* Translated by permission of Agencja Autorska, Warsaw, for the authors(110).
Marin, Sanda, *Carte De Bucate.* Published by Editura "Cartea Românească." Bucharest(139, 147).
Martin, Peter and Joan, *Japanese Cooking.* Copyright © 1970 Peter and Joan Martin. First published 1970 by André Deutsch Limited, London. By permission of The Bobbs Merrill Co., Inc.(94).
Mei, Fu Pei, *Pei Mei's Chinese Cook Book.* Published by T. & S. Industrial Co., Ltd., Taipei. By permission of T. & S. Industrial Co., Ltd.(96, 145).
Meijden, J. M. J. Catenius-van der, *Groot Nieuw Volledig Indisch Kookboek.* Translated by permission of B. V. Uitgeverij W. van Hoeve, Amsterdam(142).
Menon, *La Cuisinière Bourgeoise.* Paris, 1745(125, 160).
Miller, Gloria Bley, *The Thousand Recipe Chinese Cookbook.* Copyright © 1966 by Gloria Bley Miller. Published by Grosset & Dunlap, New York, 1970. By permission of Gloria Bley Miller(115).
Miller, Jill Nhu Huong, *Vietnamese Cookery.* Copyright in Japan, 1968, by The Charles E. Tuttle Company, Inc. Published by The Charles E. Tuttle Company, Inc., Tokyo. By permission of The Charles E. Tuttle Company, Inc.(120, 122).
Molokhovets, Elena, *Podarok Molodým Khozyaĭkam.* Published in St. Petersburg, 1892(118).
Montagné, Prosper, *The New Larousse Gastronomique.* English translation © 1977 by Hamlyn Publishing Group Limited. Published by Crown Publishers, Inc. By permission of Crown Publishers, Inc.(98, 132).
Montagné, Prosper and A. Gottschalk, *Mon Menu — Guide d'Hygiène Alimentaire.* Published by Société d'Applications Scientifiques, Paris(107, 109).
Ochorowicz-Monatowa, Marja, *Polish Cookery.* (Translated and adapted by Jean Karsavina) © 1958 by Crown Publishers, Inc. Published by Crown Publishers, Inc. New York, 1958. By permission of Crown Publishers, Inc.(101, 102, 146).
Olney, Richard, *Simple French Food.* Copyright © 1974 by Richard Olney. Published by Atheneum Publishers Inc., New York, 1974. By permission of Atheneum Publishers, New York(104, 162).
Ortiz, Elisabeth Lambert, *The Complete Book of Caribbean Cooking.* Copyright © Elisabeth Lambert Ortiz, 1973, 1975. Published by M. Evans and Company, Inc., New York. By permission of John Farquharson Ltd., Literary Agents(112, 129, 138).
Pareren, Mrs. Lily van (Editor), *Prisma Vleesboek 2 Kalfs-en varkensvlees.* Copyright © 1977 by Het Spectrum. Published by Uitgeverij Het Spectrum, Utrecht/Antwerp. Translated by permission of Uitgeverij Het Spectrum(161).
Pascoe, Ann, *Cornish Recipes, Old and New.* Copyright © by Tor Mark Press. Published by Tor Mark Press, Truro. By permission of Tor Mark Press(157).
Peck, Paula, *Paula Peck's Art of Good Cooking.* Copyright © 1961, 1966 by Paula Peck. Published by Simon & Schuster, a Division of Gulf & Western Corporation, New York. By permission of Simon & Schuster, a Division of Gulf & Western Corporation(157).
Pellaprat, Henri-Paul, *Le Nouveau Guide Culinaire.* Copyright © 1969 by René Kramer, Publisher, Castagnola /Lugano. Published by René Kramer. Translated by permission of René Kramer, Publisher(149).
Pépin, Jacques, *A French Chef Cooks at Home.* Copyright © 1975 by Jacques Pépin. Published by Simon & Schuster, a Division of Gulf & Western Corporation, New York. By permission of Simon & Schuster, a Division of Gulf & Western Corporation(88, 128).
Petits Propos Culinaires, No. 2, August 1979, © 1979, Prospect Books. Published by Prospect Books, London and Washington, D.C. By permission of the publisher(128).
Petrov, Dr. L., Dr. N. Djelepov, Dr. E. Iordanov, and S. Uzunova, *Bulgarska Nazionalna Kuchniya.* © Dr. L. Petrov, Dr. N. Djelepov, Dr. E. Iordanov and S. Uzunova, c/o Jusautor, Sofia, 1978. Published by Zemisdat, Sofia, 1978. Translated by permission of Jusautor Copyright Agency, Sofia(119, 139, 140, 153).
Philippon, Henry, *Cuisine de Provence.* © Éditions Albin Michel, 1977. Published by Éditions Albin Michel, Paris. Translated by permission of Éditions Albin Michel(108).
Picayune Creole Cook Book, The. Published by Dover Publications Inc., New York, 1971. By permission of Dover Publications Inc.(87, 144).
Platt, June, *June Platt's New England Cook Book.* © 1971 by June Platt. Published by Atheneum Publishers, New York. By permission of Atheneum Publishers(132).
Point, Fernand, *Ma Gastronomie.* Translated and adapted by Frank Kulla and Patricia Shannon Kulla. English language edition © 1974, Lyceum Books, Inc., Wilton, Ct., U.S.A. Published by Lyceum Books, Inc. By permission of Lyceum Books, Inc.(123, 151).
Poulson, Joan, *Old Thames Valley Recipes.* © Joan Poulson 1977. Published by Hendon Publishing Co., Ltd., Nelson. By permission of Hendon Publishing Co., Ltd.(86).
Re Dei Cuochi, Il, Published by Adriano Salani, Editore, Florence, 1891(103).
Read, Miss, *Miss Read's Country Cooking.* © 1969 by Miss Read. Published by Michael Joseph Ltd., London. By permission of Michael Joseph Ltd.(155).
Rice, Bill, *Far Flung Food.* © Copyright 1974 Paul Rice-Chapman. Published by Siam Communications Ltd., Bangkok. By permission of Siam Communications Ltd.(136).
Robaglia, Suzanne, *Margaridou, Journal et Recettes d'une Cuisinière au Pays d'Auvergne.* Published by Éditions CRÉER, 863340 Nonette, 1977. Translated by permission of Éditions CRÉER(158).
Rombauer, Irma S. and Marion Rombauer Becker, *Joy of Cooking.* Copyright © 1931, 1936, 1941, 1942, 1943, 1946, 1951, 1952, 1953, 1962, 1963, 1964, 1975 by The Bobbs Merrill Company, Inc., New York. Reprinted by permission of The Bobbs Merrill Company(114).
Rossi, Emmanuele (Editor), *La Vera Cuciniera Genovese.* Published by Casa Editrice Bietti, Milan, 1973. Translated by permission of Casa Editrice Bietti(142).
Rundell, Mrs., *Modern Domestic Cookery.* Published by Milner and Company, Limited, London(133).
Saint-Ange, Madame, *La Bonne Cuisine de Madame Saint-Ange.* Copyright 1929 by Augé, Gillon, Hollier-Larousse, Moreau et Cie. (Librairie Larousse), Paris. Published by Librairie Larousse, Paris. Translated by permission of Éditions Chaix, Grenoble(92, 108).
Salvation Army Women's Auxiliary, The, Rochester, N.Y., *Rochester Heritage Cook Book.* Reprinted by permission of the Salvation Army Women's Auxiliary, Rochester, N.Y.(116).
Sarvis, Shirley, *Woman's Day Home Cooking Around The World.* © Copyright 1978 by Fawcett Publications, Inc. Published by Simon & Schuster, a Division of Gulf & Western Corporation, New York. By permission of C.B.S. Publications, Inc., New York(98).
Schoon, Louise Sherman and Corrine Hardesty, *The Complete Pork Cookbook.* Copyright © 1977 by Louise Sherman Schoon and Corrine Hardesty. Published by Stein and Day Publishers. Reprinted with permission of Stein and Day Publishers(100, 113).
Sheridan, Monica, *My Irish Cook Book.* Copyright © 1965 Monica Sheridan. Published by Frederick Muller Limited, London. By permission of Doubleday & Company,

Inc., New York(132, 154).
Sho, Michiko, *Joy Cooking — Pork Side Dishes.* © Shufunotomo Co., Ltd., 1978. Published by Shufunotomo Co., Ltd., Tokyo. By permission of Shufunotomo Co., Ltd.(121).
Singh, Dharamjit, *Indian Cookery.* Copyright © Dharamjit Singh, 1970. Published by Penguin Books Ltd., London. By permission of Penguin Books Ltd.(141).
Snaglewska, B. and I. Zahorska, *Potrawy Staropolskie I Regionalne.* Published by ZWCZSR, Warsaw, 1976. Translated by permission of Agencja Autorska, Warsaw, for the authors(134).
Spanko, Vojtech, *Slovenská Kuchárka.* Published by OBZOR, Bratislava, 1968. Translated by permission of LITA, Bratislava(154).
Spizzotin, Pier Antonio (Editor), *I Quaderni del Cuchiaio d'Argento — Gli Arrosti.* © Editoriale Domus SpA., Milano, 1979. Published by Editoriale Domus SpA. Translated by permission of Editoriale Domus SpA.(104, 109).
Stockli, Albert, *Splendid Fare: The Albert Stockli Cookbook.* Copyright © 1970 by Albert Stockli, Inc. Published by Alfred A. Knopf, Inc., New York, 1975. By permission of Alfred A. Knopf, Inc.(106, 162).
Susanne, *Danish Cookery.* Copyright 1950 by Andr. Fred. Host & Son. Published 1961 by W. H. Allen & Co., Ltd., London in association with Andr. Fred. Host & Son, Copenhagen. By permission of W. H. Allen & Co., Ltd.(143).

Technique of Chinese Cooking, The. Published by Tang's Publishing Company, Taiwan. By permission of Tang's Publishing Company(95).
Tobias, Doris and Mary Merris, *The Golden Lemon.* Copyright © 1978 by Doris Tobias and Mary Merris. Published by Atheneum Publishers, New York, 1978. By permission of Atheneum Publishers(105).
Troisgros, Jean and Pierre, *The Nouvelle Cuisine of Jean & Pierre Troisgros.* Copyright © 1978 in the English translation by William Morrow and Company, Inc. Originally published under the title *Cuisiniers à Roanne.* Copyright © 1977 by Éditions Robert Laffont, S.A. Used by permission of William Morrow and Company, Inc.(126).
Tyndall, Ruth R., *Eat Yourself Full.* Copyright © 1967 by Ruth R. Tyndall. Reprinted by permission of the David McKay Company, Inc.(117).
Valente, Maria Odette Cortes, *Cozinha Regional Portuguesa.* Published by Livraria Almedina, Coimbra, 1973. Translated by permission of Livraria Almedina(96, 107).
Vaughan, Beatrice, *The Old Cook's Almanac.* Copyright © 1966 by Beatrice Vaughan. Reprinted by permission of The Stephen Greene Press(118).
Venesz, József, *Hungarian Cuisine.* © by Mrs. József Venesz. Published by Corvina Press, Budapest. By permission of Artisjus, Budapest, for Mrs. József Venesz(86, 90, 116, 153).
Voltz, Jeanne A., *The Flavor of the South.* Copyright ©

1977 by Jeanne A. Voltz. Published by Doubleday & Company, Inc. Reprinted by permission of Doubleday & Company, Inc.(105, 131, 150).
Waldo, Myra, *The Complete Round-The-World Cookbook.* Copyright 1954, by Myra Waldo Schwartz. Published by Doubleday & Company, Inc., New York. By permission of Doubleday & Company, Inc.(103, 104).
White, Florence (Editor), *Good Things in England.* Published by Jonathan Cape Limited, London, 1968. By permission of Jonathan Cape Limited(88).
Willinksy, Grete, *Kochbuch der Büchergilde.* © Büchergilde Gutenberg, Frankfurt am Main, 1958. Published by Büchergilde Gutenberg. Translated by permission of Büchergilde Gutenberg(119, 149).
Witty, Helen and Elizabeth Schneider Colchie, *Better Than Store Bought: A Cookbook.* Copyright © 1979 by Helen Witty and Elizabeth Schneider Colchie. Published by Harper & Row, Publishers, Inc. Reprinted by permission of Harper & Row, Publishers, Inc.(87, 89).
Wright, Carol, *Portuguese Food.* Copyright © 1969 by Carol Wright. Published by J. M. Dent & Sons Ltd., London. By permission of Deborah Rogers Ltd., Literary Agency, London(92).
Zuliani, Mariù Salvatori de, *La Cucina Di Versilia e Garfagnana.* Copyright © by Franco Angeli Editore, Milano. Published 1969 by Franco Angeli Editore, Milano. Translated by permission of Franco Angeli Editore(136).

Acknowledgments

The indexes for this book were prepared by Louise W. Hedberg. The editors are particularly indebted to: Pat Alburey, Hertfordshire, England; John Davis, London; Tim Fraser, London; Samuel J. Gadell, Tyson's Frozen Food Locker, Vienna, Va.; Monette and Robert Harrell, Suffolk, Va.; Ann Norman, National Pork Producers Council, Des Moines, Iowa; and Jimmy W. Wise, Meat Quality Division, U.S. Dept. of Agriculture, Washington, D.C.

The editors also wish to thank: Herbert C. Abraham, Daniel Englejohn, Everett Lail, U.S. Dept. of Agriculture, Washington, D.C.; R. Allen & Co. (Butchers), Ltd., London; Jane Anderson, Linda Gray, American Meat Institute, Washington, D.C.; Skeffington Ardron, London; Dr.

Bradford W. Berry, Judy Quick, Dr. John Sink, Beltsville Agricultural Research Center, Beltsville, Md.; Dr. Thomas Blumer, North Carolina State University, Raleigh; Sarah Bunney, London; Harley Caldwell, Georgette Parsons, Magruder's Inc., Rockville, Md.; Claire Clifton, London; T. Cole, A. P. Guyatt, H. I. Hutton, Harrods Meat and Charcuterie Department, London; Ann Daro, Meat Promotion Executive, London; Jennifer Davidson, London; Pamela Davidson, London; W. J. Duncum, Hertfordshire, England; C. D. Figg, J. W. Strother, Meat and Livestock Commission, Milton Keynes, England; Julie French, Good Housekeeping Institute, London; The Gadell Family, Tyson's Frozen Food Locker, Vienna, Va.; Frank Gerrard M.B.E., London; Diana Grant, London; Fayal Green, London; Henrietta Green, London; Dr. Thomas G. Hartsock, University of Maryland, Dept. of Animal Science, College Park; Maggie Heinz, London; R. Hibbin, F. J.

Mallion, College for Distributive Trades, London; Christie Horn, London; Judith Howlett, London; Marion Hunter, Surrey, England; Brenda Jayes, London; H. Kenneth Johnson, Gay Starrak, Maura Stockman, Mark Thomas, Hilda Wagner, National Live Stock and Meat Board, Chicago; Maria Johnson, Hertfordshire, England; Douglas Jones, Harry Segal, Ace Beverages, Washington, D.C.; Dr. Edwin A. Kline, Dr. Joseph G. Sebraner, Iowa State University, Dept. of Animal Science, Ames; John Leslie, London; Christopher Maynard, London; Elizabeth Moreau, Buckinghamshire, England; Maria Mosby, London; Mariana Nasta, London; National Farmers Union, London; Dilys Naylor, Surrey, England; Jo Oxley, Surrey, England; Marie Powell, Arlington, Va.; Joanna Roberts, London; Shirley Sarvis, San Francisco; Greg Schaler, Silver Spring, Md.; Alexa Stace, London; Anne Stephenson, London; Gabrielle Townsend, London; Maja Turçan-Parfitt, London.

Picture Credits

The sources for the pictures in this book are listed below. Credits for each of the photographers and illustrators are listed by page number in sequence with successive pages indicated by hyphens; where necessary, the locations of pictures within pages are also indicated — separated from page numbers by dashes.

Photographs by Tom Belshaw: 4, 15 — top right, 18, 19 — top and bottom, 20, 21 — top left and bottom right, 22, 24 — bottom, 25 — bottom left and center, 27 — bottom, 28-29 — top, 32, 34, 36 — top, 37 — top left, center and bottom, 38-49, 54, 55 — top, 60, 66-69, 74-75 — top, 76-77 — bottom, 79.
Photographs by Aldo Tutino: 10-11, 12 — right, 13-14, 15 — left and center, 21 — top center and right, bottom left and center, 36 — bottom, 37 — top right, 52-53, 58-59, 62-65.
Other photographs (alphabetically): Alan Duns, 15 — bottom right, 16 — top, bottom left and center, 25 — bottom right, 26, 27 — top, 28-29 — bottom, 35, 50, 55 — bottom, 56-57, 70, 72-73, 80-81, 84. John Elliot, 19 — center, 24-25 — top, 76-77 — top, 78. Eddy Ely, 16 — bottom right, 17. Louis Klein, 2. Bob Komar, cover, 30-31, 74-75 — bottom, 82-83.
Illustrations (alphabetically): Biruta Akerbergs, 12 — left. From Mary Evans Picture Library and private sources, *Food & Drink: A Pictorial Archive from Nineteenth Century*

Sources by Jim Harter, published by Dover Publications, Inc., 1979, 89-167. Richard Lovell, 8-9.

Library of Congress Cataloguing in Publication Data
Time-Life Books.
   Pork.
   (The Good cook, techniques and recipes)
   Includes index.
   1. Cookery (Pork) I. Title. II. Series: Good cook, techniques and recipes.
TX749.T58   1980   641.6'6'4   79-24649
ISBN 0-8094-2877-6
ISBN 0-8094-2876-8 lib. bdg.

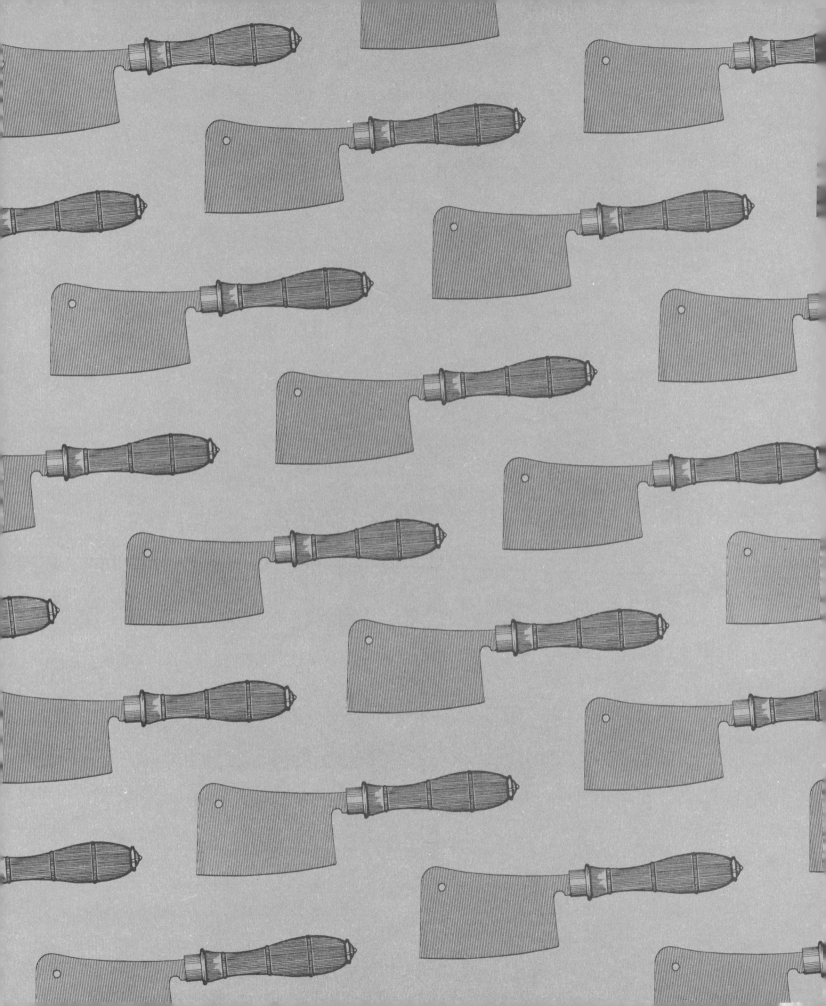